Software Requirements Analysis and Specifications

Jag Sodhi

McGraw-Hill, Inc.

New York   St. Louis   San Francisco   Auckland   Bogotá   Caracas
Lisbon   London   Madrid   Mexico City   Milan   Montreal   New Delhi
Paris   San Juan   São Paulo   Singapore   Sydney   Tokyo   Toronto

FIRST EDITION
FIRST PRINTING

© 1992 by **McGraw-Hill, Inc.**

Printed in the United States of America. All rights reserved. The publisher takes no
responsibility for the use of any of the materials or methods described in this book,
nor for the products thereof.

Library of Congress Cataloging-in-Publication Data

Sodhi, Jag.
    Software requirements analysis and specifications / by Jag Sodhi.
       p.   cm.
    Includes index.
    ISBN 0-07-157879-X (h)
     1. Computer software—Evaluation. I. Title.
  QA76.76.E93S66 1992
  005.1—dc20   92-3367
                                                        CIP

For information about other McGraw-Hill materials, call 1-800-2-MCGRAW in the
U.S. In other countries call your nearest McGraw-Hill office.

Acquisitions Editor: Gerald T. Papke
Book Editor: Sally Anne Glover
Director of Production: Katherine G. Brown
Book Design: Jaclyn J. Boone   TPR4

Contents

Part III
Implementing
Software requirements

Appendices

Acknowledgments

I thank Gerry Gotvald of Teledyne Brown Engineering, Huntsville, Alabama, who convinced me of the need for this book. He also contributed to the book's development.

I owe a great debt to friends who contributed to the development of this book: Frederick Lizza, AI Corp., Waltham, MA; David Peirce and Joyce Turk, American Management Systems, Arlington, VA; Lois Valley, Software Productivity Solutions, Melbourne, FL; Joanne Dowson, CADRE Technologies, Providence, RI; Paul Raymond, GEC-Marconi Software Systems, Reston, VA; Allen Gooch, MAGEC, Plano, TX; Robert Poston, PEI, Tinton Falls, NJ; James Besemer, SAGE Software, Beaverton, Oregon; Richard Jordon, Synthesis Computer Technologies, Long Beach, CA; Gary Rippen and Sharon Allen, Transform Logic Corporation, Scottsdale, AZ.

I express my appreciation to friends who contributed in different ways toward the completion of this book: Sanford Cohen, Software Engineering Institute, Carnegie-Mellon University, Pittsburgh, PA; Judah Mogilensky, CONTEL Federal Systems, Chantilly, VA; Edward Berard, Berard Software Engineering, Gaithersburg, MD; Thomas Webb, RATIONAL, Arlington, TX.

I thank wholeheartedly all my friends, students, and colleagues who helped with this book in many different ways. It's not easy to identify all of the people who contributed to the development of this project. I thank all the people at the publishing company who were involved in the editing and production of the text.

Finally, I commend my wife, Lynda, who diligently supported me so this project could be finished successfully. Without the love and support of her and my children, I would not have completed this book.

Preface

Software Requirements Analysis and Specification covers the software development forefront, in which software developers study the user/customer's requirements and understand them completely. Failure to understand the requirements in the beginning results in incorrect software and probable delays in delivery. Requirements must be well-written, well-defined, analyzed, and understood to produce cost-effective software of high quality.

Requirements analysis and specification encompasses the early software development activities that culminate in the creation of:

- System requirements specifications.
- System engineering design.
- Software requirements specifications (SRS).

Requirements analysis and specification also involves the ongoing activities of constant updates to the SRS, which result in learning more about the software solution. The SRS assures that the requirements are right before the products are designed. A customer's requirements must be analyzed thoroughly and completely understood before design is started. This book will help you efficiently design software and smoothly take you on the journey of software requirements implementation. The book explores the famous saying in the industry, "Trust me." It also covers how to establish meaningful relationships among the requirements, user/customer, and system/software developer.

This book provides comprehensive information that will help you track the customer's requirements throughout the software development process. The book addresses the customer's automation needs, establishment of requirements, feasibility, definition, specification, and analysis of requirements. Prototyping and CASE tools are liberally discussed. In appropriate chapters, I have included CASE tools that are specific to the needs of a particular topic. Many examples and case studies illustrate the application of the techniques to real problems.

This book's main goal is to present high-quality information that covers a wide range of selected subject areas, such as: the requirements life cycle, requirements determination, requirements reliability and feasibility, requirements specification, requirements traceability, requirements engineering and planning, software requirements analysis methods, structured functional methods, real-time impact, the object-oriented approach, artificial intelligence methods, emerging software requirements analysis methods, software requirements implementation, documenting software requirements analysis, software design, the implementation process, software requirements validation and verification, and CASE tools. This material can certainly help you understand the importance of software requirements and help you select a suitable method and CASE tool for your needs.

The book is intended for both beginners and experienced computer professionals—analysts, designers, programmers, engineers, and managers. The focus throughout the book is on practical software technology that covers material from "cradle to finish." The book can be an asset to university courses in computer sciences, software engineering, and other branches of a computer curriculum. This book can also be used as a supplement to my other works, which are *Software Engineering Methods, Management, and CASE Tools* (1991), *Computer System Techniques: Development, Implementation, and Software Maintenance* (1990), and *Managing Ada Projects Using Software Engineering* (1990).

The success of my previous books in the computer market motivated me to write this book. Comments that I received from my readers also encouraged me to accept the task of writing an additional book. My friend Gerry Gotvald, of Teledyne Brown Engineering, convinced me that there's a need for this book in the computer market.

The book presents state-of-the art material; you can be assured it reflects what's currently happening in the software requirements and specification field. I encourage you to use the book's appendices for a list of vendors and further discussion.

The information and data that's contained here has been compiled from various sources and is intended for reference purposes. Neither the publisher nor the author warrants the accuracy of the information and data. The opinions and findings that are contained in this book are those of the author's.

Introduction

This book consists of three parts and four appendices. Part I reviews the requirements life cycle. Chapter 1 discusses:

- The importance of understanding requirements.
- Types of requirements.
- Relationship criteria among user/customer, analyst, and software developer.
- The "trust me" myth.

Requirements play a vital role in the software development process, and it's important that the requirements are understood completely before a costly decision of "what to build" is made.

Chapter 2 explains the requirements determination process, requirements elicitation, requirements identification, requirements models, prototyping, rapid prototyping, and related CASE tools. The requirements determination process determines what is desired by the user/customer. The primary purpose of defining requirements at early stages is to draw blueprints and document them so that any potential confusion and misinterpretation can be eliminated.

Chapter 3 deals with requirements reliability, feasibility, and cost/benefits analysis. Ambiguous and incomplete requirements will create problems sooner or later in the software development life cycle. Requirements reliability confirms the correctness of the requirements as they were defined. To meet the defined requirements, the software development project should be feasible technically, operationally, and economically.

Chapter 4 covers system requirements specification, characteristics of a good requirement specification, contents of a requirements specification document, and the formal requirements specification review. This document captures and records the requirements of both software and hardware. The document establishes the baseline for testing the system requirements, which will be validated and verified before the customer accepts the product.

Chapter 5 presents requirements for the traceability process, selection criteria for good requirements CASE tools, and the Requirement Tracer CASE tool of Teledyne Brown Engineering. The traceability CASE tool ensures that the information contained within the requirements specification documentation is neither created nor destroyed while requirements are being allocated. The CASE tool produces comprehensive reports that explain how each requirements specification documentation sentence has been interpreted by the software developer.

Chapter 6 covers requirements and system engineering, and the RqT CASE tool by CADRE. By this time, the software developer should have understood the requirements, and design of the system should start. The software developer identifies hardware and software that will be used and allocates the requirements to a computer software configuration item.

Chapter 7 deals with managing requirements and the GEC-Marconi CASE tool. It's important that the management aspects of software development are planned. In this plan, the software developers describe their complete plan for conducting and following software development. This plan includes risk management, total quality management, software configuration management, and software acceptance procedures.

Part II presents a variety of methods and CASE tools for software requirements analysis. Chapter 8 covers conventional versus modern approaches, modeling techniques, formal and informal methods, and the MAGEC CASE tool. Before the software requirements analysis is properly specified, it's vital that some study be given to the available methods and CASE tools for software requirements analysis. This chapter also includes a few practical prototyping methods for software requirements analysis.

Chapter 9 includes a formal requirements specification method, structured functional requirements analysis environments, multiple views of a software requirements model, and requirements specification languages. In addition, this chapter covers the reusability of requirements specification techniques.

Chapter 10 deals with real-time requirements analysis and specification, Ada language, and the Transform CASE tool. Real-time requirements of a system are accuracy, reliability, and immediate response. Real-time systems should have predictable timing characteristics and should be robust under stress.

Chapter 11 covers object-oriented methods and the Software Productivity Solutions CASE tool. Software requirements are defined in terms of objects that comprise a system and the behavior of those objects. Instead of writing instructions, object-oriented programming involves interconnecting reusable software components. This chapter also covers object-oriented requirements analysis models.

Chapter 12 presents artificial intelligence methods. Artificial intelligence is a computer science that's concerned with analyzing requirements so intelligent computer systems can be built. Expert systems are tools that let software developers analyze, design, and implement customers' requirements. Knowledge-based systems use established methods to analyze customer requirements.

Chapter 13 deals with emerging software requirements analysis methods, fuzzy logic, selection criteria for a suitable model, effective dialogue, the software factory, the smart way, unified software requirements methods, and the Synthesis CASE tool. Effective dialogue must be established between the customer and software developer for harmony so the project can be completed. It's well known that no two applications are identical. The requirements analysis approach to each system is unique. For each of these applications, an analyst must decide the most effective method or combination of methods for the software requirements analysis.

Part III deals with software requirements implementation. Chapter 14 covers documenting software requirements analysis. A requirements specification document describes the behavior of a software, which includes external and internal software interfaces. This document establishes the baseline for software design and testing.

Chapter 15 presents the software design process. This chapter shows the logical internal structure of software design. It discusses the external data formats and the hierarchical partitioning of software requirements into manageable components. The software developer uses ingenuity, imagination, creativity, and expertise to create a correct and logical design.

Chapter 16 deals with the software requirements implementation program. This chapter includes writing logical instructions that the computer will process. The output result must match the specified requirements. The Logiscope CASE tool and the quality and metrics of a well-structured computer program are discussed.

Chapter 17 presents the software requirements validation and verification process. Building a system is a technique that integrates the correct and tested software components into the system. Before it's accepted, the system software product is validated and verified by the customer for its correctness and fulfilment of the requirements.

The names in parentheses throughout the book refer to the references that are listed in Appendix C. All abbreviations and acronyms used in the book are also defined at the end of the book in Appendix A.

Part I

The life cycle of requirements

1
Requirements taxonomy

Requirements play a vital role in the software development process. This process evolves from an initial statement of requirements that are needed for the completion of a software engineering product. There's always a need to engineer system software that will:

- Meet user requirements and expectations within available resources.
- Accommodate change throughout the software life cycle.

It's important that the requirements are understood before making a costly decision of "what to build." This process involves determining, defining, and specifying requirements before analyzing them.

What are requirements?

Requirements are created by a customer for some specific purpose. This purpose may sometimes be simply to satisfy a user's needs. Thus, requirements are needed so that a problem can be solved or an objective can be achieved. These requirements are capabilities or conditions as stated by the customer/user. Requirements can be functions, constraints, or other properties that must be provided, met, or satisfied so the needs are filled for the system's intended user(s) (1986 Abbott).

Requirements are the conditions that must be met for a software product to be acceptable to its customer/user. Requirements can be totally new for a new software development project or requirements can be for improving an existing system. This improvement can be possible either by changing requirements in the existing software, enhancing the existing requirements, or correcting requirements in order to solve a problem in the existing software.

Importance of understanding requirements

Many problems are encountered when using the English language to specify the needs and requirements of complex systems. The following is an example of a simple requirement.

Example 1

A customer needs to build a new concrete road from the city of Apache to link with the city of Mt. Genesis. The road should be 10 feet wide and 38 miles long and fitted with all the necessary signs and facilities/amenities. The road should be completed in 60 days time.

Solution 1

After accepting the lowest bid, the project was contracted to a corporation. The project was completed as scheduled and is illustrated in FIG. 1-1.

Generally, most of the requirements are vague and not clear in the beginning. They're written in ambiguous language. Maybe the originator understands them, but often the people who have to implement those requirements

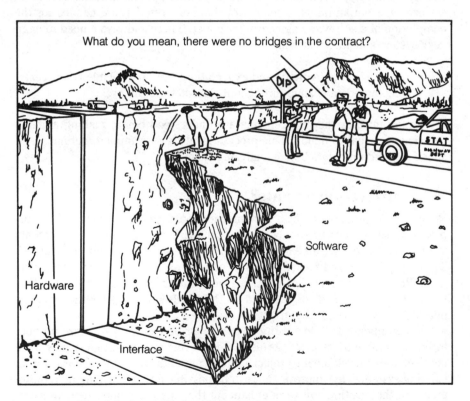

Fig. 1-1. A result of unclear requirements. Teledyne Brown Engineering

don't understand them. Often the problems in the computer industry are that the requirements are either not complete or the originator is frequently changing the requirements. It's important that a considerable amount of time is spent defining and specifying the requirements, and making them more clear.

Software requirements

It's very important that the requirements are understood before commencing an expensive and critical software project. The user's requirements analysis is the prime phase in software development, as shown in FIG. 1-2. The require-

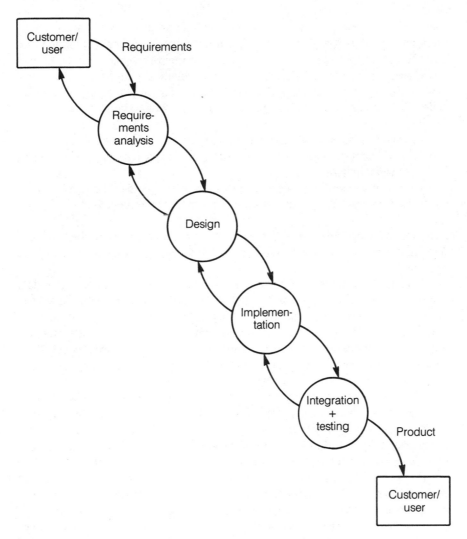

Fig. 1-2. Software development's major phases.

ments must be understood and analyzed thoroughly before commencing the work. Requirements fall into four classes (1985 Ross):

- Functional requirements.
- Nonfunctional requirements.
- Inverse requirements.
- Design and implementation constraints.

Functional requirements specify a function that a software must be capable of performing. These can be stated from either a static or dynamic perspective. The dynamic perspective describes the behavior of a software under specified circumstances. These can be fundamental processes or transformations where the software should perform on inputs in order to produce outputs. It's sometimes necessary that the requirements are specified on inputs, processing, and outputs. Functional requirements stated from an external dynamic perspective are frequently written in terms of externally observable states. Functionality can be considered as having three components:

- Transformations are carried out on inputs that produce outputs.
- Dynamic requirements are concerned with requirements for sequencing and parallelism.
- Exception handling is concerned with those aspects of the requirements that are outside the mainstream of normal system behavior.

Functional requirements, stated from a static perspective, describe the functions performed by each entity and how it interacts with other entities and the environment.

In order for functionality to be defined, data has to be defined. Such data can be categorized as inputs and outputs, stored data, and transient data (temporary results, etc.). Data definitions should have levels that define just the lowest-level attributes or data items in an unstructured form that's manageable. If definitions are structured, then grouping of the lowest-level items should be clear and hierarchical. Examples of common groupings are entities, data groups and data dictionary entities.

Nonfunctional requirements are those that relate to performance, reliability, security, maintainability, availability, accuracy, error-handling, capacity, ability to be used by a specific class of users, anticipated changes to be accommodated, acceptable level of training or support, or the like. Nonfunctional requirements state characteristics of the system that will be achieved and are not related to functionality. For example, in a real-time system, performance requirements may be of critical importance, and functional requirements may be sacrificed so that minimal acceptable performance is achieved.

Inverse requirements describe the constraints on allowable behavior. They explain what the software shall not do. In many cases, it's easier to state that certain behavior must never occur than to state the requirements guaranteeing

acceptable behavior in all circumstances. Software safety and security requirements are frequently stated in this manner (1986 Leveson).

Design and implementation constraints are boundary conditions on how the
required software must be constructed and implemented. They're development guidelines within which the designer must work.

Relationship criteria

The primary phase of a software development process is to determine requirements that state "what" is required. The customer/user establishes the
requirements. The requirements are analyzed, and an analyst determines
what the developer will have to deliver; the analyst also forms the basis for
acceptability of the product by the customer. The requirements life cycle is
like a three-ring circus, as shown in FIG. 1-3. The major participants are cus-
tomer/user, analyst, and software developer. Each of them has their related
responsibilities in completing a software project.

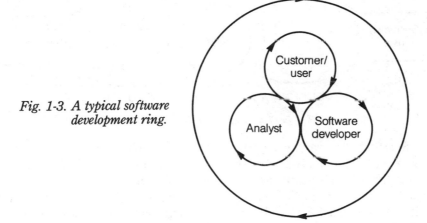

*Fig. 1-3. A typical software
development ring.*

The *customer/user* creates the requirements for developing software. Normally the customer/user contracts the software project for development. It's
assumed that the customer/user is responsible for accepting the software
product. Usually the requirements in the beginning are fuzzy. The allotted
budget and time is not adequate. The management of the requirements for
traceability is not mature. Unlike other types of engineering, in software engineering, the customer can't physically see any developed product until the
software project is completed. These problems can be surmounted somewhat
by establishing reviews and check points for the customer during the software
development life cycle. Customers should educate themselves enough to be
able to trace the requirements through the software development process.

Customers should believe in the requirements and understand what they
are. They should be knowledgeable enough in software engineering so that

they can comfortably present requirements to technical professionals. Customers should provide necessary information for clarification. They should be good in communication and not lose their temper. They should patiently listen to open dialogue. They should work easily with people.

An *analyst* is an experienced member of a software development team. Sometimes, depending on the volume of the requirements, the analyst can form a team with a few analysts that can assist. The analyst should understand the requirements from the customer's perspective. The analyst acts as a catalyst by identifying requirements from information gathered from many sources. The analyst also structures the information by building models, and the analyst communicates draft requirements for different audiences, as depicted in FIG. 1-4. It's important that the analyst gain the confidence of the customers who are providing funds to carry on the project. Good rapport and effective communication with customers will help achieve success.

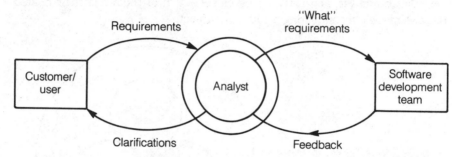

Fig. 1-4. The role of an analyst.

Since there's a variety of participants in the requirements life cycle process, requirements analysis must be presented in alternative but consistent forms that are understandable by different audiences. It's not surprising to find that some of the audience may not be expert in requirements or computer software. At minimum, a good analyst is a thinker, knowledgeable, and analytical. The analyst should be articulate in dealing with the customer and extracting information that's needed in order to understand the requirements. The analyst should be technically oriented and able to translate the requirements to professionals for successful implementation. The analyst should communicate well and work easily with people. The analyst increases mutual trust between the customer and the software developer professionals. The analyst believes in satisfying the customers with results. A good analyst achieves an agreement on the requirements, provides a basis for software development, and also provides a reference point for software validation.

Software developers are a group of professionals who are contracted to develop software that meets the requirements. The software development team is headed by an experienced manager. The manager keeps a good track record of software development and meets the requirements. The manager should be well versed in state-of-the-art techniques and able to analyze the user's requirements, develop software, and deliver the finished product to the satisfaction of the user. A good manager must recognize what tools are required and then use them in a knowledgeable manner. The manager must lead the team so that they plan, estimate, schedule, and develop the project's complete work structure without guesswork or reliance on an individual's memory or experience. A manager is a leader who communicates effectively with a group and guides with a vision for success. A manager makes practical decisions and recognizes the importance of objectivity, vision, and initiative for sound, quality decisions. A manager encourages teamwork and infuses confidence to understand the requirements, develop software, test the requirements, and document them properly. A manager establishes priorities and uses available resources effectively. A manager identifies risk and defines risk avoidance alternations. He or she finishes the project on time, within budget, and meets all the requirements.

"Trust me" myth

Contractors in the computer industry often say "trust me." They often reiterate that they understand the requirements exactly as the customer stated them and that they will build the product to customer's entire satisfaction. Contractors often insist on getting the contract right away so they can start soon and deliver the best product. Here's a typical example.

Example 2

Mr. Smith is a successful businessman and has very little time for anything but his work. He lives in an apartment that has two bedrooms. His family grows and he is now in dire need of a big house. One day, he calls his friend who knows a home builder. The builder accepts the contract of building a beautiful house for Mr. Smith. The requirements are stated verbally as follows.

- Mr. Smith needs three bedrooms to accommodate his three boys.
- He also needs a master bedroom with an attached bathroom.
- Since his children are growing, Mr. Smith wants his children's rooms away from his master bedroom so he can enjoy peace in isolation when he comes home from work.
- He also wants the children to have a common bathroom of their own.
- Mr. Smith wants his house on one acre of land.
- Mr. Smith doesn't want to copy any existing plans of houses.
- He is ready to spend $100,000.00.
- He wants a house with his own unique requirements.
- Mr. Smith doesn't have any time to look at the progress of the house.
- He just wants the house finished in six months so he can move in and live happily.

Solution

The contractor promises that he knows exactly what Mr. Smith wants. He has all the experience for building good homes. The contractor also thinks that he can finish the house in six months. The contractor agrees that Mr. Smith should trust him and when the house is ready then the contractor will invite Mr. Smith for inspection.

Mr. Smith enquired a few times about the house by telephone. The contractor always reiterated the same words, "Trust me." The house is progressing right on schedule. The contractor always welcomes Mr. Smith to visit the site of the house, but cautions that Mr. Smith will not be able to appreciate much since the house is not complete yet.

To make a profit the contractor hired a subcontractor to finish the house. The subcontractor, out of necessity, hired young part-time help to make more profit. The requirements were understood literally. The experience of building a house was never put into practice. No effort was made to understand the customer's requirements.

The work started as scheduled and was completed on time in accordance with Mr. Smith's requirements as understood by the contractor's assistants, as illustrated in FIG. 1-5. The contractor did meet the requirements, but he did not satisfy the customer.

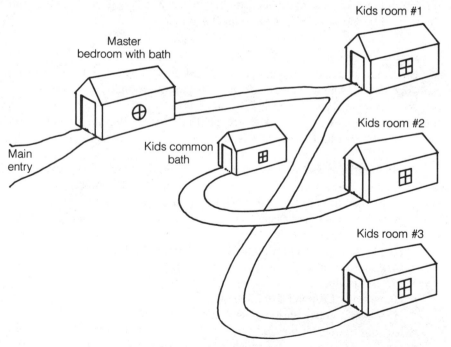

Fig. 1-5. Mr. Smith's home requirements, as understood by the contractor.

Lessons learned

Here's how to avoid such incidents. Requirements should be clearly, precisely, and unambiguously identified, defined, and specified. The customer/user should be kept in the loop throughout the life cycle of software development. Requirements should be properly managed and tracked for validation and verification. These topics will be discussed in detail in the following chapters.

2

The requirements determination process

The requirements determination process determines what is desired. Determining what's desired involves subprocesses, such as the customer defining the requirements, and the software developer learning those requirements. The primary function of defining requirements is to draw blueprints and document them to eliminate any potential confusion and misinterpretation. Requirements need to be stated clearly, rigorously, and precisely before proceeding to other software development phases. The software requirements definition subprocess consists of identification, representation, communication, and preparation for validation.

Who knows "exactly" what the requirements are?

Does the customer know exactly what the requirements are? Is the user solely knowledgeable about the requirements? Does the analyst know exactly what the requirements are? Does the software developer understand the requirements enough to develop software that will produce the desired result?

The answer is that a combination of all of these people can determine the requirements. At the beginning, requirements are always fuzzy. As time passes, the requirements mature because all of these members provide the necessary input. Each member of the team provides his or her input and makes the requirements clear and understandable.

A customer knows his or her point of view if he or she is the sole originator of these requirements. In case the customer has a user who created these requirements, then the user knows about the requirements from his or her point of view. A user is also called an end user, since he or she is the one who actually uses the product of the requirements at completion. In this particular case, the customer must first understand the user's requirements before the customer can explain them to an analyst. At best, a customer tries to present requirements, provide input sources, and determine the acceptance criteria for the software products.

An analyst belongs to the software development team. He or she must extract the best knowledge of the requirements from the customer. An analyst must understand the customer's way of thinking and provide expert knowledge on the subject. An analyst must also thoroughly understand the customer's requirements and clearly explain them to the software development team. This process is illustrated in FIG. 2-1.

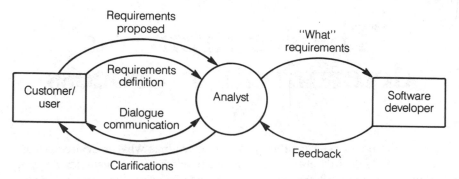

Fig. 2-1. Understanding requirements.

Requirements elicitation

Requirements elicitation is a process performed by analysts, who gather and understand information (1988 Leite). This process involves the following factors:

- Fact-finding.
- Validating the customer's understanding of the gathered information.
- Communicating open issues for resolution.

Fact-finding uses mechanisms such as interviews, questionnaires, and observation of the operational environment of which the software will become a part. Validation involves creating a representation of elicitation results in a form that will focus attention on open issues that can be reviewed with those who provided the information. Possible representations include summary documents, usage scenarios, prototypes, and graphic models. Requirements elicitation is achieved by a requirements proposal, requirements communication, and requirements definition, as shown in FIG. 2-2.

Requirements proposal

A *requirements proposal* outlines the need for customer requirements. The proposal requests an update that modifies or corrects an error in existing software or develops new software. A requirements proposal is sometimes referred to as a statement of work. It states what is required from a contractor. It's an agree-

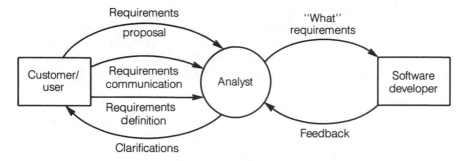

Fig. 2-2. Requirements elicitation.

ment that the customer and software developer will abide by in the future. The requirements proposal may ask for a software developer's ability to meet projected growth and operational changes. It can also ask for detailed costs, estimates of installation manpower, and an implementation plan. It may ask for a contractual agreement that will include responsibilities, delivery schedules, penalty clauses for missed deadlines, and explicit definitions of what constitutes software acceptance.

Requirements communication

Requirements communication involves the iterative elicitation and refinement of information from a variety of sources, which provides the customer with divergent perceptions of what is needed. An analyst learns the applications and attributes of the product for delivery to the customer. The form of communication is generally meetings and phone conversations between the customer and the analyst.

Frequent review of the evolving requirements by analysts who have a variety of backgrounds is essential to the convergence of this iterative process. The goal is to reach an agreement on the requirements definition. The result of the requirements definition is presented to a diverse audience for review and approval. Even though the customer and analysts are frequently expert in their own areas, they are often less experienced in each other's domain, and that makes effective communication particularly difficult.

The result of requirements communication is frequently further iteration through the requirements definition process so an agreement can be reached on a precise statement of requirements. The documents generated supplement graphic diagrams of various sorts: prototypic and graphic models. Requirements documents must facilitate communication with the customer, as well as with analyst/software developers and others who will test the software after it's developed.

Defining requirements

Defining requirements is not an easy process. Requirements may not be mature enough to be defined. The requirements may only be an idea in the customer's mind. A customer must sit down and write explicitly what his or her requirements are. The requirements definition document thus produced by the customer will ensure that the software developer understands the customer's requirements, needs, and objectives. This understanding and agreement will eliminate potential confusion and misinterpretation in software development.

Requirements definition will usually include an understanding of the environment in which the software can operate and how the software will interact with that environment. Some type of explicit approval to proceed with requirements definition completes the elicitation process. The audience who must approve the requirements should agree that all relevant information sources have been contacted.

Requirements identification

Requirements identification is a step in the requirements definition during which software requirements are elicited from a heterogeneous audience. An important precursor to requirements definition is the context analysis process, which is depicted in FIG. 2-3. Context analysis answers the following questions.

- Why is the software to be created?
- What is the environment of the software to be created?
- What are the technical, operational, and economic boundary conditions that an acceptable software implementation must satisfy?

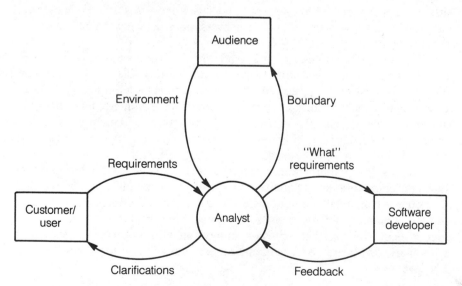

Fig. 2-3. The context analysis process.

Requirements representation

Requirements representation is a step in the requirements definition during which the results of requirements identification are portrayed. Requirements have traditionally been represented in a purely textual form. However, techniques such as model building and prototyping, which demand more precision in their description, are being used more.

Requirements models

Requirements models are a simplified version of reality. They don't attempt to capture every detail of the requirements. Instead, requirements models are built during requirements definition so specific characteristics of the software can be defined. Specific characteristics are the functions that software will perform and interface to a software environment. This graphical form can be more easily understood and analyzed than a textual description. It's important at this stage for the analyst and the customer/user to work together, since it's the user who knows what must be done and the analyst who analyzes how to do it.

Figure 2-4 shows a sample requirements model. A good requirements model reduces the amount of complexity that must be comprehended at one time. This requires the analyst to use all of his or her experience, education, and creativity. It's well known that undetected errors that occur in the requirements analysis are the most costly to fix in later phases of the software development. Compared to the real thing, it's inexpensive to build a model and modify it. The model facilitates the description of complex aspects of the real thing. Requirements models portray the results of requirements elicitation. The models help analysts identify the potential problems early in the requirements definition process.

Once a requirements model is created, it's used to provide many answers to the customer/user. The model may further need to optimize or simulate in order to satisfy the customer/user. In optimization the user implements a mathematical technique that will determine the best possible solution to model. Optimization can be constrained or unconstrained. If constrained, the range of possible solutions is restricted.

Some models are too complex for optimization techniques to be used. Simulation technique is used when the requirements are studied. Simulation models employ a series of values that simulate the situation under study. Simulation is also used when more information on the models is needed for customer/user satisfaction. Sometimes a model must be prototyped for understanding and defining complex requirements.

There are many benefits with the use of graphical models. A model reveals misconceptions about functions and work done by the software developer. A model produces suggestions on how the work should be organized. A

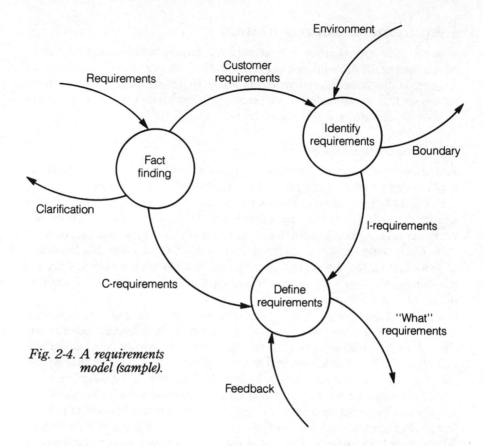

*Fig. 2-4. A requirements
model (sample).*

model can be felt and seen by the user/customer and analyst for discussion. It gives participants a clearer perception of the expectations of each other. It encourages participants to explore anxieties about losing control when the system is implemented. A model in front of them will lead participants to bring issues into the open at an early phase in the project. A prototype model can simulate almost any real picture. Rapid prototyping can bring the customer/ user and analyst closer to the reality of the requirements solution. Models assist by enhancing the understanding of the requirements.

Requirements prototyping

Requirements prototyping uses a model to analyze requirements, and it enhances direct communication between customer/user and analyst/software developers. Requirements prototyping is used to provide early feedback to customers/users. This improves communication of requirements between customer and software developers. Many customers find it difficult to visualize how software will perform in their environment when it's based only on a non-executable description of requirements.

A prototype can be an effective mechanism that conveys a sense of how the software will work. Hands-on use of a prototype is particularly valuable to customers, since not all of them have participated in the requirements definition process. This is especially true for embedded systems software. The idea of building a protoype of a software requirement is commonly accepted in the industry. A prototype can give to the customer and to the analyst early visibility of the likely functional and operational behavior of the software. Now, particularly for database-oriented software, fourth-generation tools are available that enable the analyst to very quickly construct software that possess the functionality specified in the requirements. The type of products include relational database management systems, fourth-generation languages (4GLs), code generators, report writers, query languages, rapid screen design tools, application generators, functional exercisers, and collections of specialized, reusable software components.

Although a prototype is not a substitute for a thorough written specification, a prototype does allow representation of the effect of some requirements. A sample prototype is shown in FIG. 2-5. Models developed after the requirements elicitation can be useful in deciding what functionality should be included in such a prototype.

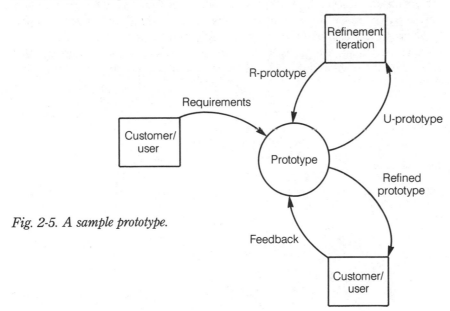

Fig. 2-5. A sample prototype.

Rapid prototyping

Rapid prototyping is a technique for constructing requirements models rapidly and cheaply. This technique accelerates the development of software that meets the user's requirements. This is especially useful where the requirements are perfectly stated, but it's not known how the software should be developed for the system design. This is often useful for research and development projects in which the knowledge of how to build a current state-of-the-art system is not clear. This approach is used as a learning process.

Rapid prototyping can also be used for improving the progress of software quality during the software life cycle. Often, the user discovers that the requirements he or she originally defined need revision in light of the experience that's been gained with a working model of the system. The defined requirements are incrementally improved. As the requirements shift, the software development phases need redevelopment. Rapid prototyping assists in learning about stable, accurate requirements as early as possible in the life cycle. Rapid prototyping prevents downstream waste as much as possible and prevents poor morale among the software developers due to shifting requirements.

The basic benefits of rapid prototyping are twofold. One benefit deals with quick response in changing requirements after a software has been developed and with initial articulation of correct and complete requirements. The second benefit is early exposure to the user for requirements in which three to five years are spent in software development.

Often, if the optimization constraints are relaxed, models can be built more rapidly and with less expense. Thus, partial models of the system can yield samples of system behavior at a fraction of the cost of the real system. These partial models can be adequate for determining the software's responsiveness to the user requirements. In rapid prototyping, you don't need to model everything. Model only that which is relevant to the functionality requirements as viewed by the user. A sample rapid prototype model is illustrated in FIG. 2-6.

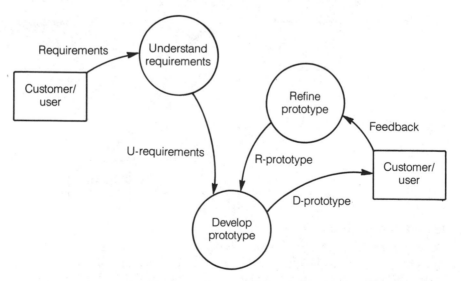

Fig. 2-6. Rapid prototyping.

Computer Aided Software Engineering tools

Computer Aided Software Engineering (CASE) tools are support environments that are necessary for automating the customer requirements for software development. These tools assist in prototyping and modeling, which enhance understanding of the requirements.

CASE tools are not a replacement for any of the methods of software development. CASE tools are supplements for the methods and are enhancements for generating quality products. This approach saves time and money in software development and achieves efficiency and quality in the final products. A CASE tool links the software and requirements engineering with a central database. (See FIG. 2-7.) There are many CASE tools available that will assist in automating models and prototypes. Some of these CASE tools will be discussed in the following chapters.

External interfaces for requirements

External interfaces establish the link with other systems. The user will describe the impact the requirements will have when they interface with exist-

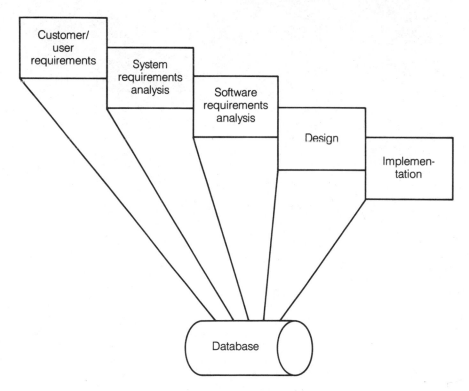

Fig. 2-7. A generic CASE tool diagram.

ing systems. The purpose of each interface and the relationship between each interface will be detailed. Each interface will be specified in detailed quantitative terms that explain dimensions, tolerances, loads, speeds, and communications protocol. In addition, there can be data flowing across the interface that includes direction, frequency, and timing. The media of flowing data are files, reports, and any other method of communication. These will be constrained on any proposed solution for the requirements.

3

Requirements reliability and feasibility

Requirements reliability confirms the correctness of the requirements as defined. The feasibility study is conducted to explore whether or not the requirements are worth solving. To meet the defined requirements, the software development project must be feasible technically, operationally, and economically.

Requirements reliability

Requirements reliability depends upon the soundness of the defined requirements. Requirements are assessed for stability. A stable requirement addresses a need that's not expected to change during the software life cycle. These are mandatory requirements and must be included in the software before it's acceptable to the customer.

An analyst conducts the necessary analysis and establishes the reliability of the requirements definition. The tools used are graphical modeling, prototyping, and rapid prototyping. This process includes the assessment of potential problems and risk factors, and the evaluation of requirements feasibility. These steps are frequently iterated until all issues are resolved.

Assessment of potential problems

Requirements are assessed for the following potential problems:

- Ambiguity.
- Incompleteness.
- Inconsistency.

Ambiguous and incomplete requirements are not understandable. These requirements create problems sooner or later in the software development process. The earlier these requirements are understood, the better. Cost-effective software can then be developed. Graphical representations are used for clarity so requirements can be completely understood. A narrative text only explains these requirements, and they can often be interpreted differently by a heterogeneous audience. Any inconsistency in understanding the requirements should be resolved in the early stages. Inconsistency can create a high risk factor if carried on longer during the software development phases.

Risk factors

Risk factors should be carefully calculated. A list of the risk factors should be created and maintained at regular intervals until the completion of the software development project. Different levels of risk factors should be recognized. Risks can be low-level, moderate-level, and high-level. The high-level risk factors should be prioritized and resolved first. Risk factors can arise that are due to changes in the requirements, environment, technology, organization, personnel, and unforeseen events.

Software hazards and safety are related to the software risk factor. A hazard is a set of conditions that can lead to an accident in certain environmental conditions. Safety is defined in terms of hazards. Software can contribute to system hazards, and hazardous software behavior must be eliminated or controlled in order to reduce or prevent accidents. Risk can be reduced by decreasing any or all three of the following risk factors.

- The likelihood of a hazard occurring.
- The likelihood that the hazard will lead to an accident.
- The worst possible potential loss associated with such an accident.

Software can potentially contribute to risk through the effect of the software on system hazards. Therefore, software safety should ensure that the software executes within the system context without resulting in unacceptable risk. System software safety involves such factors as identifying hazards, assessing hazards risk, and controlling hazards.

Identifying the hazards should begin at the earliest stages of software development, during requirements definition. An initial risk assessment should be made, which identifies the safety-critical areas and functions, identifies and evaluates hazards, and identifies the safety design criteria that will be used in the remainder of the software development phases.

Hazard assessment can be viewed as falling along a continuum in terms of severity. One approach establishes a cutoff point on this continuum. Only the hazards above this point are considered in further system safety procedures. The other approach uses several cutoff points that establish categories of hazards. These categories can be negligible, marginal, serious, or critical when differing levels of time and effort are applied.

Hazard control can be introduced during the software requirements analysis, and techniques can be designed to attempt to prevent or minimize the occurrence of a hazard. The objective of software safety requirements analysis is to ensure that the requirements functionalities are specified and implemented, and that they are consistent with the safety constraints as shown in FIG. 3-1. Ideally, this is accomplished by verifying that the software requirements satisfy the safety constraints and that the software correctly implements the requirements.

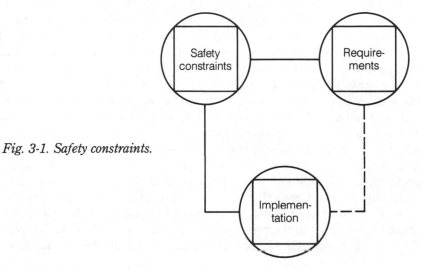

Fig. 3-1. Safety constraints.

The advantages of safety analysis steps are that errors are caught earlier and thus are easier and less costly to fix. The information from the early verification activities can help design safety features into code and provide leverage for the final code verification effort. The verification effort is distributed throughout the development process instead of being concentrated at the end. Ideally, each step merely requires that newly added detail doesn't violate the safety verification of the higher level abstraction at the previous step. Each level is consistent with the safety related assumptions made in the analysis at the next higher level. These verification activities may have both formal and informal aspects; static analysis uses formal proofs and structured walk-throughs, and dynamics analysis involves various types of testing that provides confidence in the models and the assumptions used in the static analysis.

The first step in any safety verification procedure verifies that the software requirements are consistent with or satisfy the safety constraints. This analysis is important so that the code ensures and satisfies that these requirements will be safe; the analysis also identifies important conflicts and tradeoffs early, before design decisions have been made. Decisions about tradeoffs between safety and reliability or other software qualities, and between safety and functionality, must be made for each project on the basis of potential risk, acceptable risk, liability issues, and requirements.

This analysis is accomplished by the requirements, which must be specified in a formal language. This formal language is defined as having a rigorously and unambiguously defined semantics. It must be emphasized that the performing of this type of safety verification doesn't negate the need to verify the correctness of the software in some formal or informal way.

Evaluation of requirements feasibility

Evaluation of requirements feasibility determines whether there exists a viable, effective solution. The purpose of a feasibility study is to gather enough information and knowledge about the business functions, environment, and systems plans to determine whether real benefits will be gained from a significant change; the feasibility study also identifies the possible course of action for a solution. Evaluation of requirements feasibility evaluates whether or not the requirements can be met with the current technology. The requirements are evaluated according to whether the software can be used by existing professionals in their environments. Further, the requirements are evaluated on whether or not the cost of software development is acceptable to the customer. The evaluation of the requirements is summed up according to whether the requirements are technically, operationally, and economically feasible. The primary objectives are to confirm that the requirements are reliable and that there are viable solutions available for software development. In such an evaluation, the software development team creates alternative solutions and selects the one that meets all the requirements and is acceptable to the customer.

Technical feasibility

Technical feasibility confirms that software can be developed with current technology and that the software can meet the defined requirements. The hardware and software either already exist or can be developed in time for implementation of the requirements. The analyst is convinced that the hardware and software will meet the requirements.

Operational feasibility

Operational feasibility means that the software can be developed within the constraints that have been placed on the operating environment. Operational feasibility ensures that the software that has been developed is compatible with the operating environment and meets the requirements for response time and capacity.

Economic feasibility

Economic feasibility means that developing the software for the requirements is an economically wise decision. In evaluating economic feasibility, the analyst considers software development costs, operating costs, and benefit estimations. A separate economic analysis is conducted for each alternative solution under consideration. Some of the recognized financial techniques such as break-even analysis, return on investment, or discounted cash flow are used in the economic feasibility study.

Cost/benefits analysis

The cost/benefits analysis involves analyzing the monetary and nonmonetary costs and benefits of satisfying the requirements and solving the problem. If this cost/benefit analysis shows that the costs will outweigh the potential benefits, the analyst will recommend that the project be scrapped. Use of the analyst's report will help to decide whether or not to go ahead.

There may be several approaches that will satisfy the requirements. So that a reasonable recommendation is made as to which approach should be followed, it's necessary to estimate the costs, benefits, and risks associated with each alternative. The purpose of defining potential alternative solutions is to determine that there's at least one approach that will satisfy the requirements and provide a reasonable benefit. A comparative evaluation of the possible alternatives determines and recommends which approach will provide the best balance of benefits against the costs and risks involved. The following information should be developed for each alternative.

1. Software development costs are estimated. They're a major input in the economic evaluation of alternative approaches. Since the software development costs can't usually be estimated with a high degree of accuracy at this time, these estimates should not be considered as a firm project budget. Models such as a prototype and a rapid prototype can assist in this estimation. The main purpose at this time is to ensure that the project as a whole is economically feasible and to provide financial comparison between different alternatives.

   Total costs of developing software or acquiring software can be separated into direct or indirect costs. The direct costs are cash outlays for the sole purpose of software development in a new project. It's the spending of the allotted fund all at once or incrementally. The indirect costs are those already in existence. These are salaries of the current professionals. Figure 3-2 depicts the value of benefits in relation to costs.

2. Operating cost estimates provide the second major input to the economic evaluation of any proposed solution. Estimating operating costs also ensures that the project as a whole is economically feasible and provides a relative, if not completely accurate, financial comparison between different alternatives. These estimates are quite speculative and will be refined as the software development project progresses.

3. Estimated benefits provide the third major input to the economic evaluation of any proposed solution. Benefits are not easily measured. The benefits can be generally examined in three categories of increasing

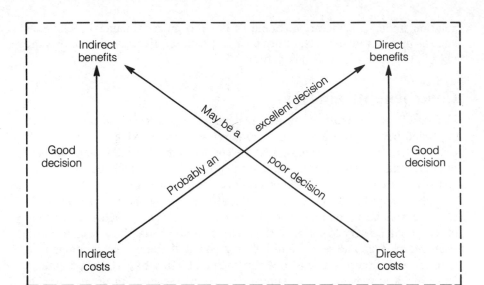

Fig. 3-2. Benefits and costs.

risk and decreasing measurability; these categories of benefits are: quantitative, qualitative, and intangible.

Software development costs, operating costs, and estimated benefits are usually considered when analyzing how to meet the defined requirements. These analyses should contain a low-cost "bare-bones" solution that meets the minimum requirements, an intermediate solution that meets all the requirements, and an expensive solution that extends beyond the current needs of the user.

Feasibility study objective

The feasibility study objective comes to an initial understanding of the requirements and decides whether or not it's feasible to proceed with a full-scale study of the requirements. There's no attempt by an analyst to actually find a solution to the requirements. He or she can use the additional assistance of a prototype and graphic models that present proposed solutions. A feasibility study ensures that the user is in agreement with the analysis of the requirements. A feasibility study identifies the objectives of the system by investigating functional objectives, by analyzing costs, by analyzing management's decision making, and by identifying weaknesses in present control systems.

The feasibility study typically requires 5 percent of the total project costs and takes four to twenty weeks for completion. The effort required depends on the size, complexity, and risk of the proposed solution and the extent of justification needed for the project's future development.

Planning the feasibility study

Planning the feasibility study is an important phase in understanding the requirements for software development. This planning is the prime phase, which lets the project go ahead or be scrapped. The major steps in planning this phase are establishing objectives, selecting tasks/activities, developing a logical network, breaking the network into work-units, arranging resources, and sizing the project as follows.

- Select required phases, tasks, and activities for the details of the project.
- Develop a detailed logical network for the phase.
- Estimate resources required for performing the tasks and activities as shown in the network.
- Break down the feasibility study network into work-units that should not exceed a given limitation, such as ten workdays each.
- Based on work-units, prepare a detailed schedule and budget for the feasibility study.
- Arrange resources and define responsibilities.
- Size the total project and estimate the likely impact of a potential solution.
- Develop procedures for controlling the feasibility study.

There are three normal aspects of good phase control. These are as follows.

- Quality.
- Time.
- Cost.

The quality ensures that the results meet expectations. The time ensures that the results are obtained within the planned time schedule. The cost ensures that the results are obtained within the authorized phase budget. It's not necessary that these steps be performed sequentially. Iteration will be necessary for some of these steps.

Feasibility verification

Feasibility verification evaluates the alternatives and recommends which of the alternatives will best meet the project objectives and satisfy the customer's requirements. The verification will provide the best balance of costs, risks, and benefits. The evaluation of the alternatives requires a comparative analysis of project objectives, technical feasibility, operational feasibility, economic feasibility, and risks. The analyst selects the one best alternative solution and presents to the customer. He or she develops the recommendations on the basis of a reasonable balance of feasibility, costs, benefits, and risks.

A good technique displays the evaluation criteria and the solution alternatives in the form of a matrix. Low, medium, and high are then entered into the boxes, depending on how highly a particular alternative is rated against the evaluation criteria. The development of recommendations usually involves an element of compromise. For example, a particular alternative may be very attractive from an economic standpoint, but may be eliminated because of high risk.

Requirements feasibility review

A requirements feasibility review is conducted by the analyst and presents the findings and recommendations of the requirements reliability and feasibility study. The audience consists of decision makers that decide whether or not to proceed into the subsequent phases. The documented results of this phase are organized and formalized into the requirements reliability and feasibility report. This report is reviewed by management and the customer, and any pertinent issues are resolved at the review meeting. The basic elements of the report are tabulated in TABLE 3-1.

Table 3-1. Reliability and
Feasibility Report Basic Elements

Title page
Contents page
Management summary
Problem statement
Findings
Availability of existing related system software
Existing operating costs
Alternatives considered
  Description
  Economic analysis
  Risk analysis
Recommended solution
Future plans
Appendices

Sometimes more than one study is presented and the best one is selected, which is the most technically, operationally, and economically feasible one. The analyst presents alternative solutions along with his or her findings of technical, operational, and economic feasibilities. He or she recommends the best solution on the basis of cost/benefits. He or she uses many techniques, such as prototype models, in the presentations. The prime concern at this phase is that the user's agreement to the proposed approach is approved.

4

The
system requirements
specification process

The requirements specification process captures and records the requirements that have been defined so far. A requirements specification document is created and signed as an agreement between the customer and the software developer. This document ensures that the software developer has understood the requirements. The document also contains the baseline for functional, performance, interface, and design constraints. Any unresolved items should be reviewed, discussed, and resolved at this time.

Requirements specification

Requirements specification enables the software developer to understand exactly what the customer desires. The understanding of the requirements establishes the basis for agreement between the customer and the software developer concerning what is required. (See FIG. 4-1.)

Requirements specification provides a clear, concise, precise and unambiguous statement of the requirements. It covers all aspects of the functionality, performance, interfaces, and design constraints. The requirements are stated so that it's possible to objectively verify whether the delivered software will meet the requirements. TABLE 4-1 addresses the major components of requirements specifications. These are also illustrated in FIG. 4-2.

A *performance requirements specification* specifies system operation capacity, response times, system management, and availability. The capacity depends on the number of simultaneous users and networking requirements. The response times are especially for enquiry functions and online updating. The availability or usability depends on fault recovery, which includes fallback procedures and data reconstruction. The availability also includes the exception handling.

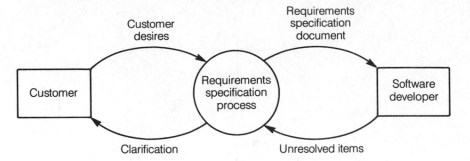

Fig. 4-1. The requirements specification process.

**Table 4-1. Major Components
of Requirements Specification**

- Performance requirements (operation concepts) specification
- Design requirements specification
- Interface requirements specification
- Testing specification

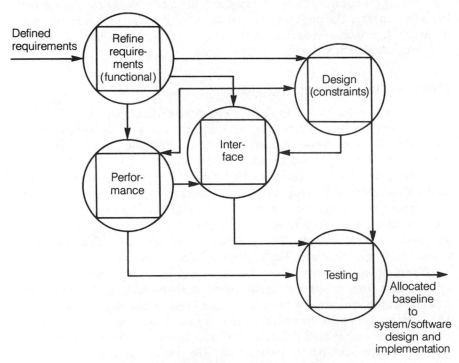

Fig. 4-2. Components of a requirements specification.

The *design requirements specification* includes constraints on specific technical design solutions so that certain requirements are met. These cover software, hardware, and user design constraints. The software design constraints are applicable standards and languages. This also includes the following standards.

- Analysis.
- Design.
- Implementation language.
- Data naming.
- Audit tracing.
- Communication.
- Interfaces.

The constraints include program size and data handling capabilities. The hardware design constraints include requirements that use specific types of hardware, details of the working environment, hardware reliability requirements, and mechanical and physical constraints. The user design constraints include the features of the operator/user and the environment in which the system will be functional.

The *interface requirements specification* describes the hardware and software interfaces across which the system communicates or interacts with its environment and with other systems. This specification should clearly define the boundary between functional inputs/outputs and interfaces. In addition, the boundary between the requirements and design should be explored. Basically, there are three interfaces, and they're specified as follows.

- Man-machine interfaces (MMI).
- Hardware interfaces.
- Software interfaces.

Man-machine interfaces support and enhance human capabilities. The interactive devices are user dialogues, graphics, and screen formats. The conversation between the person and the system is a complex protocol. These should be defined in terms of what response is created, to what inputs, in what combinations of situations. This covers ergonomic (human engineering) requirements for equipment and hardware devices.

Hardware interfaces include all kinds of interfaces via hardware to the external world. This covers maintaining precise timing requirements, analog measurements, and analog control. Communication interfaces are special cases of hardware interfaces. These include input and output communication ports, communication protocols and procedures, message formats, and throughput. Their specific problem is how to combine the following:

- Complex protocol.
- The timing and parallelism of other hardware interfaces.
- The need to maintain continued communication and data integrity under all circumstances.

Software interfaces are the procedure-call or language interfaces to other pieces of software. This includes any requirements for a specific operating system, a database management system, and an application package. The interfaces clarify the logical connection between data constructs that will be generated within the system and those in any other interacting system.

A *testing specification* identifies the risks and presents a process that can reduce these risks. Tests are designed to identify and reduce risks. Types of risk are as follows:

- Technical.
- Programmatic.
- Supportability.
- Cost.
- Scheduling.

Technical risks are associated with evolving a new design that will provide a greater level of performance than was previously demonstrated. These technical risks are in testing, modeling, integration interface, software design, requirement changes, operating environment, system complexity, unproven technology, fault detection, safety, and related properties. There are programmatic risks associated with obtaining and using applicable resources and activities. These are personnel skills, requirement changes, communication, security, safety, and environmental impact. Supportability risks are associated with fielding and maintaining systems that are currently being developed. These are reliability, maintainability, training, technical data, and safety. Cost and scheduling risks are associated with setting unreasonably low cost and scheduling objectives. Sources of cost risks are technical, programmatic, supportability, error estimating, and scheduling. Sources of schedule risk are technical, programmatic, supportability, scheduling, number of critical paths, and error estimating.

Risk can be high, medium, or low. High risks are difficult to solve. The high-risk problems are of significant importance. They can cause serious disruption in schedule, increase in cost, and degradation in performance. The medium-risk problems are less significant and are solvable, but with consequences. The medium-risk problems can cause disruption in schedule and degradation in performance. The low-risk problems are easily solvable. They can cause some minor disruption in schedule, increase in cost, and degradation in performance.

Risks and defects are directly related. During the early stages of requirements specification, it's cost-effective to identify defects that can cause risks. Requirements defects are very expensive if not detected before the formal or system test. Such defects lead to various degrees of risks. The percentage of software defects occurrence is depicted in FIG. 4-3. The correction of defects will cost more if not corrected when they occur, and this will cause risks, as illustrated in FIG. 4-4.

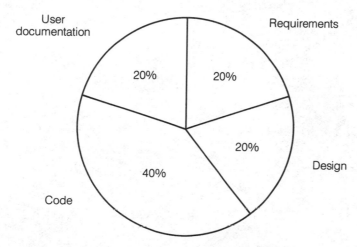

Fig. 4-3. Occurrences of software defects.

Characteristics of a good requirements specification

The characteristics of a good requirements specification are that the requirements have been specified uniquely. There's no duplication or overlapping of the requirements. The requirements are needed for further analysis. The requirements are feasible, implementable, and are not outside the capability of current technology. The requirements have been stated unambiguously and consistently. They can be evaluated. The requirements are complete and traceable. TABLE 4-2 outlines the characteristics of a good requirements specification.

Unambiguous   There should be only one interpretation of every stated requirement. The many ambiguities in natural language must be guarded against, and ambiguity can be avoided by using a formal requirements specification language.

Complete   Every significant requirement that's concerned with system function, performance, attributes, interfaces and design constraints should be included. Completeness also requires conformity with any specified standards. The terms and units used should be defined and all sections of the specification should be fully labeled.

Verifiable   Requirements can be verified if they're stated in concrete or absolute terms and involve measurable quantities.

Fig. 4-4. Defects were not corrected when they occurred.

Table 4-2.
Characteristics of a Good
Requirement Specification

- Unambiguous
- Complete
- Verifiable
- Consistent
- Modifiable
- Traceable
- Usable after development

Consistent   Stated requirements should not use conflicting terminology when referring to the same system element or call for different forms of logical or data structure.

Modifiable   The specification should be structured and annotated so that changes to requirements can be made easily, completely and consistently.

Traceable   The origin of each requirement should be clear, and the format of the specification should facilitate referencing both forwards and backwards.

Usable after development   After the system goes into operation, it should be possible to use the specification for the identification of maintenance requirements and constraints.

Requirements Specification Document

The Requirements Specification Document (RSD) is prepared by the software developer. It specifies the complete requirements for a system and becomes the functional baseline for the system. The format of the document is outlined in TABLE 4-3.

The *title page* contains the necessary information with regard to system name, number, who is preparing the document, and for whom the document is

Table 4-3.
Requirements Specification
Document Structure

1. Cover
2. Title page
3. Table of contents
4. Scope
5. Applicable documents
6. System requirements
   - Definition
   - Characteristics
   - System quality factor
     a. Reliability
     b. Maintainability
     c. Availability
   - Environmental conditions
   - Transportability
   - Flexibility
   - Portability
   - Design and construction
   - Documentation
   - Logistics
   - Personnel and training
   - Qualification
7. Quality assurance provisions
8. Preparation for delivery
9. Notes
10. Appendices

being prepared. This page also contains signatures of the person who approves the document and the person who is authenticating it.

The *table of contents* contains the title and page number of each paragraph and subparagraph. It also contains a list of page numbers for each figure, table, and appendix.

The *scope section* consists of the indentification number, title, and abbreviation, if applicable, of the system to which the document applies. The system overview consists of a brief summary, purpose of the system, and summary of the purpose and contents of the document.

The *applicable documents* section contains specifications, standards, drawings, and other publications such as manuals, regulations, handbooks, and bulletins.

The *system requirements* section specifies the requirements for the system. It consists of the following major paragraphs.

- Definition.
- Characteristics.
- Design and construction.
- Documentation.
- Logistics.
- Personnel and training.
- Qualification.

The definition paragraph provides a brief description of the system. This description addresses pertinent operational and logical considerations and concepts. This also includes a system diagram.

Characteristics paragraphs describe the requirements for system performance and physical characteristics. The performance characteristics specify the system's capabilities in the context of the states in which the system can exist and the modes of operation within each state. Each capability of the system is specified in uniquely identified subparagraphs in order for objective qualification to be provided. The *state name* identifies and provides a brief description of a state in which the system can exist, such as idle state, ready state, and deployed state. The *mode name* identifies and provides a brief description of the mode of operation, such as surveillance, and a threat evaluation within the system state. These subparagraphs specify a capability of the system by name and describe its purpose. They also identify the applicable parameters that are associated with the capability and express them in measurable terms.

The characteristics also include system capability relationships and external interface requirements. The external interface requirements describe requirements for interfaces with other systems. If necessary a separate document is created that provides the detailed information. The system external interface description identifies an external system with which this system interfaces. This subparagraph identifies the purpose of each interface and describes the relationship between each interface and the states and modes of the system. When possible, each interface specifies in detailed quantitative terms, such as dimensions, tolerances, loads, speeds, and communication protocol.

The physical characteristics specify the requirements for themselves as to weight limits and dimensional limits of the system. Additional considerations for determining physical requirements include transportation and storage, security, durability, safety, vulnerability, and color. Protective coatings specify requirements that assure protection from corrosion, abrasion, or other deleterious action.

System quality factors specify applicable requirements that pertain to system quality factors. These consist of the following factors:

- Reliability.
- Maintainability.
- Availability.

Reliability specifies requirements in quantitative terms and defines the conditions under which the reliability requirements are to be met. This subparagraph includes a reliability apportionment model that supports the apportionment of reliability values. These values are assigned a portion of system capabilities to help achieve desired system reliability.

Maintainability specifies quantitative maintainability requirements. The requirements apply to maintenance in the planned maintenance and support environment. Some examples are detailed as follows:

1. Mean and maximum down time, reaction time, turnaround time, mean and maximum time to repair, and mean time between maintenance actions.
2. Maximum effort required in the location and fixing of an error.
3. Maintenance work-hours per flying hour, maintenance work-hours per specific maintenance action, operational ready rate, maintenance hours per operating hour, and frequency of preventative maintenance.
4. Number of people, skill levels, and variety of support equipment.
5. Maintenance costs per operating hour, and work-hour per overhaul.

Availability specifies the degree to which the system shall be in an operable and committable state at the start of a mission that is called for at an unknown point in time.

Additional quality factors specify system quality requirements such as integrity, efficiency, or correctness of the requirements of the system.

Environmental conditions specify the environmental conditions that the system must withstand during transportation, storage, and operation, such as:

- Natural environment.
  a. Wind.
  b. Rain.

    c. Temperature.
    d. Geographic location.
- Induced environment.
    a. Motion.
    b. Shock.
    c. Noise.
    d. Electromagnetic radiation.
- Miscellaneous.
    a. Overpressure.
    b. Explosion.
    c. Radiation.

Transportability specifies any special requirements for transportation and material handling. In addition, all system elements that have operational or functional characteristics are unsuitable for normal transportation methods and should be identified.

Flexibility and *expansion* specify areas of growth that require planning for system flexibility and expansion. In addition, this subparagraph shall specify particular system elements that require spare capacity to support flexibility and expansion.

Portability specifies requirements for portability that are applicable to the system and permit employment, deployment, and logistic support.

Design and *construction* specify minimum system design and construction standards that have general applicability to system equipment, are applicable to major classes of equipment, or are applicable to particular design standards.

Materials specify those system-peculiar requirements that govern the use of materials, parts, and processes in the design of system equipment.

Safety specifies those requirements which are basic to the design of the system with respect to equipment characteristics, methods of operation, and environmental influences. It also specifies those safety requirements that prevent personnel injury and equipment degradation without degrading operational capability.

Human engineering specifies requirements for the system or for specific configuration items. It includes those specific areas, stations, or equipment required for concentrated human engineering attention due to the sensitivity of the operation or the importance of the task. Such areas might include those where the effects of human error would be particularly serious.

System security specifies requirements that are basic to the design of the system with respect to the operational environment of the system. It shall also specify those security requirements necessary for the prevention of compromise in sensitive information or materials.

Documentation specifies the requirements for system documentation such as specifications, drawings, technical manuals, test plans and procedures, and installation instruction data.

Logistics specifies logistic considerations and conditions that apply to the operational requirements. These considerations and conditions include maintenance, transportation modes, supply-system requirements, impact on existing facilities, and impact on existing equipment.

Personnel and training specify the requirements for personnel and training. It specifies requirements that must be integrated into system design. These requirements shall be the basis of determining system personnel training, training equipment, and training facilities.

Qualification states the requirements for, as applicable, verifying or validating capabilities in a specific application. Each qualification test shall be identified in a separate subparagraph, and the specific application shall be described. Requirements shall be included for the condition of testing, the time (program phase) of testing, period of testing, number of items to be tested, and any other pertinent qualification requirements.

Quality assurance provisions specify how the requirements so far defined and understood shall be satisfied. This will assign responsibilities for the performance of inspections of delivered products, materials, or services, and determine the compliance with all specified requirements. Special tests and examinations shall specify any special tests and examinations that are required for sampling, lot formation, qualification evaluation, and any other tests or examinations as necessary. Each test and examination shall be described in a separate subparagraph. Requirements with cross reference shall correlate each system requirement to the quality assurance provisions specified. This paragraph may refer to a requirements cross reference table that should be provided as an appendix to this specification.

Preparation for delivery specifies requirements for the preparation of the system and all its components for delivery, which includes packaging and handling.

Notes contain any general information that aids in understanding the document, such as background information and a glossary. This section contains an alphabetical listing of all acronyms, abbreviations, and their meanings as they were used in the document.

Appendices provide information published separately for convenience in document maintenance. As applicable, each appendix shall be referenced in the main body of the document where the data would normally be provided.

Formal requirements specification review

A formal requirements specification review is conducted so any differences in understanding the Requirements Specification Document (RSD) can be resolved. The presentation of a requirements specification includes both informal and formal parts. *Informal* means nondefinitive parts and *formal* means definitive parts. They're complementary, but they should be clearly delineated from each other. Whenever there are any doubts about the informal specifications, the formal ones should be used to resolve the doubts. The use of notations may be reasonable, with different degrees of formality for different types of requirements within a specification.

The presentation of requirements specification must at all times foster and promote communication among the attendees. An informal diagrammatic notation may help understand or reduce the time taken to achieve good communication. A formal mathematical notation with defined syntax and semantics will reduce the probability of errors of inconsistency and ambiguity. CASE tools are available that permit the expression of an underlying formal requirements model in a notation that neither intimidates nor requires extensive training and experience for understandability.

The outcome of the review is the approval of the Requirements Specification Document. It's agreed that the requirements have been understood completely, unambiguously, and clearly by the software developer and the customer. The budget and schedule should be adequate for successful completion of software development.

Benefits of requirements specification

Requirements specification provides a firm foundation for the system design phase. It further enables the planning of validation, verification and acceptance procedures that are to be done against a baseline for compliance. Requirements specification provides a starting point for all subsequent control and management of the software development project and includes estimates of cost, time, and resource scheduling.

5

The requirements
traceability process

The *requirements traceability process* tracks the specified requirements of the
Requirements Specification Documentation (RSD) throughout the software
life cycle. A table that shows this correspondence is called a *traceability matrix*.
The matrix confirms that the corresponding deliverable components correctly
satisfy the requirements. CASE tools are available that provide requirements
traccability for the convenience of customer and software developer. The
traceability CASE tools ensure that the information contained within the RSD
is neither created nor destroyed while allocating requirements. The CASE tool
produces comprehensive reports that explain how each RSD sentence has
been interpreted by the software developer.

Requirements traceability

Requirements traceability means that specified requirements are mapped onto
deliverable components throughout the software engineering process, as illustrated in FIG. 5-1. Traceability should also be forward and backward, and covered in all the software development documents. The mapping process is
called *allocation*. Allocation means that a particular software component
should satisfy a particular requirement. Well-defined requirements are properly allocated to targets. The requirements allocation assigns each requirement to the targets that should satisfy it. Ideally, every target has at least one
allocation. Targets with no allocations are unnecessary.

Importance of requirements traceability

The importance of requirements traceability is that the software developer
demonstrates the traceability of the requirements in software development

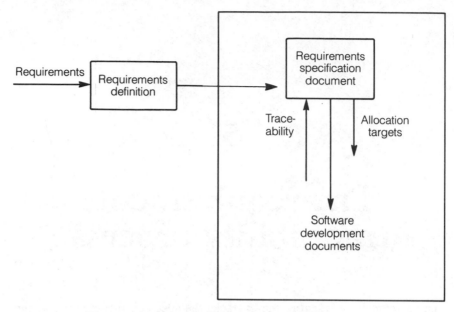

Fig. 5-1. Mapping a requirements specification document.

documentation, both forward and backward. It's especially important in defense systems, where multiple documents that contain thousands of pages of written requirements are produced. By following standards such as DOD-STD-2167A, the software developers must show at each milestone that their deliverables satisfy requirements for payment. At the end, the software developer not only completes the project on time and within budget but delivers products that satisfy requirements. The system is tested thoroughly in accordance with these requirements.

Many times, requirements interpretation depends upon the opinion of the analysts who view them. Normally, the interpretation of a requirements sentence is heterogeneous and not homogeneous. For example let's consider a typical requirements sample, as follows.

Example 5-1

"We need coast-to-coast coverage. The system will be deployed in California and New York. The system must be ready for service at 5:00 a.m. and shut down at 6:00 p.m."

Discussion Does the sentence mean 5:00 a.m. and 6:00 p.m. in each respective time zone, or is it Eastern Standard Time (EST) or Pacific Standard Time (PST)? Different analysts could make different assumptions. A careful analyst might actually call the customer and ask for an opinion. In a tight schedule, the analyst may simply create an implied requirement that would state his or her assumption and verify it with the customer later. (The implied requirements are implementation independent.)

After the software development enters the design phase, the software developer may decide that, ''The system shall contain a real-time clock that tells the date and time-of-day'' rather than rely on a human operator who would start the system. The requirement should be derived from the RSD, which determines the system's daily hours of service. Figure 5-2 depicts the relationship between sentences in the document and true requirements. This figure reveals the difficulty of managing the requirements analysis and allocation procedures. The goal of analysis should be to build a consensus about what's nonessential text, implicit requirements, and derived requirements. TABLE 5-1 categorizes the sentences of the previously discussed requirements example.

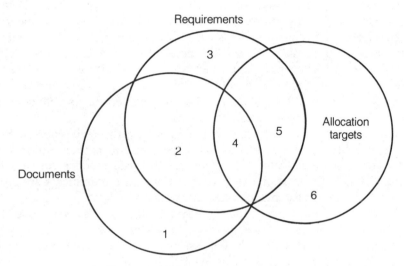

1. Nonessential text
2. Explicit, unallocated requirements
3. Implied or derived, unallocated requirements
4. Explicit, allocated requirements
5. Implied or derived, allocated requirements
6. Unnecessary components

Fig. 5-2. Requirements classification.

Table 5-1. Category of Sentences in Example 5-1

Category #	Category Description	Sentence
1.	Nonessential text	''We need coast-to-coast coverage.''
2.	Requirement	''The system will be deployed in California and New York.''
3.	Requirement	''The system must be ready for service at 5:00 a.m. and shut down at 6:00 p.m.''
4.	Implied requirement	''Eastern Standard Time will be used to determine when the system is operational.''

Each sentence in a document may or may not represent a requirement. To make matters worse, some sentences contain many requirements. For example, the requirement "It must be big, red, and eat rocks" can be split into three separate requirements for clarity and understandability.

Requirements traceability CASE tools

Requirements traceability CASE tools are emerging in the computer industry. The best CASE tools are those that trace the requirements to deliverables and back again and provide products that satisfy requirements. Once the software is developed, it must also be maintained throughout its life cycle. Requirements will modify, delete, and update the defects during the life cycle. Determine which components are responsible for defects and which components will be impacted by enhancement requests. If requirements can be traced to deliverables and back again, the needs of development and maintenance engineers can be met. The size and complexity of today's software development presents enormous challenges to software developers who try to control them. CASE tools are needed for automating the mapping documents onto deliverables so that requirements traceability is feasible.

Many in-house tools are available and can trace the requirements. But these tools suffer from the lack of formal support, documentation and maintenance. Text editors are commonly used, and they can produce traceability matrices because the start-up costs are low. Here the requirements are typically identified in one list and allocated in others.

A text editor doesn't ensure that all the requirements have been defined as stated in the Requirements Specification Document. There's no automated check that verifies that all requirements are allocated. This situation is aggravated when there are many-to-many relationships between document sentences and requirements. There is no convenient way of recording different interpretations of the documents so an accurate consensus can be built. When documents or requirements change, the process of updating all of the obsolete references is labor-intensive and error-prone.

IBM-PC equivalents that run user-friendly Data Base Management System (DBMS) software are a common and inexpensive platform that builds requirements traceability tools, as shown in FIG. 5-3. Software developers use the 4GL of the DBMS and build a trace tool on top of it. Here, the requirements are commonly identified in one table; targets are identified in another table, and allocation is done in a third table. The single-user DBMS offers no help in defining or determining requirements that all have been accurately entered into the database. There's no convenient way of recording different interpretations of the documents so an accurate consensus can be built. Usually, the schemas of such databases support neither the many-to-many relationship between sentences and requirements nor the many-to-many relationships between requirements and targets. There may be no backup and restore regimen that will ensure database roll-back or recovery. There may be storage capacity and performance

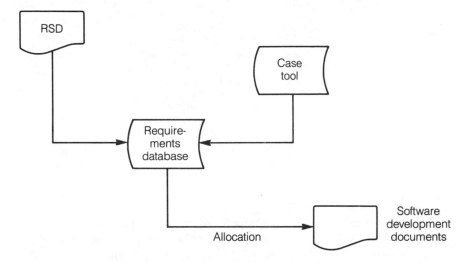

Fig. 5-3. Allocating requirements to targets.

problems for large systems. The trace database may not be integrated with the file systems where the design, code and/or test procedure database resides. Thus verification of the allocated requirements is difficult.

As an alternative, a multiuser DBMS enables the software developers to work in parallel on a given database, provides adequate storage capacity for large systems, and usually makes the trace database accessible on the same platform that's used in the development of targets. Otherwise, the drawbacks of this approach are the same as for the single-user DBMS case described previously.

Another approach is that the software developer will take soft copies of the source documents and insert tags in the appropriate places so requirements and record allocations are uniquely identified. A scanner generates a database that cross-references requirements and targets. Here the software developer can't work in parallel on the same source document. It takes too much time for the scanner to regenerate the entire database after an update. There's usually no syntax checking performed when entering the tags. Data entry errors are detected slowly during the scan and then corrected. Then the scan must be restarted.

Selection criteria
for a good requirements CASE tool

The selection criteria for a good requirements CASE tool are that it consists of the minimum properties, as tabulated in TABLE 5-2. *Integrity traceability* assures that the information contained within the Requirement Specification Document is neither created nor destroyed while allocating requirements. The tool must produce comprehensive reports that tell the customer how each sentence was interpreted.

Table 5-2.
Properties of a Good
Requirements CASE Tool

- Integrity traceability
- Document analysis
- Allocation minimizing
- Consensus achievement
- Allocation schemas
- Platform choice
- Changing requirements
- Entire life cycle integration

Document analysis is a prime property of the CASE tool. The tool should present a document so that the software developer merely points and clicks with a mouse to record a judgement about a sentence in the document. The integrity of the document must not be compromised. Only a baselined or frozen document should be analyzed. Otherwise, allocations based on changing text would be undermined in an uncontrolled fashion. In order for the support of point-and-click document analysis, the tool must parse the document into the elements of allocation: sections, paragraphs and sentences. The parser should be rule-based and accommodate various input formats with embedded control sequences. It must be possible to override the results of automated parsing.

Allocation minimizing is essential for efficiency of the CASE tool. For example, if there are 10 requirements and 10 targets in each of the 10 project phases, 1000 allocations might be maintained. Every requirement that's eliminated could reduce the maintenance burden by 100 allocations. Therefore, it's essential that the trace tool helps minimize the number of requirements for allocation. Every sentence in a document doesn't represent an individual requirement. Adjacent sentences often support each other. It should be possible to bundle contiguous sentences into mutually exclusive regions to more concisely restate the requirement represented by a given region.

Consensus achievement can resolve the disharmony by adopting the dominant judgement. The CASE tool should allow different users to record their analyses of the same document separately. There should be a report that itemizes any disagreements between analysts.

Allocation schemas should easily display a given target in order to evaluate the quality of its allocations. The trace tool should support dynamic navigation to targets so that an allocation can quickly display its target. Conversely, given a target, it should be easy to cause the trace tool to display either target's allocations.

The process of finding which requirements apply to a given target could become very labor-intensive as the number of requirements grows. The CASE tool should enable and associate user-defined key words with each requirement, and the tool should classify and query the key words. The granularity of key word classifications becomes too coarse as the number of targets grows. Fortunately, a given target, A1, is usually part of a larger target, A, and the requirements that apply to A1 are a subset of those that apply to A. The CASE tool should allow leverage to the hierarchical relationships between targets so that allocation can easily migrate top-down or bottom-up. A software developer in the early stages of a project will allocate large groups of requirements to macro components that then "trickle down" to subcomponents. The software developer who begins requirements allocation in the later stages of the development will allocate requirements to low-level components and then consolidate upwards.

The link that enables allocations to be visible between parent and child targets is called an *allocation channel*. A given target may have an allocation channel from multiple parents. Targets that represent reusable components will have many parents within the same phase. The CASE tool should navigate through these allocation channels.

The *platform choice* is a network of workstations. The large bit-mapped graphics display of workstations allows the requirements and their allocation targets to be seen simultaneously in multiple windows. This makes verifying the accuracy of the allocations easy. The network gives multiple software developers the same requirements database.

Changing requirements assimilates document revisions. A revision may be in the form of a complete replacement or changing sheets. The impact of such changes on the previous analysis and allocation efforts should be limited to those portions of the database that depend on the individual sentences that are changed or deleted. Before the changes are applied, it should be possible to produce a report that predicts the impact of the change. Otherwise, it will be difficult to accurately predict how much the change will cost in time and resources. The targets of requirement allocations are in constant flux. When a target is updated or deleted, all allocations to that target must be inspected or reallocated.

Entire life cycle integration includes hardware and software designs, source code, and test plans. The CASE tool should allocate requirements to any type of target. The tool should have an open architecture that will support such features as point-and-click bidirectional navigation to targets that are managed by other tools. Couple navigation to and from external objects that have the ability to navigate through allocation channels should effectively integrate all phases of the software life cycle.

Requirements Tracer (RT) tool

Requirements Tracer (RT) tool, developed by Teledyne Brown Engineering, is an automation aid for system developers. The RT traces the system requirements as defined in the Requirements Specification Document. From a database of natural language requirements for which various criteria have been defined or an attribute assigned, relationships between requirements can be established. The RT then creates a requirements traceability matrix that assists the user in verifying proper requirements allocation. The RT operation is based on a user-friendly "point-and-click" interface that consists of pop-up menus and templates that provide simplicity of use for system developers. The RT output includes a variety of listings and requirements reports.

RT methodology

The Requirements Tracer (RT) tool provides automated support for requirements tracing activities. These activities include extracting requirements from a specification, assigning unique identification numbers, tracing requirements through different specification levels, and creating a trace matrix. With the RT, requirements can be extracted from a source specification, or manually entered by the user, for storage in the RT database. Any number of specification levels can be included for a single system. Attributes and keywords can be assigned to each requirement statement. For example, an attribute might be a file name for an engineering drawing or source code module. Key words, such as communications, Block-1-Build, or algorithms might be assigned according to a user-defined cataloguing taxonomy.

Requirement tracing is based primarily on parent/child relationships in a requirements hierarchy. Other criteria assist in the tracing task, including optional mapping to a function/subfunction hierarchy and attribute and key word values. Tracing results in creation of a requirements trace matrix.

Figure 5-4 shows an RT system diagram composed of four specifications: SPEC A, SPEC B, SPEC C, and SPEC D. As indicated, the four specifications originated from separate source documents. The lines interconnecting the specification blocks represent requirement traceability.

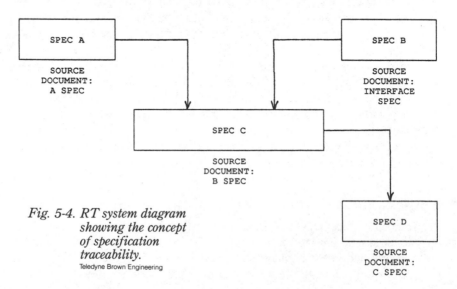

*Fig. 5-4. RT system diagram
showing the concept
of specification
traceability.*
Teledyne Brown Engineering

A *specification*, in RT technology, is a set of requirements taken from a source document. A system is a collection of one or more specifications stored in the RT database. Specifications represent various levels of requirements for the same application.

Requirement fields

A requirement is composed of the following fields: SPEC (specification), ID, Function, Date, Paragraph, Requirement Number, Paragraph Title, and Requirement Text. Not all fields are required. The SPEC field identifies the specification to which the requirement belongs and the Requirement Text field contains the actual requirement. These two fields are user-defined and mandatory. The ID field contains an integer value assigned to the requirement, and the Date field contains the date the requirement was entered or last modified. The ID and Date fields are mandatory and are generated by the RT. The remaining requirement fields are optional. The Function field contains the function, if any, to which requirements are assigned. The Paragraph and Paragraph Title fields are user-defined identifiers, usually taken from the requirement source document. The Requirement Number field is another user-defined identifier, associated with the indicated Paragraph, and must be unique within the paragraph. The Paragraph field contains the actual paragraph number from the source document containing the requirement. The Paragraph Title field is a string of characters identifying the same source paragraph. The Requirement Number field identifies requirements within a paragraph. A meaningful format can be selected because the field is user-defined. For example, the user can choose to use the paragraph number followed by a dash (-) and another number representing a breakdown of the paragraph. However, the actual format can be individually established by the user, although some restrictions must be observed. Optional fields can be entered as the requirement is entered, or later. An overview of this requirements definition philosophy is shown in FIG. 5-5.

Working set

A *working set* is the current set of requirements available during an interactive session. The working set is a subset of the RT database but can include the entire database. The user can reduce the number of working set requirements based on any of the following criteria: specification, function, subfunction, attribute value, key word, requirement text, or paragraph. Reductions can be made repeatedly to any number of levels. For example, a user may wish to view the requirements from a particular specification that concern a specified function. These requirements can be defined as the working set. From that working set, the user may be interested in a particular subfunction. The current working set can be reduced to include only those requirements allocated to the specified subfunction. If more than one subfunction is specified, the "or" operation is in effect. That is, a requirement is included in the working set if that requirement is allocated to at least one of the specified subfunctions.

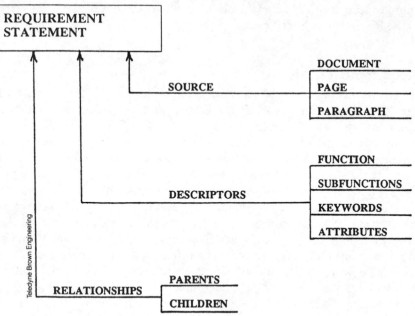

Fig. 5-5. RT approach to cataloging requirements statements.

If desired, further reductions can be made. This concept is shown in FIG. 5-6. Any working set definition can be saved for later use.

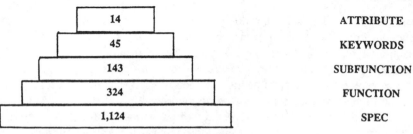

Fig. 5-6. Using the working set to identify unique requirements cataloging. Teledyne Brown Engineering

Requirement associations

Before requirements can be traced, some method must be used to associate the requirements. The RT provides three such methods: parent/child relationships, function/subfunction hierarchy, and attribute/key word values.

Parent/child relationships

The basis of requirements tracing is the parent/child relationship. A *child* of a given requirement is one that must be satisfied before the parent requirement can be satisfied. A child can belong to any number of parents and a parent can have any number of children. A parent requirement with multiple children is not satisfied until all of the child requirements are satisfied. The collection of parent/child relationships for a specific system establishes the requirements hierarchy for that system. Each requirement in the hierarchy depends upon all of its descendants (lower-level requirements) and is depended upon by all of its ancestors (higher-level requirements). The RT assists the user in defining the parent/child relationships and thus establishing the requirements hierarchy. Figure 5-7 is a graphical description of a parent/child relationship. In this example, SPEC A contains a requirement whose specifications rely on requirements stated in SPEC B and SPEC C. The interconnecting lines represent requirement traceability. Example requirements statements are included to provide a clear representation.

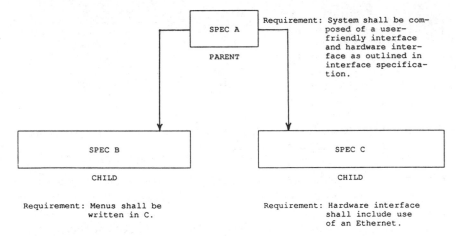

Fig. 5-7. A parent/child relationship diagram showing top/down requirements specification traceability. Teledyne Brown Engineering

Function/subfunction hierarchy

Functions/subfunctions are trace criteria that assist the user in defining parent/ child relationships. *Functions* are major system divisions to which a requirement belongs; *subfunctions* are a level of system division below functions. A requirement can be assigned to only one function but can be allocated to multiple subfunctions. A parent/child relationship can be defined only if the child requirement function is a parent requirement subfunction. However, function/subfunction hierarchy use is optional; parent/child relationships can be defined when no such hierarchy exists. The system function/subfunction hierarchy must be consistent with the requirements hierarchy as defined by the parent/child relationships. Function/subfunction assignments can be made before or after the parent/child relationships are defined. If assignments are made after the relationships are defined, the RT will not allow any assignments that conflict with the requirements hierarchy, as defined by the relationships. Conversely, if parent/child relationships are defined after function/subfunction assignments are made, the RT will not allow any relationships that conflict with the function/subfunction hierarchy.

Figure 5-8 is a graphical description of a functional hierarchy with the parent/child relationships respected. The System Specification functional area

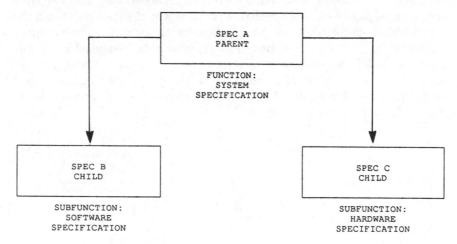

Fig. 5-8. A functional hierarchy diagram showing top/down functional decomposition traceability. <small>Teledyne Brown Engineering</small>

contains two subfunction areas: Software Specification and Hardware Specification. In FIG. 5-8, at least one requirement in SPEC A must be allocated to the subfunction Software Specification, and at least one requirement must be allocated to the subfunction Hardware Specification. It's possible for one SPEC A requirement to be allocated to both subfunctions. Although only two levels are shown, a function/subfunction hierarchy has no limit to the number of levels allowed. The only restriction regarding levels is that the functional hierarchy and requirements hierarchy must be consistent with each other.

Attribute/key word values
Attributes and key words provide techniques for associating requirements, whether or not parent/child relationships exist between the requirements.

Attributes and key words are independent of any functional or requirements hierarchy.

An attribute consists of a user-defined label and a value. Any number of attributes can be defined. A value can be assigned to each attribute for each system requirement. The values can be assigned as requirements are entered, or later. Attributes can be used as an aid in the tracing process. Two requirements can be associated if both have the same specified attribute value. However, this association doesn't establish any formal relationships between the requirements. If a parent/child relationship is desired, the user must specifically define the relationship.

A *key word* is a text identifier that can be actual text from a requirement or a derived word (phrase) describing a requirement. Key words are user-defined, and any number are allowed. Key words can be assigned to a requirement when the requirement is entered in the system or later. As with attributes, key words are used as an aid in tracing. Requirements can be associated using key words, but no parent/child relationships are established unless specifically defined by the user. Figure 5-9 is a list of possible attributes, possible associated values, and a list of possible key words for a given requirement. Both lists are based on the same requirement.

```
Requirement: System shall be composed of menus for user interfaces
             and hardware interface outlined in interface
             specification.
```

ATTRIBUTE	POSSIBLE VALUES
USER INTERFACE	MENU SHELL DRIVEN
HARDWARE SYSTEM	WORKSTATION PC MAIN FRAME

KEYWORDS
SYSTEM
INTERFACE

Fig. 5-9. Attribute and key-word list assignments to a requirements statement.
Teledyne Brown Engineering

Requirement trace process

The requirement trace process consists of two preliminary activities, and actual requirements tracing. The preliminary activities are requirement definition and function assignment.

Requirement definition

Requirements can be defined (entered in the system) by extraction from a source document or by manual entry. For extraction, the RT uses two windows. The source document is displayed in the lower window and, as each requirement is extracted, text is entered in the requirement text field in the upper window. Alternatively, text can be manually entered by the user in the requirement text field. Figure 5-10 shows an RT display screen.

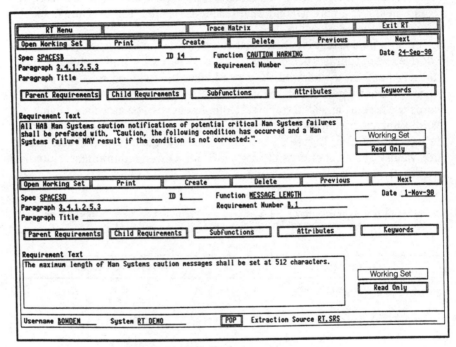

Fig. 5-10. RT display. Teledyne Brown Engineering

If the extraction process is used to extract requirements from a source document, the document must exist as an ASCII file. This file can be created using any appropriate procedure, such as an optical character reader (OCR) or a text editor.

Function assignment

Following requirement definition, function assignments and subfunction allocations can be made. A requirement can be assigned to only one function. The RT allows the user to manually enter the desired function for a requirement or select a function from a previously entered list of acceptable functions.

Requirements are allocated to subfunctions in the same manner as function assignment, either direct entry or selection from a previously defined list. However, one requirement can be allocated to any number of subfunctions.

The subfunctions at one level will become functions at the next lower level of the requirements hierarchy.

Function assignments and subfunction allocations can be made in either a top-down or bottom-up manner. In the top-down approach, requirements at the highest level of the requirements hierarchy are assigned to functions and allocated to subfunctions. The same procedure is then performed at the next lower level, where the subfunctions already allocated become functions to which requirements can be assigned. Subfunction allocations are also made, and these subfunctions become functions for the next lower level. The process continues until all levels are complete. In the bottom-up approach, requirements at the lowest level are assigned to functions. These functions become subfunctions for the next higher level of the hierarchy. Requirements at that level are allocated to the subfunctions and also assigned to functions, which then become subfunctions for the next higher level. The process continues until complete.

Requirement tracing

Requirement tracing is the creation of parent/child relationships between a specific requirement (the parent) and its associated child requirements. To determine whether a relationship should be established between two requirements, the user can view any or all of the following: functions, subfunctions, attributes, and key words. The only restriction on establishing a parent/child relationship is that the relationship not violate the functional hierarchy, if such a hierarchy already exists. The user can also examine previously created parent/child relationships and delete any that are not appropriate.

As parent/child relationships are established, RT builds a trace matrix based on those relationships. The user can view the trace to determine what dependencies exist among the requirements. This helps resolve issues such as whether all high-level system requirements have been included in a lower-level specification, or whether all high-level requirements have been tested.

6

Requirements and system engineering

Upon acceptance of the RSD, the requirements are tentatively frozen by the user. The software developer is expected to have understood these requirements, and design of the system should start. This chapter presents the highest level of system engineering, in which the software developer identifies hardware and software that will be used and allocates the requirements to computer software configuration items. RqT, a CASE tool by CADRE, is also discussed in this chapter.

Building a system

The building of a system requires identification of hardware for which the software will be developed. The requirements for the system will be derived from the RSD. Identification of hardware depends on the customer, who provides the necessary tools and instruments that will be used by the software developers. This process assists the software developers so the software is tested in accordance with the requirements. Any further discussion of hardware is beyond the scope of this book.

Identification of software depends on whether it's a new development, a re-use of the available existing software, a re-engineering of the software, or a reverse engineering process. A lot of commercial off-the-shelf (COTS) software is available that can suit the requirements. The knowledge and experience of the system analyst/engineer plays a major role in this selection decision. The selection must be the right software for the right requirements.

New development

In new development, it's customary that various software development phases are met. These are stated in FIG. 6-1. The major phases are requirements anal-

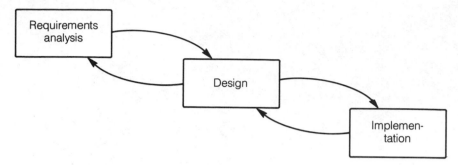

Fig. 6-1. Software development phases.

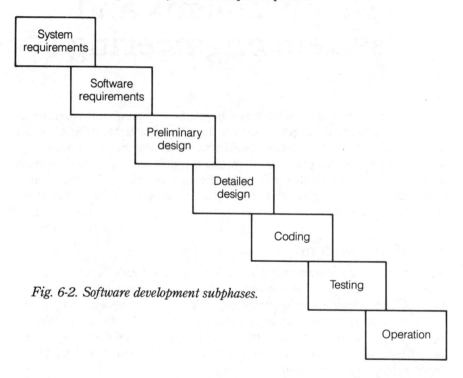

Fig. 6-2. Software development subphases.

ysis, design, and implementation. These can be further divided into sub-phases, as shown in FIG. 6-2. Most of these phases are reiterative and exemplify a typical waterfall model. Various models have been discussed in detail in my book, *Software Engineering Methods, Management, and CASE Tools*.

New development normally follows a set of prescribed standards, methods, and CASE tools. Traditionally, the process moves from high-level abstractions, logical implementation, and independent designs to the physical implementation of a system. It follows a sequence that goes from requirements through the design of the implementation. It leads forward to new development of software throughout the life-cycle phases. It starts from the initial phase of analysis of the new requirements and moves forward to the development of all phases of analysis until completion of the project.

Reusable software means that software that's been developed in response to the requirements for one application can be used, in whole or in part, to satisfy the requirements of another application. The system analyst should find a way to use existing software, which is pretested and thus saves cost and time. The basic approach is configuration and specialization of preexisting software components into viable application systems. Studies suggest that initial use of reusable software during architectural design specification is a way to speed implementation.

Reverse engineering

Reverse engineering extracts design artifacts and builds or synthesizes abstractions that are less implementation dependent. This process implements changes that are made in later phases of the existing software and automatically brings back the early phases. It starts from any level of abstraction or at any stage of the life cycle. It covers a broad range that starts from the existing implementation, then recaptures or recreates the design, and finally deciphers the requirements that are actually implemented by the system.

Re-engineering

Re-engineering is the renovation, reclamation, examination, and alteration of the existing system software for the changing requirements. This process will reconstitute the existing system software into a new form and the subsequent implementation of the new form. Re-engineering dominates during the software maintenance life cycle. It helps identify and separate those systems that are worth maintaining from those that should be replaced.

System engineering requirements characteristics

System engineering consists of requirements for the hardware and software. Requirements characteristics specify their uniqueness and completeness. The software developer ensures that the requirements do not overlap and are not duplicate. The requirements are necessary in the development of system engineering. They're feasible and implementable. The requirements must not be outside the capability of current technology. They must be consistent and stated unambiguously. These requirements must be evaluated. There must be a feasible way to determine that the requirements have been satisfied and are traceable forward and backward. The requirements must state "what" will be implemented, not "how" to implement them.

Three types of requirements are generally identified from the Requirement Specification Document, which is the system functional baseline. The requirements are identified as explicit, implicit, or derived. The explicit requirements are part of the functional baseline; whereas, the implicit requirements are implied by nature or by special knowledge of the system, although not stated or expressed in the functional baseline. Implicit requirements may include requirements that are derived from a specified technical understanding of the system. The derived requirements are also unstated in the functional baseline but may be deduced from structure, relationship, or nature of the system. These requirements will be correctly and seamlessly mapped in the system design.

Computer software configuration item selection criteria

A computer software configuration item (CSCI) is not easy to select. The software developer must conduct a proper analysis and select one or more CSCIs. The selection criteria depend on the following factors:

- System requirements.
- Hardware.
- Software.
- Requirements allocation.
- User acceptance.
- Schedule.
- Cost.

It's better that the system requirements are partitioned and allocated to the lesser number of CSCIs for effective cost and time. The more the number of CSCIs, the more work in the creation of the volume of documents, which further leads to more manpower that's needed in the checking of the documents. This schema will definitely need more time and cost. The ideal number of selection is from one to three CSCIs.

Allocating requirements to CSCI

The software developer will determine the best allocation of system requirements to a CSCI. The software developer will define a set of engineering requirements for each CSCI by showing the system architecture and its interfaces. The operational concepts of the system will be explored. Its functional and operational environments will be discussed.

A sample system architecture is illustrated in FIG. 6-3. It represents the allocation of system hardware and software resources. Graphically, it represents the picture of the system when built. It's the top-level model that shows all the interfaces with external entities. The context of the system is presented graphically. If more than one CSCI has been selected, it's better that the system architecture be shown for each CSCI for clarification. It's important that meaningful names be given to the CSCI and interfaces. These names will be

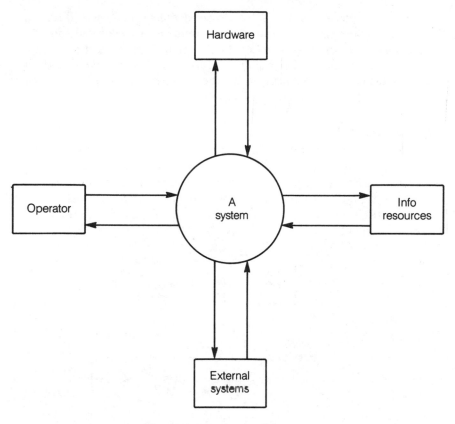

Fig. 6-3. A system architecture.

carried out throughout the software development life cycle. This top-level graphic becomes the foundation of system software development.

The requirements must be segregated between automated and manual. Only the automated requirements will be allocated to the CSCI for software development. The automated requirements also consist of environmental and operational requirements. All of these requirements are derived from the RSD.

RqT

RqT is a CASE tool developed by CADRE Technologies Inc. It amalgamates with Teamwork and tracks large systems requirements that must adhere to rigorous quality standards. Tightly integrated with Cadre's workstation-based full life cycle CASE environment, Teamwork/RqT helps the software developer automate the requirements engineering. Then, through requirements traceability, the CASE tool tracks project progress and completeness and shows relationships between system requirements and actual deliverables throughout all phases of the software development life cycle. From the Requirements Specification Document, requirements are allocated and specified by work breakdown structures such as analysis, design, test procedures, and code. Teamwork/RqT helps automate this entire process and ensures that all requirements have been met and that the final software products will meet all requirements.

RqT discussion

Figure 6-4 presents the context diagram and shows the integration of Teamwork and RqT CASE tools. RqT has its own database that's separate from teamwork. An RqT project can allocate requirements to targets whose external objects reside in a multiple teamwork database. The context diagram shows how RqT interfaces with its environment. Figure 6-5 represents the data flow diagram.

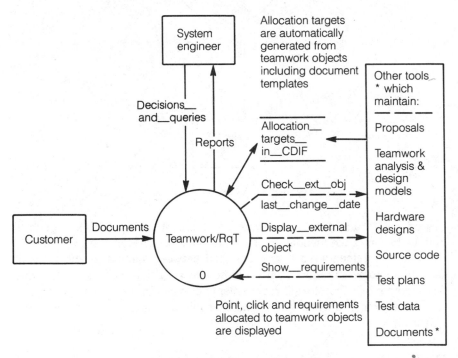

Fig. 6-4. A context diagram of Teamwork/RqT. Cadre Technologies

Teamwork/RqT takes soft-copies of the requirements source documents as input and automatically parses them into section, paragraphs and sentences, as shown in FIG. 6-6. The parser is rule-based so that RqT can be extended and accept ASCII documents with embedded mark-up commands. RqT presents a WYSIWYG (What You See Is What You Get) display of a parsed document so that the user can interactively override RqT's parsing

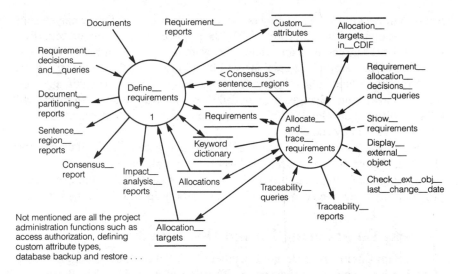

Fig. 6-5. A data-flow diagram of Teamwork/RqT. Cadre Technologies

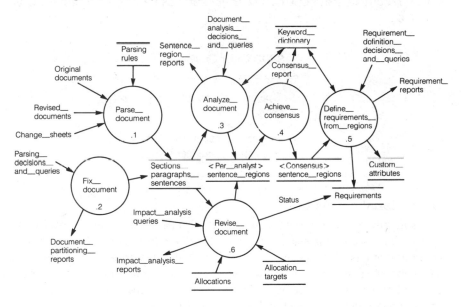

Fig. 6-6. Parses into section, paragraphs and sentences. Cadre Technologies

decision. Parsed requirements documents can then be displayed and analyzed interactively so the essential requirements can be extracted and consolidated. Actual requirements may be taken directly from the document text or may be summarized and restated from the RSD. Redundant sentences found in the documents can be represented by a single requirement for allocation. Allocation labor is thus reduced without losing any data.

RqT manages the process of building a consensus among software analysts/engineers as to the meaning of the source documents. Each analyst/engineer votes on his or her interpretation of the requirements document text. RqT reports the disagreements and allows the system analyst/engineer a choice as to which of the conflicting opinions will be adopted. RqT also accepts document revision, which allows the software developer to map the changes onto the original. Before changes are applied, a report can be generated that will tell the software developer all of the requirements, allocations and targets that will be impacted by the change.

An allocation target can be linked to multiple parents as well as multiple children. Teamwork structured analysis objects can be mapped onto structured design objects across multiple models. The same links that are used in propagating allocations can be used for navigation up and down the life cycle.

System Engineering Design Document

The System Engineering Design Document (SEDD) contains the highest level of design information for the system. The SEDD describes the allocation of system requirements to CSCIs. The major outlines for the SEDD are listed in TABLE 6-1.

Table 6-1.
SEDD Major Outlines

1. Operational concepts
2. System architect
3. System design
4. Processing resources
5. Requirements traceability

Operational concepts

The software developer summarizes the user's needs that must be met by the system. The primary mission of the system will be described. The operational environment describes the environment in which the system will be employed. The support environment describes the operational system during the production and deployment phase of the life cycle. It covers the use of multipurpose or automated test equipment and maintenance criteria.

System architecture

System architecture describes the internal structure of the system. The CSCIs and HWCIs will be identified and their purpose summarized. The purpose of each external interface will be explained. A graphical system architecture will be included for clarification.

System design

System design consists of the identification of each HWCI, CSCI, and manual operation of the system. A description of the relationships of HWCIs, CSCIs, and manual operations within the system will be described. Each CSCI will be named uniquely. Each requirement from the RSD to the CSCI will be identified. Each external interface to the system that's addressed by the CSCI will be recorded as follows:

- Bits per second.
- Word length.
- Message format.
- Frequency of messages.
- Priority rules.
- Protocol.

Any design constraints on the CSCI will be described. The internal interfaces to the system will be described, and system state and mode will be discussed.

Processing resources

Processing resources covers hardware, programming, design, coding, and use characteristics of the processing resource. These characteristics include the following parameters:

- Memory size. Amount of internal memory (absolute, spare, or both) of the computer.
- Word size. Number of bits in each computer word.
- Processing speed. Computer processor capacity (absolute, spare, or both).
- Character set standard.
- Instruction set architecture.
- Interrupt capabilities of the hardware.
- Direct Memory Access.
- Channel requirements.
- Auxiliary storage.
- Growth capabilities of any part of the processing resource.
- Diagnostic capabilities.
- Allocation of pertinent processing resources to each CSCI.

Requirements traceability

Requirements traceability provides traceability of the requirements that were allocated to the HWCIs, CSCIs, and manual operations back to the requirements of the RSD. The traceability should be tabulated in a requirements traceability matrix. This traceability will carry out forward and backward throughout the software development documents.

System engineering design review

The system engineering design review is a formal review in which the SEDD (Systems Engineering Design Document) is accepted by the customer. The software developer conducts and presents the necessary design documents for formal review. The software developer conducts the review, and the customer evaluates the correctness of the allocation of the requirements to the CSCI. The review encompasses the system engineering parameters, as tabulated in TABLE 6-2. Once the SEDD is reviewed by the customer and accepted, the software developer uses this design information in subsequent phases as the basis for developing software.

Table 6-2. SEDD
Review Parameters

- System engineering
- Operations
- Maintenance
- Test
- Training
- Software
- Facilities
- Personnel
- Logistic support
- Security
- Safety
- Risk
- Optimization

7

Planning
software engineering
management

Planning software engineering management can start at any time, in parallel with the phases that I've discussed in the previous chapters. It's important that the management aspects of software development be planned. In this plan, the software developers describe their complete plan for conducting software development. This plan will assist the customer in monitoring the proce dures, management, and contract work of the organization that's performing the software development. In this chapter, I discuss the GEC-Marconi CASE tool, which covers forecasting, planning, personnel, and control of the project.

What is a software engineering management plan?

A software engineering management plan can be defined as detailed information that deals with the contractor's management of the project. The software developers describe their complete plan and intention for conducting software development. This includes details of their organization, equipment, documents, facility, and training program. The plan starts with scope, which details the system overview and capabilities. This plan will assist the customer in monitoring the procedures, management, and contract work of the organization that's assigned to perform the software development successfully within the given time and budget.

The software development management plan presents the project organization, resources, schedule and milestones for each activity, as listed in TABLE 7-1. This includes risk management, security, safety, external interfaces, reviews (formal and informal), and all related items. The plan includes a soft-

Table 7-1. Major Activities

- System requirements analysis
- System design
- Software requirements analysis
- Preliminary design
- Detailed design
- Coding and unit testing
- CSC/CSCI integration and testing
- System integration testing and testing

ware engineering relationship between the organization and resources, personnel, and software engineering environment. Included in the plan is the use of any standard or procedure while various activities are conducted. The plan explains formal and informal testing schema. It also includes software product evaluation procedures and tools. The plan covers configuration management and quality management factors in detail. Finally, the plan covers the software engineering products acceptance plan.

Establishing a software engineering plan

The software developers establish their plan for conducting the software development. They provide to the customer the insight into the organization that's responsible for performing the software development. These methods and procedures should be followed by the organization during the software development process. The plan covers, at a minimum, the topics listed in TABLE 7-2.

Table 7-2. Software Engineering
Management Plan's Major Topics

- Organization
- Equipment
- Documents
- Facility
- Training

Organization The software developers describe the project organization structure. This identifies the authority and responsibilities of individuals in the organization. The plan includes the total estimated number of personnel needed for the completion of the software development. This also includes the number of personnel that are assigned to various duties and tasks. The work breakdown structure covers tasks that belong to managers, supervisors, team leaders, system analyst/engineers, software engineers/designers, software programmers, software testers, software products quality evaluators, and software configuration managers. Figure 7-1 presents a sample graphical representation of a hierarchy chart that displays responsibilities and duties.

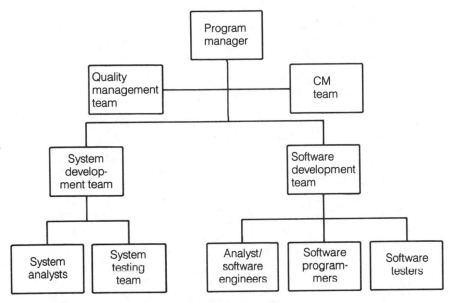

Fig. 7-1. Hierarchy chart.

Equipment   This plan covers the necessary equipment that will be furnished by the customer for the software developers. A schedule is given that details when the equipment is needed.

Documents   For references, a list of documents that will be used in the software development is described in the plan.

Facility   The software developers describe the facilities that will be used in the software development. The plan includes the location of specific project resources, such as the software engineering environment and software test environment. The plan states whether any secure area is needed for such activities.

Training   The software developers formulate a training plan to educate their personnel and achieve success in the software development. This is especially applicable for a complicated system that uses evolving methods and newly developed languages.

Characteristics of a software engineering management plan

The software engineering management plan characteristics cover the schedule of all the activities and milestones that will be achieved. It's a fact that no two projects are alike. This underscores the project manager's need to prepare the project plan. The plan describes each software development activity of the project and its associated schedule, which reflects the master schedule. An example that shows the principles of a project master schedule is drawn in FIG. 7-2. The development schedule also indicates all significant events, such as reviews, audits, and meetings. A graphic schedule is provided for clarity. The schedule indicates each activity's initiation and completion, along with the availability of draft and final copies of documentation and any high-risk areas.

Project XYZ	Assign to	1989		1990		1991
		J F M A M J J A S O N D		J F M A M J J A S O N D		J F M A M J J A S
System-A	John	Requirements analysis Preliminary design Detailed design Coding & CSU testing CSC/CSCI testing System integration testing				Documentation
System-B	Sara		Analysis Design Coding			Testing
System-C	Sue	Requirements analysis Preliminary design Detailed design CODING & CSU testing CSC/CSCI testing System integration testing				Documentation
System-D	Anita	Coding Testing Documentation				

Fig. 7-2. Master schedule sample.

The main reasons for schedules are time and work activity control. Preparation of a schedule is necessary so the entire project can be thought through the steps and can be fitted together in an integrated manner. Thus, the job can be gone through mentally step by step. This planning is invaluable in understanding the full scope of the project, the interrelationships among the many steps, and the sequence that must be followed. The plan covers any sequential relationship among the activities of the project. This plan includes those activities that impose the greatest time restriction on project completion and those activities with an excess of time for completion. The plan also identifies and describes the source of the required resources of software, firmware, and hardware for the software development effort. All relevant aspects of the system must be taken into account, not just the cost of the biggest item. The life cost analysis of the items, such as hardware, software, and firmware are established. Such an analysis takes into account all reasonable factors, such as reliability, maintenance costs, operating costs, ease of modification and ease of expansion. The budget estimate and the schedule can be refined from time to time as more and better data becomes available. A plan provides that the required resources be obtained and indicates the need date and availability of each resource item.

For simple projects, a list of key dates may suffice. Larger, more involved projects often use the Critical Path Method (CPM) diagram, along with a CASE tool for status and reporting. For success, a project manager must form a plan that combines the right tools and the know-how for the creation of a successful project.

Planning software engineering development

The software engineering development plan includes the life cycle aspects. It covers all aspects that relate to the operational life of the system. The following items must be included in this plan:

- The educational qualifications and experience levels of personnel who will be involved in the software development during various activities and phases.
- Standards that will be required for documentation structure and format.
- Requirements for individual testing of components, integrated testing, and maintenance.
- A software test plan that covers formal qualification testing. This includes the organizational structure for the testing. There should be personnel responsible for the testing and the test approach schema.
- The correct product produced in each activity.
- A review to be conducted at the end of each activity to determine whether to go or not go to the next activity.
- The schema planned for the development and maintenance of the software development files and database.
- A plan for any particular method or methodology that will be used in the software development.

Configuration control and version control systems necessary for the management of a large, complex, developing system should be clearly specified in the plan. The systems should be integral to the chosen requirements analysis and specification method and any supporting tools used in the plan.

The support services, which should be identified in the plan, include spares, tools, test equipment, back-up equipment, emergency maintenance staffing, and licenses. The changes and expansions that are envisaged during the useful life of the system need to be specified in the plan so that the design that's produced will allow for these revisions.

Installation aspects of the plan should cover hardware installation and where and when the new system should be installed. The new system may be a replacement for a previous system, in which case the requirements for the conversion from one to another must be specified. The necessary training requirements for operators and maintenance staff should be identified in the plan.

The plan also includes an agreed list with delivery dates of items throughout the development life cycle. The acceptance should be designed with testing so the new system behaves according to the requirements specification and can be completely mapped to the requirements.

In addition, the plan includes an appropriate project management environment that's conducive to the acquisition of information that's needed for decision making. There should be an establishment of procedures for error detection, correction, and change control. Schema should minimize the technical risk. There must be a plan for monitoring and controlling the use of resources. The plan should include an agreement between the customer and the software developers for project milestones, the products of each phase, and acceptance criteria for products.

The plan should cover quality assurance. Project management carries the responsibility for the combination of skills and talents for quality assurance. A total quality plan that incorporates the acceptance criteria must be developed in parallel with the requirements definition process. This plan identifies specific quality assurance activities throughout the project life cycle. The project must have intermediate products and phases. This allows for the requirements definition process to be monitored and subjected to proper quality control.

Risk management plan

The risk management plan describes the software developers' procedures for managing areas of risk in order to complete a successful project. The plan identifies the areas of risk and prioritizes them. It also identifies constituent risk factors that contribute to the potential occurrence of each risk. The plan documents procedures for monitoring the risk factors and provides guidelines for the reduction of potential recurrence of each risk. As appropriate, the plan identifies contingency procedures for each area of risk.

The project must be monitored to ensure that it proceeds according to the established plan with a minimum risk. This confirms that management has better control of the success of the project. This can be achieved by scheduling milestone meetings for the review of one stage of work before proceeding to the next stage.

Planning total quality management

Total quality management means building quality into a software product up front, instead of employing a quality professional to catch errors or defects at the back end. Total quality management is a tool that binds a modern management style to the mission of the organization. It's a method that empowers software developers, managers, and the total organization with the ability to meet objectives and standards and strive for even higher standards. Essentially, it's a commitment among the software developers and managers to improve the quality of the software products and services. It's a total organizational process that continuously improves the quantity and quality of the organization's products and services.

Although it requires software developers to do their best work as individuals and as a team, it relieves the managers so they have time for planning, monitoring, and being a mentor. It doesn't remove any authority from managers; but it does give to them one more tool with which they can perform one of their functions. The boss is still the boss, but the software developers have an opportunity to increase their contributions and meet the organization's objectives. It flattens management hierarchies. It enhances the commitment for quality and teaches cooperation and teamwork. The plan consists of software metrics, quality metrics, and software measurement metrics.

Software metrics deals with the measurement of the software product and the process by which it's developed. The software product is viewed as an abstract object that evolves from an initial stated requirement to a finished software system, which includes source and object code and various forms of documentation that are produced during development. These metrics and the models for software development are used in the estimation of product costs and schedules and in the measuring of productivity and product quality. Information gained from the metrics and the models is used in the management and control of the software development process, which leads to better results.

There are two types of software metrics: product metrics and process metrics. The *product metrics* are measures of the software product at any stage of its development. They measure the complexity of the software design and the size of the final program, either source/object code or how many pages of documentation have been produced. The *process metrics* measure the software development process, such as overall development time, type of methodology that's used, or the average level of experience in the professional staff.

Quality metrics for the software are correctness, efficiency, portability, maintainability, and reliability. It's difficult to find a single metric for overall software quality. For example, increased portability may result in lowered efficiency. The program's correctness can be measured by defect counts. Software reliability can be computed from defect data, and software maintainability can be measured by complexity metrics.

Software measurement metrics refer to how well a program measures the characteristics, as listed in the TABLE 7-3. These are the common set of software properties that will be measured. Many measurement approaches are

*Table 7-3. Software
Measurement Characteristics*

- Reliability
- Maintainability
- Sustainability
- Transportability
- Interoperability
- Efficiency

used for total effort, number of failures during system test, line of codes, number of modules, number of defects found in inspection, machine time, and number of open problems.

Reliability relates to how well a program performs with required precision over a given period of time. Reliability engineering not only detects and corrects errors, but it also tries to compensate for unknown software errors and for problems in the hardware and data. The errors can be measured as the number of changes in the software design. It can also be measured by the number of errors that are detected by code inspection and the number of errors that are detected in the program tests. The number of code changes also affect the measurement. This data is used to model and compute software reliability. This will measure and predict the probability of failure during a particular time failure.

Maintainability relates to how easy it is to find and correct software errors; for hardware, mean-time-to-repair is analogous. Although there's no way that we can measure or predict maintainability, certain attributes do make maintenance of the software easier. These attributes are modularity, self-documentation, code readability, and structured coding. Modularity increases both reliability and maintainability.

Sustainability is the software's capacity, and it can accept improvement.

Transportability is the factor that shows how well a set of software moves to a new hardware or operating system environment. It's also known as portability. It's the ability of a software item to be installed in a different environment without change in functionality.

Interoperability is the exchange and mutual use of information between two or more software systems. It's the ability of separate systems to exchange database objects and their relationships without conversion.

Efficiency relates to the amount of resources used for a software function. It's the minimum use of computing resources that's required for the performance of a function. The resources that need to be assessed are as follows:

- Processor.
- Memory.
- Communication.

The processor takes a certain amount of time to complete a task. The memory is the secondary storage required to complete a task. The communication is the input/output and the network considerations for multiprocessor systems and/or multiuser problems.

Efficiency is a relative term. It's the minimum use of hardware resources by the software. By using resources efficiently, frustrating delays that waste time are eliminated.

Software configuration management plan

The software configuration management plan covers the organizational structure that manages the software configuration. It details the personnel responsible for the software configuration. They identify the configuration identification. The procedure for software configuration is established. They assign unique configuration item identifications to each contract data requirements list in the statement of work. All of the components of a computer software configuration item will be assigned a version number.

The plan consists of a configuration control process. Any problem report and/or change report process should be explained. Software trouble report handling should be planned. Any engineering change proposal must be planned and handled properly. A software configuration control board will evaluate and handle all change requests that are submitted for configured items. The plan covers storage, handling, and delivery of all project items to the customer for the software life cycle.

Planning acceptance procedures

After software engineering products acceptance procedures are designed, then tests are run on the system. The results of these tests determine if the system behaves according to the requirement specification. A well-prepared document includes criteria for each listed item, and these criteria can be used for verification and evaluation of each requirement. The plan consists of an agreed-upon list of items with delivery dates covering the entire software development life cycle. This list includes the system requirements, software requirements analysis, design, coding source and object, testing scenarios, and other agreed-upon related documentation, which can be issued in more than one sequential version.

The organization and resources for the software product evaluation are identified in the plan. Also, the plan should include personnel who will manage this task. Their responsibilities should be identified. Procedures should be established that include the requirements traceability and reviews schema. The plan should include procedures on how to conduct walk-throughs and inspections. In an informal way, these ensure the correctness of the product and maintain the quality of the product. A formal review can be conducted to review the plan. Any disagreement must be resolved before marching on to the next phase or activity.

The plan also includes verification of the product. Frequent audits can be planned, errors corrected, and quality retained. Quality-control personnel measure the quality factor of the software throughout the software development life cycle. The software quality metrics matrix provides the quality factor checklist that ensures that the product has quality.

GEC-Marconi CASE tool

The GEC-Marconi CASE tool is called GECOMO Plus. This is a project management tool for cost estimation and is based on the Constructive Cost Model (COCOMO) method that was developed by Dr. Barry Boehm. The most typical use of GECOMO Plus is at the beginning of the project, when managers and software developers are in the process of discovering more requirements for the project itself. The process begins with very little that's known, but by examining the requirements, interviewing the customer, and perhaps doing some initial experimentation with a design, then the requirements become clearer. The method uses source lines of code and statistical analysis of past projects as the basis for estimating the effort, staffing, and time requirements for a project. GECOMO Plus supports an extended version of COCOMO and provides an environment that simplifies the process of cost estimation. The main features of GECOMO Plus are listed in TABLE 7-4.

Table 7-4. GECOMO Plus Main Features

- Support for Boehm's Detailed COCOMO Model includes incremental development and the extension for the Ada Process Model.
- A staff assignment facility allows the user to adjust the calculated effort and the schedule estimate in accordance with their available staffing levels.
- Powerful graphical user interface based on the *de-facto* X-Windows and OSF/Motif standards.
- GEC-Marconi Software Systems extensions to COCOMO.

The standard COCOMO models

Three variants of COCOMO of increasing complexity are described by Boehm (1981) as the Basic, Intermediate and Detailed COCOMO models. GECOMO Plus implements the Detailed model.

The main elements of the Detailed COCOMO model are:

- The Waterfall Model of the software development life cycle, with extensions to allow for incremental development.
- A set of engineering and management activities that must be performed during the life cycle phases.
- A set of "modes" and "cost drivers" that characterize a particular project.
- A definition of the hierarchical structure of the software to be developed in terms of subsystems and modules, together with estimates of the numbers of source lines that make up these components.

The Detailed COCOMO life cycle model is shown in FIG. 7-3. It's the standard waterfall model, with extensions for incremental development; that is, the software is implemented progressively in increments of functionality. Note, however, that this model is identical to the standard waterfall model if the number of increments is set to one.

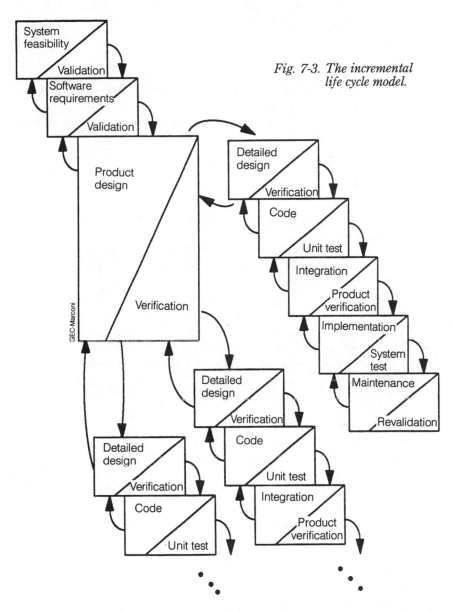

Fig. 7-3. The incremental
life cycle model.

The Detailed COCOMO Model is based upon the following engineering and management activities that compose the software development process:

- Requirements analysis.
- Product design.
- Programming.
- Test planning.
- Verification and validation.

- Project management.
- Configuration management and quality assurance.
- Production of manuals.

It's recognized in the COCOMO Model that to some extent all of these activities are performed in each life cycle phase.

The Detailed COCOMO Model characterizes software projects by their development mode. For example:

- Organic or familiar, in which small teams develop software in a familiar, in-house environment and most team members have experience with related systems.
- Semidetached or intermediate, a project that is in between the familiar and embedded modes.
- Embedded, which is characterized by tight constraints in the systems hardware and software interfaces and the procedures and regulations that govern the project.

There are three similar modes that characterize Ada projects.

The cost drivers describe those characteristics of a project that affect the development costs, such as the complexity of the software and the capability of the programmers. In the Detailed COCOMO Model the following cost drivers are used:

1. Product attributes.
   - Required software reliability (RELY).
   - Database size (DATA).
   - Software product complexity (CPLX).
   - Required reusability (RUSE).
2. Personnel attributes.
   - Analyst capability (ACAP).
   - Programmer capability (PCAP).
   - Applications experience (AEXP).
   - Virtual machine experience (VEXP).
   - Programming language experience (LEXP).
3. Programming attributes.
   - Execution time constraints (TIME).
   - Main storage constraint (STOR).
   - Virtual machine volatility host (VMVH).
   - Virtual machine volatility target (VMVT).
   - Computer turnaround time (TURN).
4. Project attributes.
   - Use of modern programming practices (MODP).
   - Use of software tools (TOOL).

- Classified security application (SECU).
- Schedule constraint (SCED).

The project manager characterizes his or her project by assigning values ranging from very low to extra high to each of these cost drivers.

From the Detailed COCOMO Model the total project effort, duration and staffing estimates are generated. These can be refined to give estimates for the design, coding and integration phases of the project. Effort and schedule estimates can also be obtained for the requirements specification phase, and the annual maintenance effort. The phase effort values can then be further refined to give figures for the effort required for each activity carried out within each phase.

GEC-Marconi software systems extensions to COCOMO

The GECOMO Plus implementation of COCOMO includes all major features of detailed COCOMO, including extensions to the model. Several other enhancements have been made to the standard model in order to make the tool more flexible and powerful. It should be noted that although GECOMO Plus contains enhancements to the detailed COCOMO model, it's still possible with GECOMO Plus to adhere to Boehm's standard model, if preferred. The principal GEC-Marconi software systems enhancements are briefly outlined in the following:

- The number of activities within each phase has been extended from Boehm's original eight to ten activities, in order to separate the configuration management and quality assurance activities and to split the programming activity into detailed design and code and unit test.
- The Detailed COCOMO Model divides a project into subsystem and module levels; GECOMO Plus allows any number of levels to be defined in a project structure. This places no restrictions on a more detailed breakdown of the project, thereby simplifying code size estimates.
- The Detailed COCOMO Model allows some cost drivers to be set at subsystem level and others to be specified at module level. GECOMO Plus doesn't restrict the levels at which the cost drivers may be set, allowing greater freedom to the user. (Although it should be recognized that some cost drivers are more appropriate at higher or lower levels.)
- In GECOMO Plus, a method of cost driver inheritance is employed, where ratings specified for a component of the project at a particular level are inherited by its children at the levels below. This provides a very fast yet simple method of setting cost drivers.
- A staff assignment facility has been devised by GEC-Marconi Software Systems. This extension to the COCOMO model allows the user to

adjust the calculated effort and schedule estimates in accordance with their available staffing levels.

General features

GECOMO Plus delivers tool support for the COCOMO method of cost estimation. The tool provides a powerful graphical user interface for entering model parameters for the project to be estimated. These are then used as the basis of analysis for calculating the effort, staffing and duration figures for the project which are, in turn, displayed or printed in a suitable format. The following list itemizes the main features of the system.

- Portability: GECOMO Plus is implemented in a portable subset of the C programming language, ensuring portability onto many different hardware configurations.
- The X-Windows System: GECOMO Plus includes a powerful graphical user interface based on the *de facto* X-Windows and OSF/Motif standards.
- Full COCOMO model: GECOMO Plus implements the full-detailed COCOMO model with Ada extensions, as described by Boehm.
- Staff assignment: GECOMO Plus includes an extension to the COCOMO model that allows the user to investigate the consequences of imposing their own staffing constraints on the project being estimated.
- Report generator: GECOMO Plus includes the ability to generate high-quality reports using either the PostScript language or standard text formatting facilities.
- Extendable: GECOMO Plus uses a popular network database for which there's an SQL interface available, thereby providing interface capability to other tools.
- Modern programming practices: GECOMO Plus has been developed using modern software engineering methods that ensure the robustness and maintainability of the system.

Architecture of GECOMO Plus

The GECOMO Plus system is made up of three major functional components:

1. The user interface.
2. GECOMO Plus cost models.
3. Report generation: each accessing data held in databases, as shown in FIG. 7-4.

The GECOMO Plus Database holds all the data used by the models, e.g., the cost driver values, the phase and activity distribution tables and the equation coefficients. In the initial release of GECOMO Plus, the database is read-

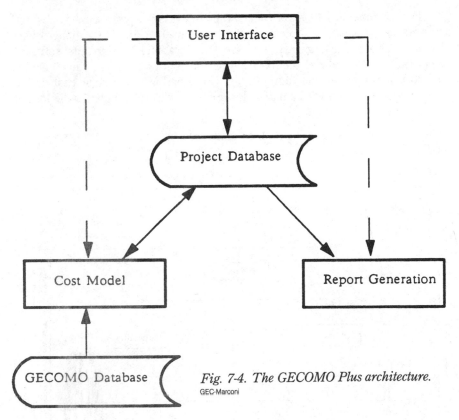

Fig. 7-4. The GECOMO Plus architecture.
GEC-Marconi

only. A later release will include an interface to the GECOMO Plus Database that will allow users to modify the data to suit their own organizations.

The Project Database is a central repository that contains both the user-specified information that defines the project, and the results of any analysis performed by the GECOMO Plus models. The project database acts as the focus of communication between the components of the system. The user interface interacts directly with the user via window, menu, mouse, and key-board facilities.

The GECOMO Plus cost models implement the cost estimation methods. The cost model implements the Detailed COCOMO method with Ada extensions. The staff assignment model adjusts the results from the COCOMO model to take account of the staffing constraints of the user.

Components

User interface The GECOMO Plus user interface is based on the X-Windows and OSF/Motif standards. The interface provides a simple yet powerful method of creating a description of a project. It follows the "what you see is what you get" paradigm, all data always accurately reflecting the current state of the project.

For example, FIG. 7-5 shows one of the project description windows, which is used for creating the project structure. As well as providing menu-driven facilities for constructing the project structure graphically, individual software units can be selected and their GECOMO Plus parameters set. This includes the cost driver values shown in FIG. 7-6. On selecting a particular cost driver, the user is presented with a menu showing the valid values applicable to that cost driver.

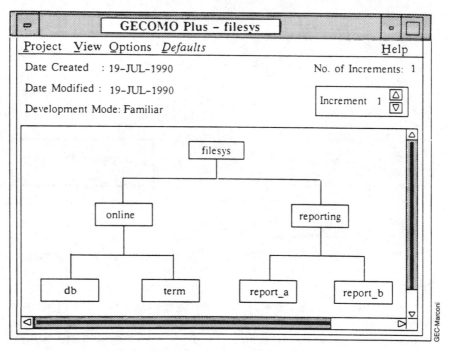

Fig. 7-5. The Project definition window.

Consistency is an important feature of the interface: common conventions are adopted throughout the product for selecting fields, pulling down menus, etc. The conventions adopted are consistent with the Motif style (a developing industry standard), and are therefore consistent with other Motif applications.

The window interface allows the display of more than one set of information at once, allowing several tasks to be performed at one time. Use of the X-Windows and OSF/Motif interfaces improves the portability of the product, allowing it to be ported to other platforms supporting X-Windows and OSF/ Motif.

In addition to interfacing with the user, the user interface acts as the control center of the system, determining the manner in which the functionality of the system is invoked. For example, the user interface adopts a lazy evaluation approach in which the cost model computations (analysis) are performed automatically, and only when necessary.

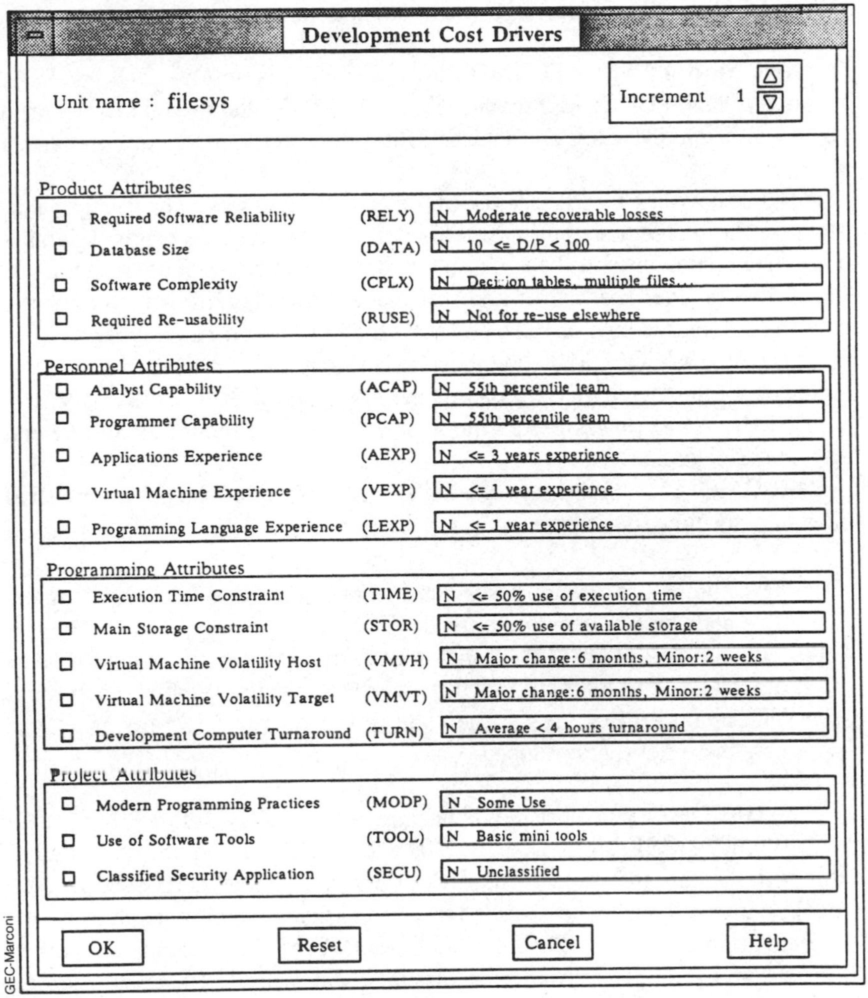

Fig. 7-6. Cost driver selection menu.

Databases GECOMO Plus database functions are provided by the database product db_VISTA III. This database system has proved very suitable for managing the hierarchical nature of the entities used and produced by GECOMO Plus. Db_VISTA also provides an applications interface via C functions and structures. GECOMO Plus has been designed to use two databases: a GECOMO Plus database pertinent to the COCOMO model that will be common across all projects, and a project database that holds sets of project-specific information.

In addition to the definition of the information to be stored in the database(s), a set of operations is defined that provides access into the databases. This interface layer facilitates integration of different database systems with

GECOMO Plus, thus ensuring a degree of independence from the database system used.

Cost model   The GECOMO Plus cost model is an extended version of Boehm's detailed COCOMO model. The GECOMO Plus model also incorporates Boehm's latest work on the use of the Ada process model and incremental development.

Studies have shown that the use of the Ada process model has a significant effect on the phase distribution of effort and schedule. The original detailed COCOMO model has thus been extended to take account of these effects. The Ada process model cost driver and phase-activity tables differ in some cases from the original values of the COCOMO model, and an Ada sigma factor is introduced to the COCOMO equations. This sigma factor reflects the project's degree of compliance with the Ada process model. GECOMO Plus can be used in either the Ada Process Model mode or conventional model mode, depending on user selection.

GECOMO Plus, following Boehm's incremental development method, takes into account the following :

- The number of development increments (up to 20 in GECOMO Plus).
- The code size of each increment.
- The starting point of each increment with respect to its own internal milestones and its relation to the milestones in the previous increment.
- The amount of change in the code of the previous increment as each new increment is developed.

The GECOMO Plus cost model has a simple, clearly defined interface to the X-Windows OSF/Motif User Interface standard. In general, it communicates with the user interface via the GECOMO Plus project database. The cost model updates all sizes and cost drivers automatically as data is entered.

Staff assignment   The Detailed COCOMO Model calculates the effort, duration, and the optimum number of staff for a project. However, the optimum number of staff may not always be available. In this case the project manager simply enters the number of staff actually available, and the staff assignment facility calculates revised effort and duration values based on this number. This facility also allows the project manager to ask "What if?" questions to investigate the consequences of different staffing levels on the project schedule and costs.

Staff assignment is a GEC-Marconi Software Systems extension to the detailed COCOMO model. It's based on communication factors between staff in projects, data for which is presented in Boehm's book (1981).

The staff assignment model is based on a method of splitting the given number of staff into teams, and calculating the number of required interactions between staff. In this way the estimates can be adjusted to take into account the communications overhead inherent in a project.

Report generation The report generation facility allows the production of hard copy reports that summarize project information, both in terms of input into GECOMO Plus and the results of analysis that are output from GECOMO Plus. Some examples of the reports available are shown in FIGS. 7-7 to 7-9. Figure 7-7 depicts the calculated effort for a project, divided between the project activities and phases. Figures 7-8 and 7-9 show examples of the Project Bar Chart and Staff Histogram reports.

Detailed Effort							
Unit Name : Test_1				Increment	1		
	Rec. Spec.	Prelim Design	Detail Design	Code & U.Test	Integ. & Test	Total	Maint. p.a.
Project Management	1.29	2.14	1.87	1.91	1.36	8.57	1.45
Technical Control	0.60	1.75	1.87	1.91	0.62	6.75	1.16
Requirements Specification	3.96	2.92	1.56	1.59	0.58	10.61	1.45
Structural Design	1.38	7.01	2.49	2.55	0.93	14.36	2.15
Detailed Design	0.15	2.18	16.27	1.85	1.98	22.43	3.48
Code and Unit Test	0.10	0.54	1.80	16.65	4.63	23.72	5.21
V.V. & T.	0.52	1.17	1.87	1.91	6.61	12.08	2.69
Manuals Production	0.43	1.36	1.56	1.59	1.36	6.30	2.07
Configuration Management	0.07	0.12	0.74	0.96	0.95	2.84	0.83
Quality Assurance	0.10	0.27	1.12	0.96	0.41	2.86	0.21
Total	8.61	19.48	31.17	31.90	19.46	110.62	20.69

| Close | Print | Help |

Fig. 7-7. Detailed effort report. GEC-Marconi

Reports are generated primarily in PostScript format and can be stored in a file or printed directly. However, if no PostScript printer is available, GECOMO Plus will create an ASCII file that can be directed to the required output printer. This ensures coverage of a wide variety of printer types.

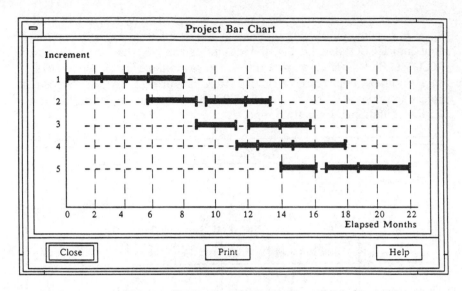

Fig. 7-8. Project bar-chart report. GEC-Marconi

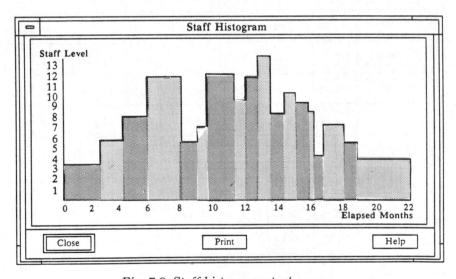

Fig. 7-9. Staff histogram report. GEC-Marconi

Installation requirements

GECOMO Plus is initially available on the following platforms:

- Sun 3/60.
- Sun SPARCstation.
- DEC VAX/VMS.
- IBM RS/6000.

- HP 9000.
- Apollo.

In total, GECOMO Plus, when supplied with X-windows and Motif, requires 20 Mb of disc space. Otherwise, GECOMO Plus can be purchased separately, in which case it requires 8 Mb of disc space.

Environment

GECOMO Plus is designed to be readily portable to a wide variety of platforms. The following design and implementation decisions enhance portability:

- Operating system: The product is written using a very portable subset of the 1989 ANSI C language and library routines, which most target machines support. This is true of all UNIX System V (HP 9000 and IBM RS/6000) and Berkeley 4.2 systems (SUNOS, Ultrix) and of VAX/VMS V5.
- Database: The database used by GECOMO Plus is db__VISTA. This is currently available for most UNIX and VAX/VMS platforms.
- User interface: The user interface is provided using the Motif package. This requires X-11 Windows release 4 or later, a bit-mapped display, and a two-button or three-button Mouse. The DECWindows product provides an implementation of the Motif software on the VAX. A range of X-terminals are available and can be connected either to DECWindows or X-11 by Ethernet or RS232. This will enable users without workstations to access GECOMO Plus.

Part II

Methods of analyzing software requirements

8

Analyzing
software requirements

The customer's requirements have been analyzed and segregated between the computer hardware and software configuration items. Before the software requirements are properly specified, it's vital that some study be given to the available methods and CASE tools for software requirements analysis. Prototyping is an important approach for developing a sample software that will satisfy the customer's requirements. Prototyping reduces actual software development costs and ensures that the software will meet the customer's requirements. But, prototyping is not appropriate for every software requirements analysis project, and sometimes prototyping is appropriate only for portions of a project. In this chapter, I present several prototyping methods for software requirements analysis, and I discuss the MAGEC CASE tool.

Conventional versus modern approaches

Conventional approaches for software requirements analysis are the ones that have been used in the computer industry for the last decade or so. Some of these approaches are: classic waterfall, structured English, flowcharts, and program design languages. These approaches are used during the software requirements analysis and specification, which is agreed upon by the customer and the software developers. A sample waterfall approach to the software development life cycle, in accordance with the United States Department of Defense standard 2167A, is shown in FIG. 8-1.

Most of the time, these approaches are manually driven and laborious when changes are made. Requirements do change during the life cycle of the software, due to either a new need or due to fixing a "bug" in the software. Any change can start a ripple effect in the model and create many more changes. Communication between the customer and the software developer is

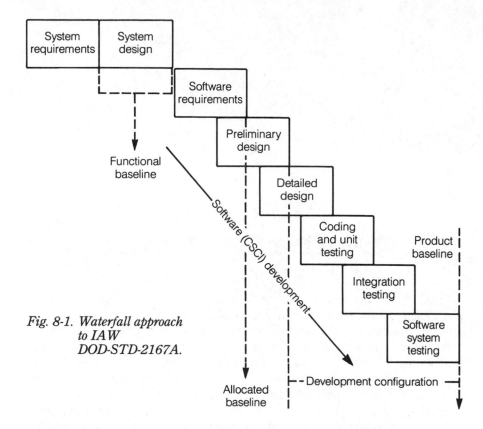

*Fig. 8-1. Waterfall approach
to IAW
DOD-STD-2167A.*

also a problem. The pictorial specification assists in eradicating the communication barrier at each phase of the software development, but it's hard to maintain the accuracy of the documents with the requirements changes.

Figure 8-2 exhibits the conventional software development process. The process follows from the customer's requirements definition and analysis to software requirements analysis, design, coding, testing, and integrated testing until the customer accepts the products. The problems with the conventional approaches are that all too often an entire project that has been developed is forced back to the beginning because of a major flaw or omission in the analysis or design phases. By this time the scheduled delivery date is near, and the software developers and the customer begin looking for a scapegoat. The truth, however, is that the process, not the people, should be blamed. The conventional process requires that participants perform essentially unrealistic tasks. The major problem is that the conventional approach is based on two false assumptions: that the customer can adequately define application requirements before actual development, and that words and pictures, as opposed to a working model, are adequate communication media. In addition, there's lack of communication between the software developers and the customer.

With the advent of CASE tools, some of these problems are solved.

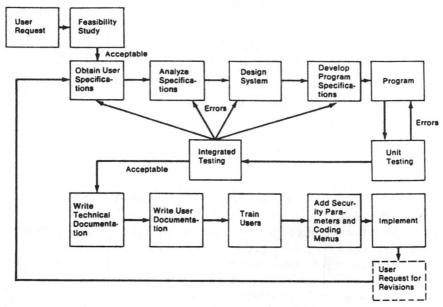

Fig. 8-2. A conventional software process.

There's surely some advantage to drawing a flowchart, logic diagram, or data diagram that uses a computer rather than a pencil; however, such an advantage can only be slight in the overall scheme of things. The shortfalls of CASE tools are that they don't solve the basic problems of the conventional approaches themselves.

In the last ten years automated application generation has come a long way. Central dictionary (repository) technology has fueled the advances in automation. Today a properly equipped software developer can actually produce in hours what would have taken weeks or months of manual coding. The resulting application will not only be as good as the manually coded one; it will be better. Automation shatters the fundamental premise on which the conventional approach was based. It opens the door for an entirely new approach based on a new set of axioms, and it takes advantage of the state-of-the-art in automation technology. These modern approaches are listed in the TABLE 8-1.

Prototyping is the iterative refinement of a model that develops a complete customer application. Because the application model is easily revised and stores all specifications and revisions, prototyping eliminates the voluminous documentation and the rigid rules and protocols of most conventional approaches. An available working model that can be easily revised encourages creative speculation about potential improvements to the initial design.

A more flexible and creative approach to prototyping encourages customers and software developers to cooperate in solving application problems. It's a fact that neither the customer nor the analyst can adequately define the requirements for a new application. It's reasonable for the customer to change

Table 8-1. Modern Approaches

- Prototyping
- Reusable software
- Throwaway prototypes
- Cornerstone prototypes
- Self-actualizing prototypes
- Evolutionary prototypes
- Operational prototypes

the requirements after they see a system model operate. Prototyping enhances the quality of communication between the customer and the software developers. An actual working system demonstrates the functions of an application better than volumes of documentation ever could. The software developer creates a mock-up of a report or screen that the customer can examine. This improves communication because the picture is worth a thousand words. This mock-up is replaced with a partial working model that has the advancement of a CASE tool. This further improves communications because a model is worth many pictures. Prototyping assists in the requirements specification process.

Reusable software configures and specializes preexisting software components into viable application systems. The process incorporates previously developed requirements specifications into newly developed software. This includes pretested code, proven designs, and any preused test plans. The software reuse approach is illustrated in FIG. 8-3.

Reusable software has many advantages. It reduces development time and saves cost. It enhances reliability by using pretested software components. The disadvantage of reusable software is that the approach is still evolving. It's not mature yet. A potentially reusable software component is not easily recognized. It needs a graphical model to improve this situation. A database can be created to store the requirements and match the reusable software components. The database needs cataloging and retrieving schema that will retrieve the reusable software components from a database repository. There are also configuration management problems for the reusable software components. Another disadvantage is the creation of a new version of the system software that modifies the reusable software. This leads to another problem of notifying all users of a new version of the reusable software component. The database should keep proper track of which version of the software component is being used. The reusable software also affects the establishment of functional, allocated, developmental, and product baselines.

Throwaway prototypes are software programs that are created in a quick and rough manner. They're used to validate the requirements and experience that's necessary to uncover any new requirements. A sample throwaway prototyping of the software development life cycle is shown in FIG. 8-4. Only those

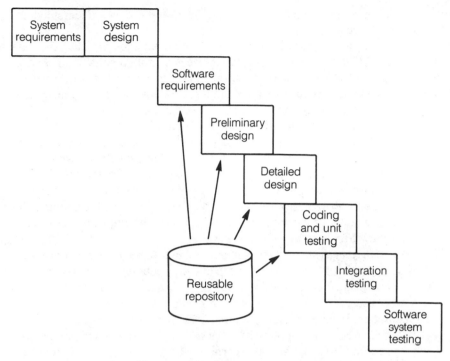

Fig. 8-3. Software reuse approach.

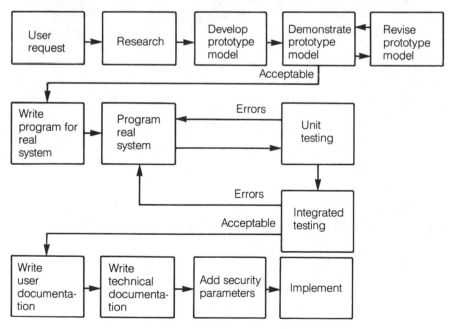

Fig. 8-4. Throwaway prototyping process.

parts of the software requirements that are fuzzy and not well understood are further developed.

When throwaway prototyping is used, the advantages are that the customer gains satisfaction at early stages and sees sample results showing that the developed software meets the requirements. The risk of software development is considerably reduced when complex systems are built. Throwaway prototyping definitely reduces software development costs, due to less changes in the requirements. It enhances communication between the customer and the software developers, which further leads to the success of the software development project. The disadvantages are that throwaway prototyping throws away something that has created expenses for the project. Sometimes the customer is convinced to just carry on with the throwaway prototyping rather than real development of the software. To the customer, the models appear to be production-ready applications, although they lack some very important attributes of a complete system.

Cornerstone prototyping, which is illustrated in FIG. 8-5, uses a modern, full-featured application generator that is capable of producing a finished product without scrapping or recoding the prototype. Cornerstone prototyping automates every aspect of the software development process, from analysis to final implementation. It requires an application generator that's capable of producing efficient and complete applications that accomplish all needed online functions. The application generator also permits the software developers to create security parameters and documentation during the prototyping sessions. Such features as menus and HELP keys facilitate customer participation. The advantages are that since the prototype is a complete and production-ready system, it can be implemented quickly, thus it satisfies the customer's desire for rapid use of an accepted model. This is also faster and superior to manual operations.

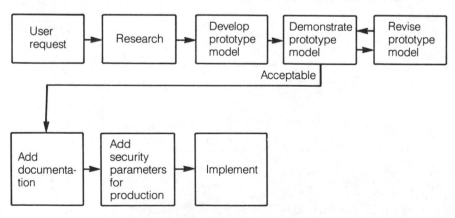

Fig. 8-5. Cornerstone prototyping.

Self-actualizing prototyping creates not only a model of the application, but also a fully functional software product that includes:

- Screens.
- Programs.
- Reports.
- Documentation.
- Security.
- Menus.
- Help keys.

The software development consists of iterative refinement of the prototype until it's good enough for production. Self-actualizing prototyping compresses all of the steps in the conventional approach into one. The major advantage is that the prototype model is not discarded. It yields tremendous productivity gains for the entire software development effort and virtually assures the customer's satisfaction. By eliminating most or all of the behind-the-scenes programming needed, self-actualizing prototyping helps reduce the opportunity for errors and produces more standardized and more easily maintained software systems.

Evolutionary prototyping is illustrated in FIG. 8-6. It validates the customer's requirements and thus gains experience; it uncovers any new requirements

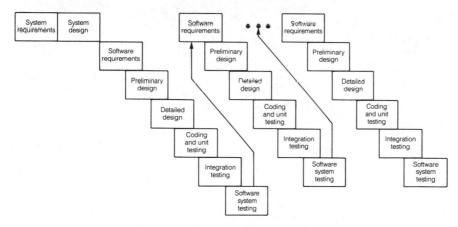

Fig. 8-6. Evolutionary prototyping.

that are needed for software development. It's repeatedly modified and redeployed whenever new information is learned. Those parts of the software requirements that are well understood are prototyped first to serve as a strong foundation for continued development of the rest of the software. Each increment is more risky than the preceding one. The experience thus gained by developing the software enhances the confidence of building the rest of the requirements software. The software quality is there from the start of the project. One disadvantage is that the customer's feedback is not received in time to incorporate it into the next iteration of the evolutionary prototype. This will hamper the inclusion of new requirements in the evolutionary prototyping. Configuration management is another problem in keeping track of requirements changes.

Operational prototyping combines the best of throwaway and evolutionary prototyping, as presented in FIG. 8-7. With operational prototyping, a stable base is constructed that uses sound software engineering principles. It incorporates only features of the requirements that are well known, understood, and

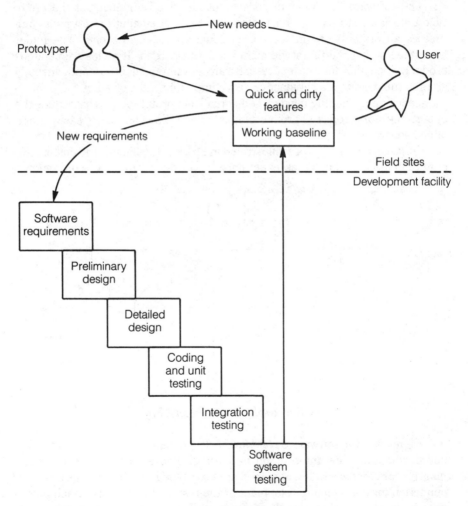

Fig. 8-7. Operational prototyping.

agreed on. This is the first step in evolutionary prototyping. This version is deployed at the customer's operational field sites. At each site, an expert prototyper observes the system in operation. As problems are uncovered, new requirements are introduced in the prototyping. When the customer is not using the prototype, the prototyper constructs a quick and rough implementation of the desired changes on top of the working baseline. The customer tests the modified system, which ensures that the prototyper understood the requirements correctly, and that the new requirements are included as desired. Eventually, the prototyper departs the field site and returns to the contractor's office; these quick changes are merged with other changes from the other field sites and then analyzed. Finally, as these changes are included in new versions of the software, new releases are baselined and redeployed with on-site prototypers, just as before, and the process is repeated.

These advantages resolve most of the problems associated with the two earlier prototyping approaches. Operational prototyping ensures a stable and quality software product. The disadvantage is hiring a unique professional who will serve at the field site and who is knowledgeable in prototyping.

MAGEC CASE tool

MAGEC stands for Mask and Application Generator and Environment Controller. This is a CASE tool that generates full COBOL applications for IBM CICS, VM/CMS, PC.DOS, and OS/2. It was developed by MAGEC Software, Plano, Texas.

MAGEC is a methodology that's based on data-driven design and a central repository concept. Figure 8-8 shows MAGEC's fully integrated environment, which revolves around the active central repository. Most editing rules, table verifications, business rules, field level HELP, and referential integrity are defined in the MAGEC data dictionary at the data item level. The requirements specifications for application, record of program changes, program source, program customization, screens, HELP data, error messages, interactive tables, and documentation are defined and stored in the MAGEC data dictionary central repository.

MAGEC automatically produces COBOL applications that out-perform hand-coded COBOL programs. This includes inquiry, update, delete, data entry, duplicate, backward/forward browse, cut and paste, and pop-up windows. A MAGEC application is best suited for real-time or batch commercial data processing tasks such as accounting systems. The following case study, "Vacation System" is discussed in detail and explains the prototyping capability of MAGEC. (See TABLE 8-2.)

Figure 8-9 presents a list of the data items that appear in the logical views of selected files. The cursor selects data items on the screen (or batch report) in the order it desires and it then appears on the screen. If you point to a group

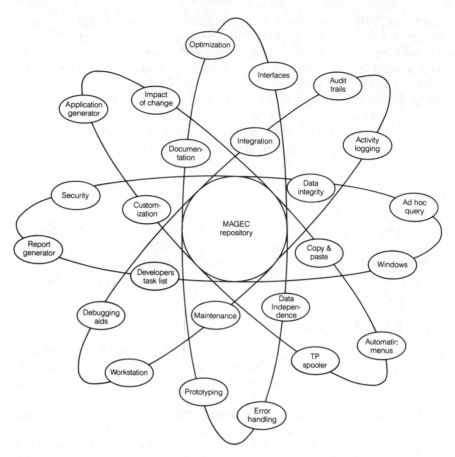

Fig. 8-8. MAGEC's fully integrated environment revolves around the active central repository. A.L. Lee & Associates

Table 8-2. A Case Study: Vacation System General Specifications

The personnel office wants an online system to help them manage and keep track of Vacation time, Sick time, and Comp time.

The following application is what the project manager has in mind when he meets with the personnel manager:

1) Inquiry   (Detailed)   Keyed by Employee Number
2) Update   "
3) Data Entry   "

Inquiry screen will be able to link or call update screen without the user retyping the Key.

Each screen will contain about 10 fields, however, the data is currently in two different files, so two files must be input.

New Standards Compliance
According to our existing standards this system must be written in structured COBOL and utilize SAA standard function keys.

Data integrity of any input data must be assured. All data items must be thoroughly edited and displayed according to our new standard. Dates and amount fields must be table verified for range accuracy. Any negative values must display a negative sign.

Table 8-2. Continued.

Dates, dollar amounts, and numeric items must be allowed to be entered any way recognizable, with or without commas, dollar signs, slashes, etc.

Fields that fail edits must cause that field to be displayed in high intensity and display an appropriate error message. For example, if, in a MM/DD/YY date, DD is 41, then the error message must say, "Invalid number of days in date field," etc.

Online user HELP data must be provided via function key request at the data item level, error message level, and function code level.

Users who are authorized by security must have the functions that they are authorized to perform added to their Menu.

Hardcopy documentation that thoroughly documents each trans-id or function in detail must be provided.

In addition to what the project manager had in mind, the personnel manager wants the following system:

1) Inquiry   (Detailed)   Keyed by Employee Number
2) Update   "
3) Data Entry   "
4) Duplicate   "
5) Forward/Backward Browse   "
6) Delete   "
7) Ability to start anywhere and list a screenful of Employees
8) Ability to list all employees that match a generic or partial name
9) Ability to use AND, OR, NOR, XOR, and NOT Logic selections (queries) to do Generic lists of Employees.

The user must be able to select, using the cursor, any item shown on any of the list screens and see the detail or update the detail. Furthermore, a method must be provided to retain the list screen for later selection of another item for detailed display or update.

User must be allowed to copy the contents of any field and later paste that value to the value of any other field on any screen desired, subject to his/her security authorization.

User department wants to see a prototype of the screens for approval before it is too late to make changes.

When a field is validated using a table lookup, the operator should be able to press the field HELP key and should be able to list the valid entries for that field. He/she should be able to then cursor select the desired one, rather than having to remember it and then type it into the screen field.

---

item, FIG. 8-10 pops up a window and asks if you want the whole group or just the item. You press PF19. After selecting all the items you want on your screen, you press PF10 to tell MAGEC to go generate the new screen. MAGEC will ask you how you would like the screen to appear, as is shown in FIG. 8-11. You will choose option 7 by placing the cursor anywhere on that line and pressing Enter.

Figure 8-12 presents MAGEC's automatically painted screen. You can modify what MAGEC automatically does for you until you're satisfied. Here I have deleted a label, moved a field, inserted some lines, and added several new fields, as shown in FIG. 8-13. Note that the PF key list at the bottom tells exactly what you must know so you can accomplish these tasks. When you finally hit Enter on your screen, MAGEC automatically senses that you have added new data fields that should be named and that may need additional attribute information defined for them. MAGEC has highlighted these new fields, placed a vertical bar on each one, and awaits your definition of this needed information. You will give the screen field some unique name, name the source/target field,

```
PAINT2 600                                  PF8=Forward/PF7=Backward/PF5=Top
              AUTO-PAINTING-FIELD SELECTION SCREEN
Grp Key                      CURSOR-SELECT Data Items                Ocr Selected
             ++TOP OF LIST++
Elt VAC01     04 VAC01-ELEMENT              X(00198)
Grp Key       05 VAC01-KEY                  X(00018)
   Key-1      07 VAC01-EMPNUM               9(09)                      ++ 01 ++
   Key-2      07 VAC01-FILLER               X(00009)
              05 VAC01-DATE HIRED           MM/DD/YY                   ++ 04 ++
              05 VAC01-EARNED-VACATION      S9(05)V9(02) COMP-3        ++ 05 ++
              05 VAC01-TAKEN-VACATION       S9(05)V9(02) COMP-3        ++ 06 ++
              05 VAC01-EARNED-SICK-DAYS     S9(05)V9(02) COMP-3        ++ 07 ++
              05 VAC01-TAKEN-SICK-DAYS      S9(05)V9(02) COMP-3        ++ 08 ++
              05 VAC01-EARNED-COMP-DAYS     S9(05)V9(02) COMP-3        ++ 09 ++
              05 VAC01-TAKEN-COMP-DAYS      S9(05)V9(02) COMP-3        ++ 10 ++
              05 VAC01-COMMENT              X(00050)              3X   ++ 11 ++
Elt SIF01     04 SIF01-ELEMENT             X(00264)
Grp Key       05 SIF01-MASTER-KEY          X(00006)
Grp Key       07 SIF01-LOVALU              X(00002)
   Key-1      09 SIF01-KEY-PREFIX          S9(04)        COMP

ENTER=select item         PF4=un-select item        PF6=Field Selections Completed
PF10=un-select ALL items                            Press PF3 to Return to JOIN01
 11 ITEMS HAVE BEEN SELECTED                        VACATION SYSTEM
```

Fig. 8-9. List of data items.

```
PAINT2 600
              AUTO-PAINTING-FIELD SELECTION SCREEN
Grp Key                      CURSOR-SELECT Data Items                Ocr Selected

Grp Key       07 SIF01-EMPNO              X(00004)
   Key-2      09 SIF01-EMPNUM             S9(09)        COMP
Grp           05 SIF01-FIRST-NAME                                    ++ 02 ++
              07 SIF01-F-INIT
              07 SIF01-FILLER                You are pointing at
Grp           05 SIF01-LAST-NAME             a GROUP item...
              07 SIF01-L-INIT
              07 SIF01-FILLER                PF18=select its
Grp           05 SIF01-LAST-ON-DT            subordinate items
              06 SIF01-LAST-ON-DT-YY
              06 SIF01-LAST-ON-DT-MM         PF19=select the
              06 SIF01-LAST-ON-DT-DD         group item only
Grp           05 SIF01-LAST-ON-TM
              07 SIF01-LAST-ON-TM-HH         PF3=return with
              07 SIF01-LAST-ON-TM-MM         NO selection
              07 SIF01-LAST-ON-TM-SS      X(00002)
```

Fig. 8-10. Group item window.

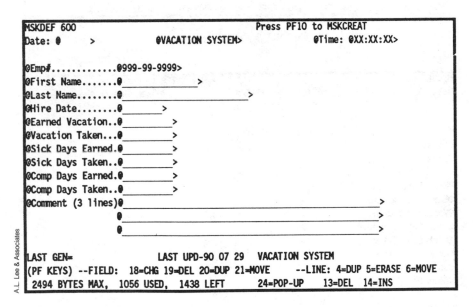

```
PAINT3 600

     AUTO-PAINT OPTIONS FOR GENERATED SCREEN FORMAT


     Select an Option using the Cursor, and Press ENTER

OPTION        1-LIST/2 -double-space, one item per line
OPTION        2-LIST/1-single-space, one item per line
OPTION        3-COMPACT/2-double-space, multiple items per line
OPTION        4-COMPACT/1-single-space, multiple items per line
OPTION        5-SUPER-COMPACT-single-space, multiple items per line, NO TITLE
OPTION        6-LIST/3-one item per line, double-space, left justified prompts
OPTION        7-LIST/4-one item per line, single-space, left justified prompts




11 ITEMS HAVE BEEN SELECTED                 VACATION SYSTEM
```

Fig. 8-11. Screen format.

```
MSKDEF 600                              Press PF10 to MSKCREAT
Date: @       >            @VACATION SYSTEM>           @Time: @XX:XX:XX>

@Emp#.............@999-99-9999>
@First Name.......@_____>
@Last Name........@_____>
@Hire Date........@_____>
@Earned Vacation..@_____>
@Vacation Taken...@_____>
@Sick Days Earned.@_____>
@Sick Days Taken..@_____>
@Comp Days Earned.@_____>
@Comp Days Taken..@_____>
@Comment (3 lines)@_____>
                  @_____>
                  @_____>


LAST GEN=                LAST UPD-90 07 29   VACATION SYSTEM
(PF KEYS) --FIELD:  18=CHG 19=DEL 20=DUP 21=MOVE     --LINE: 4=DUP 5=ERASE 6=MOVE
 2494 BYTES MAX,  1056 USED,  1438 LEFT      24=POP-UP   13=DEL  14=INS
```

Fig. 8-12. Painted screen.

set the attribute to skip protect, and indicate that the field is optional, as is shown in FIG. 8-14. Note that MAGEC determined the type of field and number of significant digits from the hit pattern that was drawn earlier. Figure 8-15 displays pop-up windows with HELP data just a *PF* key away.

```
MSKDEF 600                                    Press PF10 to MSKCREAT
Date: @      >           @VACATION SYSTEM>          @Time: @XX:XX:XX>
                         @Harbinger Company>

                           @999-99-9999>
@First Name.......@_____>
@Last Name........@_____>


@Hire Date........@_____>
@Earned Vacation..@_____>
@Vacation Taken...@_____>          <Due{z,zzz,zzz.99-}
@Sick Days Earned.@_____>
@Sick Days Taken..@_____>          <Due{z,zzz,zzz.99-}
@Comp Days Earned.@_____>
@Comp Days Taken..@_____>          <Due{z,zzz,zzz.99-}
@Comment (3 lines)@_____>
                 @_____>
                 @_____>


                 <Total Due{z,zzz,zzz.99-}

LAST GEN=              LAST UPD-90 07 29   VACATION SYSTEM
(PF KEYS) --FIELD:  18=CHG 19=DEL 20=DUP 21=MOVE     --LINE: 4=DUP 5=ERASE 6=MOVE
 2494 BYTES MAX, 1056 USED,  1438 LEFT        24=POP-UP  13=DEL  14=INS
```

Fig. 8-13. Editing screen.

```
MSKDEF 600                                -- Hit ENTER to Change --
Date: @      >           @VACATION SYSTEM>          @Time: @XX:XX:XX>
                         @Harbinger Company>

                           @999-99-9999>
@First Name.......@             >
@Last Name........@                    >


@Hire Date........@      >
@Earned Vacation..@       >
@Vacation Taken...@       >          <Due |        >
@Sick Days Earned.@       >
@Sick Days Taken..@       >          <Due |        >
@Comp Days Earned.@       >
@Comp Days Taken..@       >          <Due |        >
@Comment (3 lines)@                                >
                 @                                >
                 @                                >


                 <Total Due |        >

   SCRN FLD NM:  Svacdue  ( 000 )    ATTR:  saDRNF TYPE: - SIG: 07 DEC: 02 REQ: o
 EDIT TABLE:  000 DATABASE SOURCE/TARGET:  vacation-due
W-FLD:       ( 000 ) CLR: 0              ROW: 011 COL: 041 LGTH: 0013 LOC: 0
```

Fig. 8-14. Screen field naming.

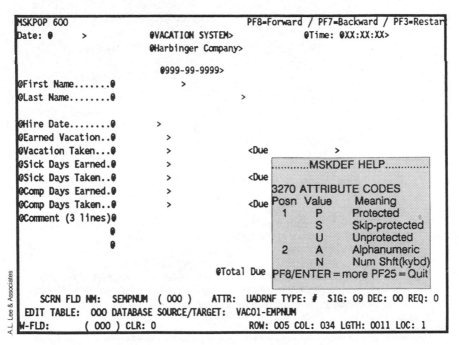

MSKPOP 600   PF8=Forward / PF7=Backward / PF3=Restart

Date: @   >   @VACATION SYSTEM>   @Time: @XX:XX:XX>
                             @Harbinger Company>

                              @999-99-9999>

@First Name.......@   >
@Last Name........@   >

@Hire Date........@   >
@Earned Vacation..@   >
@Vacation Taken...@   >   <Due   >
@Sick Days Earned.@   >   ....MSKDEF HELP.............
@Sick Days Taken..@   >   <Due
@Comp Days Earned.@   >   3270 ATTRIBUTE CODES
@Comp Days Taken..@   >   <Due Posn Value   Meaning
@Comment (3 lines)@   1   P   Protected
                  @   S   Skip-protected
                  @   U   Unprotected
                                        2   A   Alphanumeric
                                                N   Num Shft(kybd)
                          @Total Due PF8/ENTER = more PF25 = Quit

     SCRN FLD NM: SEMPNUM (000)   ATTR: UADRNF TYPE: # SIG: 09 DEC: 00 REQ: 0
     EDIT TABLE: 000 DATABASE SOURCE/TARGET: VAC01-EMPNUM
  W-FLD: (000) CLR: 0   ROW: 005 COL: 034 LGTH: 0011 LOC: 1

Fig. 8-15. Pop-up windows.

You can always return to your tasks list anytime, as is shown in FIG. 8-16. If you draw fields on your screen that don't exist in the data records, you must add code to your program so it will perform the process of computing the values and display them in those fields. You can choose any number of insertion points and insert your customer code. You will choose and insert your code immediately following a good read of your primary input file. You must insert your customer code for this process in the logical join insertion point. This insertion point is not on this screen, so you must page forward until you find it.

You will place the cursor on the logical join line and press Enter to select that insertion point, as shown in FIG. 8-17. You will indicate the line where you should add code; MAGEC will open the screen and you will enter what you want. MAGEC will align the tabs and close the screen when you hit Enter, as presented in FIG. 8-18. You have opened the screen and added the code that will perform the process, as is shown in FIG. 8-19. You have highlighted the lines you entered. Note that you always use standard COBOL. You can see that MAGEC-generated COBOL is readable by programmers. Now you can compile and test your program.

Your program is ready for use after a quick compile. The inquiry screen is shown in FIG. 8-20. Simple list-type screens were also automatically generated, as shown in FIG. 8-21. You can start at the first key or any key in the file and list all records that follow. You can also start anywhere and list backward. You can cursor select any line and see the detail screen.

```
TSKLST 600                                    PF8=Next Page   --   PF5 = PAGE 1

                        M A G E C                   TASK LIST FOR MSK600

.....................T A S K...................... PAGE 1 .......STATUS......
I.          DEFINE APPLICATION TO DICTIONARY
            1.  DEFINE SCREEN HEADER                              DONE
            2.  DEFINE MMP                                        DONE
II.         VERIFY THAT FILES/DATABASE ARE DEFINED
            1.  DEFINE MASTER KEY & NORMALIZATION RULES           DONE
            2.  DEFINE SUBORDINATE KEY(S)                       NOT DONE
III.        DEFINE SCREENS
            1.  PAINT SCREEN/DEFINE MASK DETAIL                 37 DONE
            2.  SELECT FIELDS FOR LOCATE SCREEN                  5 DONE
            3.  SPECIFY LOCATE HEADINGS                          5 DONE
            4.  GENERATE MASK (EXECUTE MSKCREAT)                  DONE
IV.         CODE CUSTOMIZATION ALGORITHMS
        A.  DATA DIVISION
            1.  DATA DEFINITION              %DATDEF            1 DONE
            2.  ADD/MODIFY FUNCTION CODES    %FUNCT        DEFAULT LOGIC USED
            3.  MODIFY (MODMAINT) FUNCTION CODES  %FUNCTM   DEFAULT LOGIC USED
Position the Cursor on an Item and Press ENTER to Select it, Press PF2 for
    Item Description       -OR-    PF1 FOR HELP
KEY=MASK NUMBER
```

A.L. Lee & Associates

Fig. 8-16. Task list.

```
TSKLST 600                                    PF8=Next Page   --   PF5=PAGE 1
                        M A G E C                   TASK LIST FOR MSK600
.....................T A S K...................... PAGE 3 .......STATUS......
IV.         CODE CUSTOMIZATION ALGORITHMS    (CONTINUED)
        D.  DATA BASE COMMANDS
            1.   INITIALIZE RECORD FOR AN ADD    %ADDINIT  DEFAULT LOGIC USED
            2.   LOGIC TO ADD DATA TO DATABASE   %ADDIT    DEFAULT LOGIC USED
            3.   LOGIC TO DELETE FROM DATABASE   %DELET    DEFAULT LOGIC USED
            4.   Logical Join-secondary files   %JOIN      1 DONE
            5.   LOGIC TO'SETL' ON THE DATABASE  %LOCKY    DEFAULT LOGIC USED
            6.   READ FOR UPDATE ROUTINE (CHANGE) %RDUKY   DEFAULT LOGIC USED
            7.   READ FOR DISPLAY ROUTINE        %REDKY    DEFAULT LOGIC USED
            8.   LOGIC TO READ FIRST RECORD      %REDLE    DEFAULT LOGIC USED
            9.   LOGIC TO READ-NEXT RECORD       %REDNX    DEFAULT LOGIC USED
           10.   LOGIC TO DROP EXCLUSIVE CONTROL %RELES    DEFAULT LOGIC USED
           11.   LOGIC TO UPDATE THE DATABASE    %UPDAT    DEFAULT LOGIC USED
        E.  SCREEN NAVIGATION
            1.   MMP EXIT LOGIC                  %GOBACK   DEFAULT LOGIC USED
            2.   LOGIC FOR AFTER A DB ADD        %GOODADD  DEFAULT LOGIC USED
Position the Cursor on an Item and Press ENTER to Select it, Press PF2 for
    Item Description              -OR-      PF1 FOR HELP
KEY=MASK NUMBER
```

A.L. Lee & Associates

Fig. 8-17. Select insertion point.

```
ALGCHG 600/JOIN/01-SIF/000              Press ENTER to Update
SEARCH ARG: ...................................................................
            Password:      M A G E C              JOIN    page
                    CUSTOM ALGORITHM DEFINITION FOR MSK 600   01-SIF  (000)
Logical Join-secondary files            TAB Option  (PF14=ON/OF): ON
....+..;10.;..+;..20....+...30....+...40...;+...50....+...60....+...70..
              IF (NOT-FOUND) GO TO JA900-RETURN.              01
;;compute vacation-due =                                     02
;;;;vac01-earned-vacation - vac01-taken-vacation.            03
;;compute sick-due =                                         04
;;;;vac01-earned-sick-days - vac01-taken-sick-days.          05
;;compute comp-due =                                         06
;;;;vac01-earned-comp-days - vac01-taken-comp-days.          07
;;compute total-due =                                        08
;;;;vacation-due + sick-due + comp-due.                      09
                                                             10
                                                             11
                                                             12
                                                             13
                                                             14
                                                             15
Move CURSOR to a line, use ERASE EOF to Delete it -or- PF20 to Insert After it
Semicolon (;) is the TAB Character     Asterisk (*) in col. 1 = suppress upcase
   Press PF2 for Instructions
```

Fig. 8-18. Screen opening.

```
ALGNXT 600/JOIN/01-SIF/000
SEARCH ARG:  ..................................................................
            Password:        M A G E C              JOIN    page
                    CUSTOM ALGORITHM DEFINITION FOR MSK 600   01-SIF  (000)
Logical Join-secondary files            TAB Option(PF14=ON/OFF):  ON
....+..;10.;..+;..20....+...30....+...40...;+...50....+...60....+...70..
            IF (NOT-FOUND) GO TO JA900-RETURN.              01
            COMPUTE VACATION-DUE =                          02
                VAC01-EARNED-VACATION - VAC01-TAKEN-VACATION. 03
            COMPUTE SICK-DUE =                              04
                VAC01-EARNED-SICK-DAYS - VAC01-TAKEN-SICK-DAYS. 05
            COMPUTE COMP-DUE =                              06
                VAC01-EARNED-COMP-DAYS - VAC01-TAKEN-COMP-DAYS. 07
            COMPUTE TOTAL-DUE = .                           08
                VACATION-DUE + SICK-DUE + COMP-DUE.          09
            MOVE REDKY                TO TWA-DB-CMD.          10
            MOVE 'SIFK1'              TO TWA-DB-KEY-NAME.     11
            MOVE 'SIF01'             TO TWA-ELT-LIST.         12
            MOVE ZERO                                        13
                   TO SIF01-KEY-PREFIX.                      14
            MOVE VAC01-EMPNUM                                15
Move CURSOR to a line, use ERASE EOF to Delete it  -or-  PF20 to Insert After it
Semicolan (;) is the TAB Character     Asterisk (*) in col. 1 = suppress upcase
   Press PF2 for Instructions
```

Fig. 8-19. Compiling and testing.

```
VACSEE  000000013
Date:  07/29/1990              VACATION SYSTEM              Time:  21:45:15
                               Harbinger Company
                                 000-00-0013

First Name.......  Jolly
Last Name........  Greengiant


Hire Date........  12/25/80
Earned Vacation..     11.00
Vacation Taken...     22.00        Due            11.00-
Sick Days Earned.      1.00
Sick Days Taken..       .40        Due              .60
Comp Days Earned.     38.40
Comp Days Taken..      2.00        Due            36.40
Comment (3 lines) Takes a vacation anytime he wants, don't give him
                  any guff or he will bean you


                                 Total Due        26.00


Press PF4 for browse (LOC) screen          Press PF13 for Hardcopy
Press PF16 to Copy field to buffer         Press PF17 to Paste data from buffer
Press PF2 for field-level HELP             Press PF24 for Pop-up Short-List
```

Fig. 8-20. Inquiry screen.

```
VACLOC 1                                    END OF LIST-PF5=Restart/PF7=Backwar


Emp#        First Name      Last Name          Hire Date   Earned Vacation

000-00-0001 Harry           Houdini             12/11/45       14.50
000-00-0002 Uri             Geller              02/27/45       16.00
000-00-0003 Merlin          The Magician        12/11/45       14.50
000-00-0004 Benny           Geller              03/02/46        3.25
000-00-0012 Demo            Programmer          12/25/80       56.00
000-00-0013 Jolly           Greengiant          12/25/80       11.00
000-00-0014 ADDED           NEWGUY              05/01/90         .00
000-00-0015 David           Copperfield         02/29/88       50.00
000-00-0017 Super           Man                 02/29/44       14.90
000-00-0018 BOBBIE          LLOYD               02/29/88       50.00
         ++++  10 Records Scanned,  10 Displayed so far -   page  1  ++++




KEY 1=Employee# (9-digits)             Press PF13 for Hardcopy
  You may Position the CURSOR on an item and Press ENTER to "SEE" it
(Browsing Forward)
```

Fig. 8-21. Detail screen.

AND, OR, and NOT logic query is also available. Here, MAGEC must find all records containing "GE" or "BO," as is shown in FIG. 8-22. Figure 8-23 presents query by example. You have told MAGEC to search for all records with a last name of GELLER. After performing any list type screen (query), you can always refer back to the old query and select another record from a pop-up window. Just move the cursor to the key that's desired and press Enter, as shown in FIG. 8-24.

If you make errors while you're updating the fields on MAGEC screens, all errors are highlighted in red, and sensible error messages will tell you what you did wrong, as is displayed in FIG. 8-25. Error-level HELP data is displayed if you request HELP while error messages are being displayed, as is shown in FIG. 8-26.

```
VACFND 1                              END OF LIST - PF5=Restart/PF7=Backward
SEARCH ARG  GE|OR| BO.......................................................
Emp#         First Name      Last Name           Hire Date  Earned Vacation
..........   ...............  ..................  ........   ..............
000-00-0002  Uri             Geller              02/27/45        16.00
000-00-0004  Benny           Geller              03/02/46         3.25
000-00-0018  BOBBIE          LLOYD               02/29/88        50.00
        ++++  10 Records Scanned,  03 Displayed so far -  page 1  ++++




KEY 1=Employee# (9-digits)                  Press PF13 for Hardcopy
  You may Position the Cursor on an item and Press ENTER to "SEE" it
(Browsing Forward)                          or Press PF4 to "CHG" it
```

Fig. 8-22. Logic query.

```
VACSCN 1                              END OF LIST - PF5=Restart/PF7=Backward

Emp#         First Name      Last Name           Hire Date  Earned Vacation
..........   ...............  geller..................  ........   ..............
000-00-0002  Uri             Geller              02/27/45        16.00
000-00-0004  Benny           Geller              03/02/46         3.25
        ++++  10 Records Scanned,  02 Displayed so far -  page 1  ++++







KEY 1=Employee# (9-digits)                  Press PF13 for Hardcopy
  You may Position the Cursor on an item and Press ENTER to "SEE" it
(Browsing Forward)                          or Press PF4 to "CHG" it
```

Fig. 8-23. Search records.

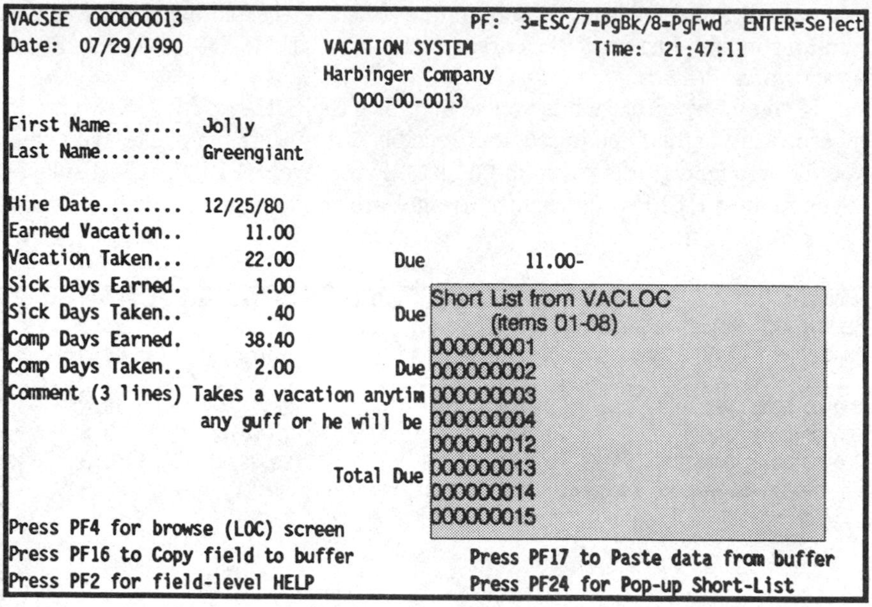
VACSEE 000000013
PF: 3=ESC/7=PgBk/8=PgFwd ENTER=Select
Date: 07/29/1990
VACATION SYSTEM
Time: 21:47:11
Harbinger Company
000-00-0013
First Name....... Jolly
Last Name........ Greengiant
Hire Date........ 12/25/80
Earned Vacation.. 11.00
Vacation Taken... 22.00 Due 11.00-
Sick Days Earned. 1.00
Sick Days Taken.. .40 Due
Comp Days Earned. 38.40
Comp Days Taken.. 2.00 Due
Comment (3 lines) Takes a vacation anytim
any guff or he will be
Total Due
Short List from VACLOC
(items 01-08)
000000001
000000002
000000003
000000004
000000012
000000013
000000014
000000015
Press PF4 for browse (LOC) screen
Press PF16 to Copy field to buffer
Press PF2 for field-level HELP
Press PF17 to Paste data from buffer
Press PF24 for Pop-up Short-List

A.L. Lee & Associates

Fig. 8-24. List-type screen.

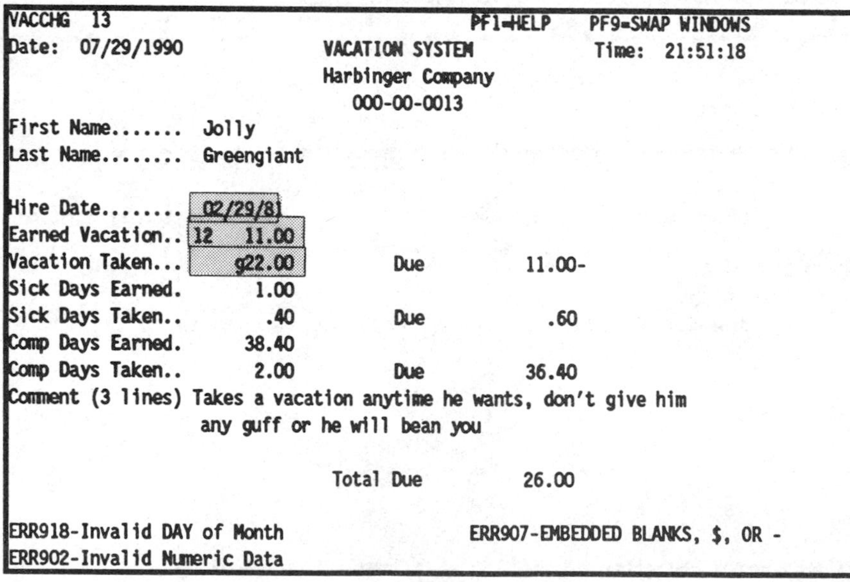
VACCHG 13
PF1=HELP PF9=SWAP WINDOWS
Date: 07/29/1990
VACATION SYSTEM
Time: 21:51:18
Harbinger Company
000-00-0013
First Name....... Jolly
Last Name........ Greengiant
Hire Date........ 02/29/81
Earned Vacation.. 12 11.00
Vacation Taken... g22.00 Due 11.00-
Sick Days Earned. 1.00
Sick Days Taken.. .40 Due .60
Comp Days Earned. 38.40
Comp Days Taken.. 2.00 Due 36.40
Comment (3 lines) Takes a vacation anytime he wants, don't give him
any guff or he will bean you
Total Due 26.00
ERR918-Invalid DAY of Month
ERR907-EMBEDDED BLANKS, $, OR -
ERR902-Invalid Numeric Data

A.L. Lee & Associates

Fig. 8-25. Updating fields.

```
                                            PRESS ENTER TO RETURN TO VACCHG

READ THIS, THEN PRESS ENTER
-----------------------------------------------------------------------------
      918      Invalid DAY of Month
The value entered into the DAY portion of a screen field defined for "date" type
editing is not valid.  It must be a numeric value, one or two digits in length, not
less than 1 nor greater than the number of days in the month.  February has 28 days
in most years, 29 in leap years.
      907      EMBEDDED BLANKS, $, or -
You have entered a numeric value incorrectly into a screen field specified for
"numeric" type editing; you have entered embedded Blanks or other illegal
characters.

      902      Invalid Numeric Data
You have entered non-numeric data into a screen field specified for numeric type
editing.  Correct and re-try.



ERR918-Invalid DAY of Month                   ERR907-EMBEDDED BLANKS, $, OR -
ERR902-Invalid Numeric Data
```

Fig. 8-26. Help data.

As shown in FIG. 8-27, you can place a cursor on a field and request field-level HELP by pressing F2. All generated HELP data may be supplemented with your words. "This is the date the employee started employment" is cus-

```
                                            Press PF3 to RETURN to Screen

      M A G E C   S C R E E N   O N L I N E   D O C U M E N T A T I O N
-----------------------------------------------------------------------------


This is a date field with a 2-digit year.  MM/DD/YY
This field is optional - may be left blank.
The database field name is VAC01-DATE-HIRED
  This is the date the employee started employment.






ERR918-Invalid DAY of Month                   ERR907-EMBEDDED BLANKS, $, OR -
ERR902-Invalid Numeric Data
```

Fig. 8-27. Online documentation.

tom HELP data. You may enter as much custom data as you think your users will read. MAGEC doesn't update the database until all errors are corrected on the screen. MAGEC always tells the user when an update has been performed, as is shown in FIG. 8-28. (Also see TABLE 8-3.)

```
VACCHG  13                                 Data UPDATED on Database
Date:  07/29/1990            VACATION SYSTEM            Time:  21:51:18
                             Harbinger Company
                               000-00-0013

First Name.......  Jolly
Last Name........  Greengiant

Hire Date........  02/29/80
Earned Vacation..     12.00
Vacation Taken...      2.00        Due          11.00-
Sick Days Earned.      1.00
Sick Days Taken..       .40        Due            .60
Comp Days Earned.     38.40
Comp Days Taken..      2.00        Due          36.40
Comment (3 lines) Takes a vacation anytime he wants, don't give him
                  any guff or he will bean you


                        Total Due          26.00



                                   Press PF24 for Pop-up Short-List
```

Fig. 8-28. Update database.

Table 8-3. Vacation System Summary

You have met or exceeded all specifications and all desires of your user.

You now have the following transactions:

VACSEE	Inquiry	Detail by key
VACCHG	Update	"
VACADD	Data Entry	"
VACDUP	Duplicate	"
VACDEL	Delete	"
VACNXT	Forward/Backward Browse	
VACLOC	Start at any location and list a screen full	
VACSCN	Query by example (generic name using wild cards)	
VACFND	Boolean AND, OR, NOT query capability	

You have prototyped for the user and you have his or her willing approval.

Your new application has real error messages that tell the user exactly what is wrong. Your new application has real HELP data for every field, every error message, and all functions.

Authorized users in the user department may even supplement the HELP data with their own words. Authorized users are automatically added to the Menu.

You have real hard copy documentation.

Your application allows generic Query with search arguments that are *not* based on the key. The Query is integrated with the detail screens. A pop-up window allows selection of another key found in a query from the detail screens.

You even have Screen swap to allow the user to easily coordinate his work.

A.L. Lee & Associates

Table 8-3. Continued.

Your application is SAA standard Structured COBOL and it performs as well as or better than the programs that you would have hand coded.

Your program is dictionary-driven for edit routines, table data, and HELP data. You are assured Data Integrity because of your centralized dictionary-driven edit routines, business rules, and referential integrity.

Your tasklist menu screen will look the same to the maintenance programmer in the future as it looks to you today. Maintenance is no longer a problem. All customization is standard COBOL. You have complete Where-Used reporting compatibility.

You can deliver this program NOW, not in months or years from now!

9

Structured
functional methods

This chapter covers the formal requirements specification method, formal specification technique, reusability of specifications, multiple views of models, the structured functional requirements analysis environment, and requirements specification languages.

Formal requirements specification method

A formal requirements specification states what a software does. It formally specifies the software development process. The informal requirement statement defines in natural language the meaning of the requirement. This statement is then translated into a precise language that's defined by formal syntax and semantics. The Software Engineering Institute of Carnegie-Mellon University has developed such a process. It has five levels of software development maturity, as is listed in TABLE 9-1.

Level 1 is chaotic due to poor management disciplines. Procedures and controls are ill defined. There are serious problems with costs and scheduling. The organization doesn't consistently apply software engineering management to the process, nor does it use modern tools and technology. 74% to 86% of all software developers fall into this category.

Level 2 repeats activities in the following order: cost estimating, scheduling, requirements changes, code changes, status reviews, and other repeatable standard methods. Costs and schedules are under control to some extent. Only 22% to 23% of all software developers are in this category.

Level 3 defines the project well. The software development process is defined in terms of software engineering standards and methods. This process includes design and code reviews and training programs. The process review

Table 9-1. Software
Development Maturity Levels

1. Chaotic
2. Repeated activities
3. Definition
4. Management
5. Optimization

is standard. Only 1% to 4% of software developers have achieved this level of expertise.

Level 4 manages the project well. The software development process is quantified, measured, and well-controlled. The tools are used more to control and manage the software development process and to support data gathering and analysis. The software developers do extensive analyses of data garnered from reviews, and they conduct tests. None of the software developers have reached this level of maturity.

Level 5 is optimization. Since a high degree of control over the process has been achieved, the project management can now focus on optimizing functionality. Comprehensive error-cause analysis and prevention studies provide the data and improve the process iteratively. No one has reached this level yet.

Formal specification technique

Formal specification technique captures both functional and nonfunctional properties of the software system that will be developed. The functional properties define the output requirements of the system, whereas the nonfunctional properties relate to the processes by which the output is obtained. Only the functional properties can be specified formally. The formal specification technique is shown in TABLE 9-2.

Table 9-2. Formal
Specification Technique

- Mechanics of specification
- Validation and verification of specification
- Reusability of specification

Mechanics of specification specifies the teams, development log, graphical aids, and documentation. Specifications of large systems are themselves large and complex, and their development is necessarily a group activity. In fact, writing a specification may take longer than building the system from that specification. Further, requirements typically change while a specification is being produced. It's essential that all assignments to members of a specification team and all requirements changes are documented in a log that the specification team keeps. A register of documentations is maintained. Such documentation contains functionality diagrams of basic data types and devices, data flow diagrams, entity relationship diagrams, a state transition diagram, and petri nets.

Validation and *verification* are the formal methods, walk-throughs, and executable specifications. The purpose of validation and verification is to show that a product or process complies with its specification. Moreover, prototype implementation of the specifications of information control systems is rather easy, and dynamic test methods can be applied to the prototype. If the prototype is derived from the specification by "correctness-preserving" transformations, then it must be consistent with the specification so that there's no need for further verification.

Reusability of specifications is a technique, a process of implementing new software systems from preexisting software, which is illustrated in FIG. 9-1.

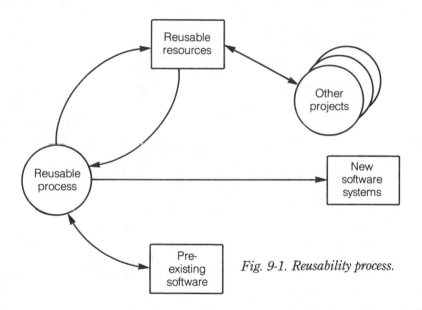

Fig. 9-1. Reusability process.

The reusability process captures commonalities and differences from the models of systems. It consists of development and acquisition of reusable resources, management, and use of those resources. The necessary steps for achieving the reusability process are listed in TABLE 9-3.

To *construct* means to reuse existing methods and products. To *collect* is to reuse the existing library and continue building it. To *catalog* is to reuse descriptive information. To *classify* is to reuse semantic and functional information. To *comprehend* means to reuse resources identification and analysis. To *customize* is to develop the application development from the reusable resources. Figure 9-2 shows the major activities of this process.

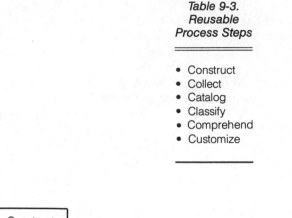

Table 9-3.
Reusable
Process Steps

- Construct
- Collect
- Catalog
- Classify
- Comprehend
- Customize

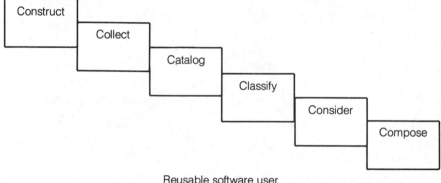

Reusable software user

Fig. 9-2. Major activities in the reusable process.

The components of the process model are adaptive, parameterized, and engineered components. The *adaptive model* for reuse is the process of modifying a system or component so it will perform its function in a different manner or on different data than was originally intended. In an adaptive model, to construct means, in this context, to build modular software while applying software engineering techniques such as information hiding and data encapsulation. Here, to collect means to organize the database of projects and project software. In this case, the catalog is the description of projects and software modules. In this model, classifying uses architectural models and applies reverse engineering. To comprehend means to maintain benchmark and other performance information that also includes test data. Customizing means using CASE tools and re-engineering support for maintenance.

Constructing, in the *parameterized process* model for software reuse, means building software as standard products and continually refining them, just like in a software factory. Here, collecting means establishing inventory for the software factory. In this case, cataloging is giving descriptive information of standard products. Classifying is semantic and functional, and tailors information on products. In this model, comprehending has rapid protoyping capability; customizing is automated customization and system generation.

The engineered process for software reuse is shown in FIG. 9-3. Domain analysis is the systematic exploration of related software systems that discover and exploit commonality. Domain analysis produces a set of features common

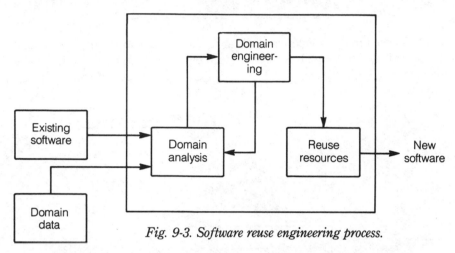

Fig. 9-3. Software reuse engineering process.

to a class of systems and represents them in an exploitable form. It also provides a method of mapping commonality to specific instances. The objectives help develop domain analysis products and support implementation of new applications by providing an understanding of domain, supporting user-developer communication, and providing reuse requirements, as illustrated in FIG. 9-4. The domain analysis consists of the components listed in TABLE 9-4. The

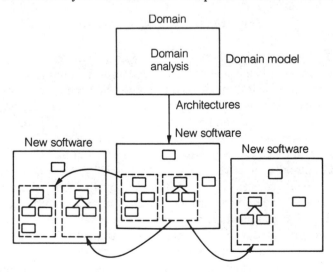

Fig. 9-4. Domain analysis products.

Table 9-4. Domain Analysis Components

- Context analysis
- Domain modeling
- Architecture modeling

methods used in the domain analysis are reused in the software development process. The domain analysis products can be further used in software implementation. Figure 9-5 shows the major features of the domain analysis methods process.

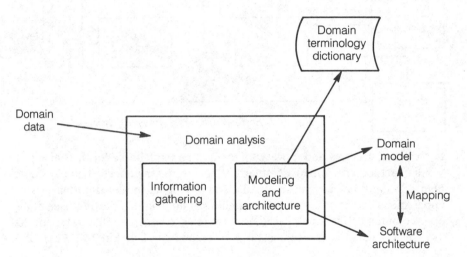

Fig. 9-5. Domain analysis methods.

Context modeling is domain scoping and analyzing the variables of external conditions. Context analysis consists of structure diagramming and context diagramming. The context model is a structure diagram that shows how the domain is placed relative to other domains. It's a top-level data flow diagram and shows external entities and data flows between the domain and the external entities. A sample context diagram is shown in FIG. 9-6. The context diagram provides the end-user's perspective on the capabilities.

Domain modeling is the analysis and modeling of domain problems. Domain modeling consists of an entity relationship model, feature model, functional model, and domain terminology dictionary. The entity relationship (ER) model is the combination of Chen's entity relationship model notation and the semantic data models. The semantic data model contains "is-a" and "consists-of" notations. A sample ER model is shown in FIG. 9-7.

The feature model provides the end-user's perspective on the capabilities of applications in a domain. These capabilities are mandatory, optional, and

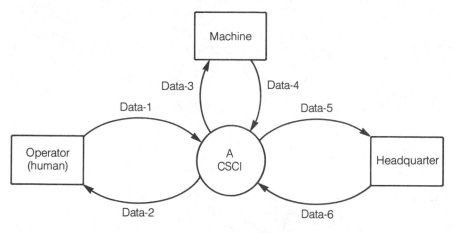

Fig. 9-6. A sample context diagram.

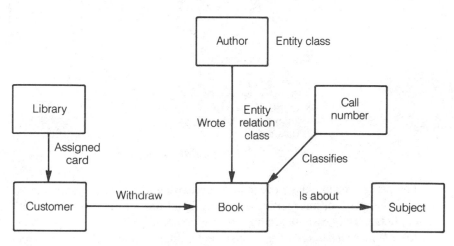

Fig. 9-7. ER model.

alternative. The capabilities of an application are defined as an instantiation of the feature model. This model is used to parameterize other models. The major components of the feature model are the features diagram, composition rules, issues and decisions, and records of existing system features.

Data flow models show the logical flow of data among the processors and data stores. The data flow model describes the internal interfaces among the components of the software system. Figure 9-8 illustrates a sample data flow model. It consists of rectangles, which are the source or destination of data outside the system. A data flow symbol (arrow) represents a path where data moves into, around, and out of the system. A process symbol (circle) represents a function of the system that logically transforms data. A data store is a symbol (open-ended rectangle) showing a place in the system where data is stored.

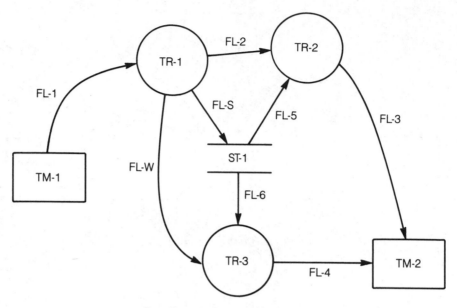

Data flow diagram

- Flows (FL)
- Transformation (TR) = processes
- Stores (ST) = files
- Terminator (TM) = data source/
  data sink

Fig. 9-8. A data-flow diagram.

The domain terminology dictionary standardizes baseline terminology. It provides the result of information gathering in all phases. The domain terminology dictionary is essential in an evolving domain.

Architecture modeling is the analysis and modeling of application architectures for the domain problems. Architecture modeling is a process that involves an interaction model and a module structure chart.

Structured, functional requirements analysis environments

A structured, functional requirements analysis environment is a collection of tools that cooperate and facilitate various activities. These tools analyze software requirements, specify software requirements, design software, test software, implement software, and manage the software life cycle during maintenance. The environment will accept any changes in the requirements without affecting its functionality and performance. It ensures that the end product will perform correctly and efficiently with the changes in the requirements. The purpose of this environment is to increase the efficiency of software production and enhance the quality of the developed software.

The environment shows the system as a set of entities that performs relevant tasks. The environment produces the inputs and consumes the outputs. The constraints on performance are imposed by the environment and function of the system. This also includes a description of the task that's performed by each entity and the way that entity interacts with other entities and the environment. Ideally, the functional aspect should complement the behavioral view. Each transaction in the latter view should be traceable through the system from the initial input through the interfaces and the functional units to the final output. The functional aspect is the normal starting point for the design process, since it's commonly the way the system is partitioned into smaller and simpler components. The functional model captures commonality of data and control flow for desired functionality. The functional model leads to requirements for architecture and reusable components.

The important nonfunctional requirement issues include performance and quality. *Performance* refers to run-time behavior issues that are related to time. Examples of performance specifications may be response times of a particular function or the reaction time that's available to an external event. *Quality* refers to software attributes such as reliability, readability, maintainability, correctness, and portability.

Multiple views of the software requirements model

Multiple views of the software requirements model are necessary so the process of software development can be understood. The models should reflect as many aspects of the software requirements as possible. The goal is twofold. The first goal is to help satisfy the customer by providing an understanding of the implementation of the requirements. The second goal is to assist the software developers with these models so the software design continues. The commonalities among these models are the types of products they eventually produce. The model differs depending upon the software development process used. The various models are listed in TABLE 9-5.

Table 9-5. Major Types of Models

- Requirements model
- User view/operational model
- Information flow model
- Implementation model

Specifications describe all subsets of the aspects of a software process. They also describe a product at some level of abstraction, from some point of view, using some degree of formalism. The desirable aspect, the desirable level of abstraction, the proper perspective, and the desirable degree of formalism are determined by the purpose and context of the particular process or product type within the software life cycle.

The *requirements model* provides at various levels a view of the software refinement process for the entire system, subsystem, or modules. The model details what requirements are essential for development of the software and what needs the proposed software system should fulfill.

The *user view/operational model* provides the requirements that are concerned with the software problems. What functions, from the customer's point of view, must the system perform so that these needs are met? The user view/operational model's main function is to communicate between the customer and the software developer. The goal is to correct any omission at the early stages, improve productivity, and increase the quality of the produced software. The model provides assistance and guidance to the customer and the software developer. It provides an understanding of the requirements in more detail and shows how they're to be implemented in development of the software.

The *information flow model* provides the necessary detailed requirements information for software development. This supplements the flow of information about what's essential from the customer's point of view. The type of information should be specified and based upon the purpose and context of the specification product.

The information is about commonality and differences. Commonality concerns the common states and transitions in the statecharts. Commonality also concerns the common activities and data flow for input and output in activity charts. The differences parameters are captured by conditions in control flow in the statecharts. The differences parameters are also captured by the optional data flow in activity charts.

The behavioral aspect shows the way the system responds to specific inputs, the states it will adopt, the outputs it will produce, and the boundary conditions on the validity of inputs and states. This includes a description of the environment that produces the inputs and consumes the outputs. It also includes constraints on performance that are imposed by the environment and function of the system. The information model includes finite state and data/object models.

The *implementation model* products actually lead and build the system in accordance with the customer's requirements. This provides the details of how a system will be built and behave as described in the software requirements analysis and specification. The code is written and tested so it can be actually implemented on the computer while a particular kind of technology is used. Any requests for change will be entertained and executed in the process. An existing system should be changed to either correct some inherent incorrectness, better fulfill changed requirements, or adapt to a changed environment of both hardware and software. Depending on the severity of the change, change requests can trigger the creation of new product versions at various levels in accordance with the changed requirements.

In the maintenance phase, the intended changes to the system need to be specified. In addition, new updated versions of various levels of existing products need to be developed. Specifications of processes and products permit the incorporation of changes in a formal way.

Requirements specification languages

Requirements specification languages allow the representation of the process and product specification. Languages provide frames within which the software requirements are defined and solved. A well-defined requirements specification language is a prerequisite for efficient and effective communication between the customer and software developer. If the functional requirements are defined better, there is more likelihood of system success. It's crucial that the customer's software requirements are well understood and analyzed so these can be further translated into an adequate set of specifications for software design and implementation.

These languages are involved in the process of eliciting, analyzing, and documenting the software requirements. These tasks are carried out in a concurrent, iterative, and interleaved manner until a set of adequate, correct, and complete requirements specifications is realized. The documented software requirements specification forms the basis of software design.

Languages include descriptive and operational aspects that analyze, manipulate, and transform the software requirements. A natural language such as English is used for description, as well as verbal reasoning and text manipulation. Graphical languages, such as data flow diagrams, entity-relationship diagrams, data/object diagrams, and flowcharts provide visual descriptions, visual reasoning, and graphic manipulation capabilities. Mathematics has its own symbolic notation, conceptual grammar, reasoning, and symbolic mechanisms.

During the software requirements specification, the descriptive model is analyzed for consistency, completeness, and correctness. The language that's used for describing and analyzing should be precise and unambiguous, and it should support operations such as checking completeness, correctness, and consistency. For software design and implementation, the language should be capable of expressing to the software developer the data logic and the software requirements in an exact and clear manner.

There are informal, semiformal, and formal languages that specify the requirements products. The formal and semiformal are complementary to each other. Informal languages are usually a combination of graphics and semiformal textual grammars that describe and specify software requirements. Graphical and natural languages provide an ideal vehicle that elicits customer requirements and communicates the software developer's understanding of the requirements back to the customer for verification.

The Problem Statement Language/Problem Statement Analyzer (PSL/PSA) is a computer-aided structure technique that's used for analysis and documentation of requirements. The methodology assists in the preparation of functional specifications for information processing systems. In the informal class, there are other methods and methodologies that are worth mentioning, such as Jackson System Development (JSD), Warnier-Orr, Structured Analysis by DeMarco, Yourdon, and Software Engineering Requirements Analysis (SERA) by the author. Some of these methods are supported by CASE tools, such as Excelerator, StP, ProMod, Teamwork, and TAGS.

Semiformal languages are based on some formal syntax that's usually graphically oriented. Formal languages are based on formal syntax and semantics. Most of the product and process representation languages used are semiformal languages that combine informal and formal components. Formal specification languages have a mathematical basis and employ formal notations that model software requirements. The formal notations provide precision and conciseness of specifications in that mathematical proof procedures can be used to test the consistency and syntactic correctness of the specification.

The Vienna Development Method (VDM) is a formal, mathematically oriented method for specifying and developing software. This method is formal because it leads to a set of interrelated formal specification documents. A formal document is written in a formal language, which is a language with mathematically defined syntax and semantics. The VDM specification language is called Meta-IV. For more detail on these methods/methodologies and CASE tools, please refer to my book, *Software Engineering Methods, Management, and CASE Tools*.

10

Real-time impact

The important features of real-time systems are accuracy, reliability, and immediate response. Real-time systems must supply correct results within specified time limits. The analytical approach should deal with transient overload, task blocking that's due to synchronization requirements, and aperiodic events. In this chapter, I discuss the impact of real-time upon Ada and run-time environments. I also discuss the transform logic CASE tool, "DesignAid II."

Real-time requirements

Real-time requirements have specific properties that a system or a particular layer of a system must satisfy. The real-time requirements of a system are accuracy, reliability, and immediate response. If the real-time system can't respond to an event instantaneously, then the event is gone forever. Real-time systems must supply correct results within specified time limits. Information that's accurate but late has no value. Real-time systems should have predictable timing characteristics and should be robust under stress.

Real-time requirements include task scheduling. Greater flexibility should be allowed in the syntactic placement of scheduling parameters. There should be a mechanism that limits the central processing unit (CPU) cycles that a task can use within a given period of time. This is needed for fault-tolerance in real-time systems. The main real-time requirement is allowing a task to use a CPU at a high priority for a limited number of cycles so that when this time budget is used up, other tasks can run.

An analysis can predict when a system will be able to meet its deadlines. The analytical approach should deal with transient overload, task blocking that's due to synchronization requirements, and aperiodic events.

It's essential that a real-time system executes a code segment within a specified amount of time. The software developer should have a mechanism that specifies the amount of time, and bounds the execution of a code segment. The software developer should have access to the time characteristics of certain critical run-time operations. These timing characteristics should be documented for future reference.

A particular task of sufficiently high priority can delay itself for a period of time with the assurance that it will resume execution immediately when the delay expires. That is, the duration of the interval should be equal to the request duration within a predictable tolerance.

The implementation-dependent timing and interprocess communication properties of the abort statement define real-time implementation. In particular, real-time implementations should require and implement the abort "immediately" for some reasonable definition. The definition should not allow the target task to run indefinitely until it reaches a synchronization point.

Real-time implementation should not generate code for subprograms that are implemented via a PRAGMA INTERFACE and explicitly placed at a specific memory location and region.

Real-time requirements analysis

Real-time requirements analysis addresses issues of logical correctness in software development. TABLE 10-1 presents a list of methods that address the timing and correctness of composition for real-time systems.

Table 10-1. Real-time Requirements Analysis Methods

- Software through Pictures (StP)
- Ward/Mellor
- STATEMATE
- Design Approach for Real-Time Systems (DARTS)
- Strategies for System Development (SSD)
- PROTOB
- ProMod
- Software Engineering Requirements Analysis (SERA)

NOTE: I have discussed these methods in detail in my book, *Software Engineering Methods, Management, and CASE Tools.*

Real-time systems are modeled not only with data flows and data stores, but also with control flows. A control flow is shown in FIG. 10-1. *Control flows* are signals or events that cause processes to be activated and other control flows to be generated.

Real-time systems are complex. Many systems include combinations of control signals that cause the activation of several different processes. These different processes can be activated in a predetermined order or as independent tasks. The activation of a process may generate a control signal, which in turn may lead to an indefinite number of other activations. Therefore, the final

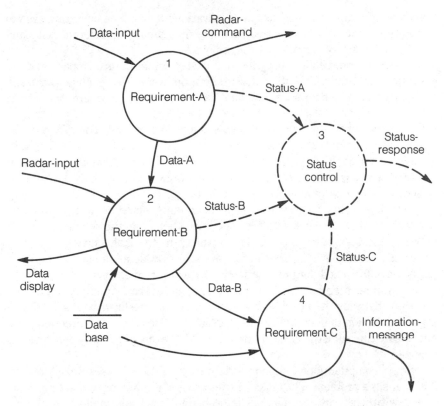

Fig. 10-1. A control-flow diagram sample.

system has thousands of possible results. All results must be completely and correctly specified by the analysis process.

Real-time and Ada language

Ada uses a multitasking facility. This facility contains Ada tasks that will be executed concurrently. In concurrent programming, several activities are proceeding in parallel. The term concurrent programming is applied to many situations in which several threads of control execute more or less in an interrelated fashion. Ada tasks are executed concurrently, which helps describe many situations where several threads of control execute in an interrelated fashion.

In order to write a program that consists of concurrent processes, you need some way to specify which processes are conceptually concurrent. In Ada, the language construct used to group a set of actions is known as a *task*. Tasks can run simultaneously on different processors in a distributed system, or they can be interleaved in a single-processor time-sharing system. Declaring a program unit as a task provides only logical concurrency; the language makes no guarantees about the speed of various tasks. The operating system or run-time processor has the responsibility for scheduling different tasks and for allocating any resources that they may need.

Tasks are independent program units; they run at their own pace and are essentially isolated unless the software developer specifies explicit *synchronization points*. A synchronization point serves as a place where one of the affected tasks can "wait" for the other process to "catch up" to it, that is, arrive at the corresponding point in its sequence of actions. The synchronization point delimits that section of code that will be executed while the tasks are synchronized. The synchronization point is known as the *rendezvous*. After the rendezvous is complete, the two tasks continue independently. Exceptions raised within a rendezvous are sometimes useful.

A task awaiting rendezvous is suspended until the rendezvous is possible. If a task must rendezvous with the scheduler, then from the scheduler's point of view, the task being blocked is equivalent to the task being suspended. When the scheduler activates the rendezvous, it awakens the task. There are many ways for scheduling to be effective by using rendezvous.

Communication between Ada tasks is asymmetrical. An important design decision that must be made with respect to system performance is determining the direction of entry calls. The decision that concerns the direction of an entry call can sometimes be made easier if the coupling between tasks is reduced.

Some compilers don't support Ada representation clauses for addresses. This causes a problem. The tasks' entries are not allowed, or they are not associated with hardware locations. This problem causes an inability for tasking and prevents hardware interrupts from being handled adequately. The only solution to this problem is to interface with the assembly program that allows adequate interrupt handling. Ada treats interrupts as entry calls to tasks.

The other problem is the lack of detailed error information when an unhandled exception occurs within a task and results in a system crash. This problem can be solved through the use of a compiler that's equipped to handle this type of problem.

Ada provides a mechanism that assigns a priority level to a task. With this mechanism, a task that has a higher priority is considered more urgent, and its processing is scheduled before those tasks that have a lower priority. A task's priority is established by a pragma that appears in its specification as follows:

```
pragma Priority (expression);
```

A concept that's commonly used in the design of real-time computer applications is that of a *monitor*. This is a software module that's responsible for controlling a resource. Its purpose is to monitor the use of that resource. For example, read and write operations to a disk are usually controlled by a monitor that ensures the integrity of data on the disk.

Ada run-time environment

The Ada run-time environment (RTE) consists of abstract data structures, code sequences, and predefined subroutines. Ada has its own unique run-time environment. The elements of the run-time environment provided by the programming language implementation must conform to the run-time environment conventions of the executive. The tailoring of run-time environments to specific applications requires unique development of the compiler and executives for the environments.

Ada includes important features for concurrent programming and storage management. Ada demands no specific supporting executive. Thus, Ada programs for embedded applications can be directly executed. Ada compilation systems provide the elements of the run-time environment. The compilation system for Ada selects the appropriate elements as they're directed by the source Ada programs and as dictated by the underlying computing resources and the resultant generated Ada program.

An Ada compilation system is responsible for providing all the elements of the Ada run-time environment. Ada provides high-level features for concurrent programming and for dynamic storage allocation. In addition to the compiler, which selects the data structure representations and enforces common code conventions, the run-time environment of an Ada compilation system accommodates the arbitrary number of Ada application interpretations that comply with the Ada language standard. The more direct support that underlying computing resources provide for the functionality of the features of Ada, the smaller the configured run-time system needs are.

Ada RTE analysis has an impact on software reuse. There are problems caused by RTE impediments to software reuse for applications with hard real-time requirements. There's a need to create standard packages that will support the RTE, classes of RTE, tailorable RTE, and provide guidelines for using the RTE for the effective reuse of the existing pretested software.

To overcome some of the problems, it's important that the RTE either modify or use compiler-dependent features in developing Ada real-time systems. This may solve the problem of immaturity in the Ada compilation systems and RTE. It's better that an Ada compiler be selected and its run-time be suitable to a particular need of an application than it is to go looking for the best one on the market. The mechanism of selection is to look for the vendor-supplied run-time routines, linker options, and pragmas. The guidelines for using an RTE focus on two essential aspects: communicating the characteristics of a configured RTE to the software development, and maintaining the configuration for future releases.

Real-time requirements specification

Real-time requirements specification is an approximation of what would actually be required if it were fully understood. A real-time requirements specification is an abstract representation of a system. A *system* is a coherent collection of computer hardware, software, communications, and possibly other components, as in a process-control system. Specifications may exist for each of the various layers of functional abstraction when they define the desired behavior of a system.

The real-time requirements specifications cover those paradigms that promote predictability, performance, and portability. The paradigms include real-time Ada tasking and monitoring for predictability and efficiency.

The specifications also include Ada run-time behavior, Ada run-time performance measurements, and Ada tasking optimization. Ada run-time behavioral specification depends upon time management, interrupt management, task management, and memory management.

Time management provides statistics on delay features. It explains under what circumstances a task can be suspended beyond its specified delay, which assumes that it's the highest priority task that's able to run. The interrupt management provides the feature for interrupt handling. Interrupt management covers under what circumstances the run-time system disables interrupts. It also explains the relationship between hardware interrupt priorities and task priorities. It presents the effects of interrupts upon the scheduling behavior of other tasks. *Task management* relates to tasks and priorities schedules. Task management presents the circumstances that determine when or if an aborted task stops executing prior to a synchronization point. The memory management relates to storage allocation algorithms.

Ada run-time performance measurements specify a set of run-time performance measurements whose values must be known so they can be completely analyzed and there can be a prediction of the average and worst-case behavior of real-time systems. TABLE 10-2 lists the measurement factors (1990 Borger and Goodenough).

Table 10-2. Ada Run-time Performance Measurements Factors

- Interrupt latency—the maximum duration of time from when interrupt request occurs until the first instruction of application code is executed.
- Interrupts disabled—the maximum duration of time when interrupts are locked out by the run-time system, other than during the servicing of an interrupt.
- Task switch—the duration of time necessary to switch from the execution of one Ada task to another.
- Run-time latency—the worst case duration of time for the execution of each run-time system service call.
- Scheduling latency—for a task whose priority is higher than the current executing task, the duration of time from when a delay expiration occurs and amount of time for a duration to resume its execution.
- Delay inversion—the worst case and average time taken to process the expiration of a delay when a higher priority task is being executed.
- Clock overhead—the amount of overhead required for the update of real-time clock.
- Rendezvous times—simple rendezvous (no parameters and no body), complex rendezvous (at least one parameter and an accept body); the additional overhead for a conditional call and a timed call of each type.
- Fetch current time—the duration of time needed so the current time can be read.

Table 10-2. Continued.

- Performance sensitivity—the effect of program performance on tasks, selective wait, entry parameters, and parameter size.
- Hidden run-time services—associated with heap management and diagnostic tests.

Ada tasking optimization specifies that context switching and tasking overhead should be kept to a minimum. It provides guidelines for optimization of compiler tasking, monitor tasks, fast interrupt calls, and run-time algorithms. The run-time algorithms include task scheduling, priority queuing, delay management, and interrupt processing.

The transform logic CASE tool

The transform logic CASE tool for real-time systems is called DesignAid II. This is a tool for the creation and management of requirements for embedded systems, behavior-dependent systems, and automated process control systems.

Real-time modeling is an integrated part of DesignAid II. This includes an interface, multiuser repository, integrated document preparation, AutoDraw, and Application Programmer's Interface (API). This provides comprehensive support for Ward/Mellor graphic notation and analysis, and Hatley graphic notation. The Process Modeling of DesignAid II supports Yourdon/DeMarco graphic notation, as well as integrated support with the Data Modeling and Real-Time.

DesignAid II Real-Time supplements structured analysis notation by adding the extensions as defined by Ward and Mellor for modeling real-time requirements. The notation is captured in Transformation Schema and State Transition Diagrams.

Transformation Schema are data flow diagrams that have been extended and allow for the specification of control. The notation used specifies control and is included in TABLE 10-3. An example of Transformation Schema is shown in FIG. 10-2.

DesignAid II checks Transformation Schema for semantic correctness and records each of the diagram objects in the repository. State Transition Diagrams (STD) allow for the specification of the behavior of the system. The

Table 10-3. Control Notations

- Control transforms
- Event flows and prompts
- Event stores
- Time-continuous data flows

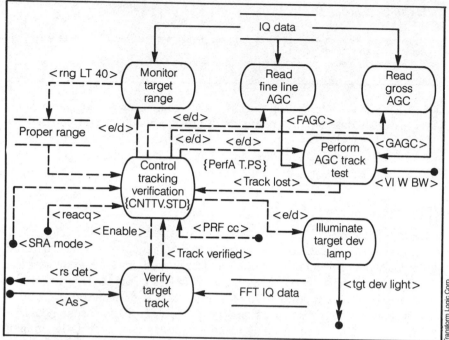

Fig. 10-2. This example of a transformation schema represents how DesignAid II allows system analysts to depict control within their system. The Design-Aid II repository automatically captures and stores all information.

notations used specify control. These are states, transitions, conditions, and actions. Conditions include text as well as events. Actions include action text as well as events and prompts. DesignAid II checks the semantic correctness of STD and records each of the diagram objects in the repository. An example of an STD is shown in FIG. 10-3.

The CASE tool also provides a balance for a parent data transform to its child Transformation Schema. It also balances a parent control transform to its child STD.

Real-time modeling technique

Real-time modeling offers extensive automated analysis features for real-time modeling techniques. This scans models and performs a rule-based analysis that validates the accuracy, consistency, completeness, and correct use of graphic syntax in real-time models. This also includes interactive error handling, locates and highlights errors in the model, and produces a detailed error report. It balances from the context schema in real-time models to all transformation schema, and balances STD with their associated Transformation

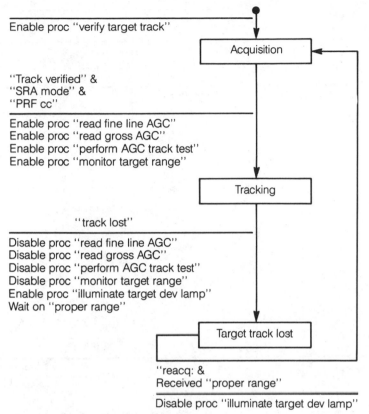

Fig. 10-3. This example of a state diagram depicts the conditions and actions that cause the system to change states. DesignAid II also provides balancing between the state transition diagram and its associated control transform. Transform Logic Corp.

Schema. Balancing locates logic errors and inconsistencies early in the development process. DesignAid II also populates the repository directly from validated diagrams and ensures consistency.

Standard reports and user-defined reporting can be used so system documentation such as functional specifications and database specifications will be generated. The repository lets the software developer prepare user-defined analytical reports on objects and relations. These reports are state matrix and impact analysis. A state matrix report is illustrated in FIG. 10-4, and it shows states and their related transition in a tabular format. The impact analysis reports form "how-used" relationships. Besides that, it also produces reports that identify redundancies and duplications in the model of the system, and locates reusable objects in the repository.

Conditions States		SRA mode & PRF cc & track lost track verified		reacq & received proper range
Entry to initial state	Enable proc verify target track Acquisition			
Acquisition		Enable proc read fine line AGC, Enable proc read gross AGC, Enable proc monitor target range, Enable proc perform AGC track test, Tracking		
Tracking			Enable proc illuminate target dev lamp, Disable proc read fine line AGC, Disable proc read gross AGC, Disable proc perform AGC track test, Disable proc monitor target range, Wait on proper range Target track lost	
Target track lost				Disable proc illuminate target dev lamp Acquisition

Fig. 10-4. The state matrix report provides an alternative representation of the state transition diagram. Transform Logic Corp.

11

The object-oriented approach

This chapter covers the evolving object-oriented approach to software requirements analysis. With this approach, software is defined in terms of:

- Objects that compose a system.
- The behavior of those objects.

The object-oriented approach is receiving wide acceptance as standard technology within the software industry. With this approach, software products can be developed in a manner that's similar to the development of hardware products. Instead of writing instructions, the object-oriented approach involves interconnecting reusable software components.

The object-oriented process

The object-oriented process identifies independent objects in the software requirements. These objects interact and operate on their components. Actions are done to objects and actions are taken by objects that communicate by messages. Actions that are taken within an object are hidden from the user. The only interface that's seen is the resulting message from the object.

The object-oriented approach is a change of mind-set. It considers the world as objects that can act. Objects can be easily identified. Let me give you a simple example. My son, Thomas, was very fond of playing with balls when he was young. When he started talking, he would look at the sky during the day, point out the moon, and say, "Ball, ball." A child speaks the truth. He saw an object that looked like his ball. Each round object has certain properties and attributes that make it unique in characteristics.

Objects, from a very high-level view, are entities that exist uniquely in time and space. In other words, objects have a state and are characterized by the actions they perform on other objects and by actions that are performed on them. The objects must communicate. The communication requirement helps with data hiding and makes possible object-oriented languages such as C++, SmallTalk, and Ada, which has the ability to treat objects as a black box.

Existing data structures are inherently part of an object. Functionality and data are not separated into programs and databases, but are encapsulated into a single whole called *objects*. A set of similar objects is called an *object class*. The attributes of one class might be inherited by any object or class and defined with the previously defined class, which includes any methods that are defined as part of the class. The actual objects are instances of an object class. An object encapsulates attributes and does functions on an entity in a single definition. The main enhancements allow for the definition of classes and functions and provide ways to control operations on them. These operations are referred to as *overloaders*, *constructors*, and *destructors*.

Inheritance can form a change that gives the most recently defined class all the attributes of the previous classes. A *class* is defined as a type with various attributes that are used so other classes and objects can be defined. Thus, a class is a general category of similar objects. An object that's created within a class also inherits the basic attributes that are common to that class. A class is a passive, defining construct. An object is the active instantiation of a class. Classes are used to relate objects and their attributes. The existence of a class allows for the inheritance of attributes and actions, which in turn allows for new objects so they can inherit attributes from older objects.

The strength of the object-oriented process is the way in which a complex system can be expressed in terms of its components and their relations rather than a system as one large process. Polymorphism is the key to the object-oriented process. A software system can be thought of as a collection of objects that forms some entity, which is an abstract machine that has specific attributes and exhibits particular behavior.

Characteristics of the object-oriented approach

The characteristics of the object-oriented approach are encapsulation, inheritance, and polymorphism. *Encapsulation* means that an object contains both a state and operations that can be performed on that state. Actions on an object's state, which are called methods, are initiated by messages that are sent to the object. With encapsulation, the user doesn't really need to worry about how an object performs its function; the user simply needs to know what the object can and can't do. Users can be confident that when adding an object to the existing code, unpredictable things will not happen to other parts of the program.

Inheritance is the ability to associate characteristics that are common to all members of a class of objects. In object-oriented programming, a subclass of objects can inherit characteristics of the class they belong to. Drawing a square or a triangle uses methods that are inherited from the method of drawing a polygon. Different types of triangles in turn inherit characteristics from the general class of triangles.

Polymorphism means that an operation that's performed on an object is determined by the type of object the operation addresses. The same command that will edit a text for this chapter, for example, would act differently when it's applied to the text of a generic letter because the characteristics of the two objects are different, as are the internal methods that act on them. But the software developer and the user need only deal with the concept of "edit." The ability to generalize behavior over many types of objects allows a higher degree of abstraction in software development since the software developer thinks about specific actions rather than the details of how they will be implemented.

Object-oriented
requirements analysis models

An *object-oriented requirements analysis model* is a graphic representation of real-world entities. The model consists of a set of symbols and rules of composition for the symbols. Each instance of a symbol reflects the entity in the problem space the symbol denotes. An object-oriented model allows for the development of software to closely match the physical world. The model consists of objects that compose the system software requirements, their description in terms of their attributes, and the interaction of those objects as they're represented by the pattern and protocol of messages.

Input to the model is customer requirements for analysis and output is the object-oriented specifications that include the complete design package and program code. This process is illustrated in FIG. 11-1. The customer requirements and object-oriented specifications are two different, yet related, models of behavior of a system.

In between these end points, a number of other models are designed. The objective is to partition complex work on a large system into steps and allow more software developers to participate in the work. Each new model gives the

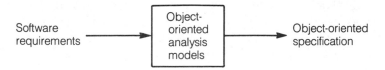

Fig. 11-1. Object-oriented analysis models.

software developers an abstraction of the system. Software developers make decisions on prototypes for getting closer to the final model of a well-formed system. Every new model gives more formal structure to the system than the previous model did.

In order for the different models to be transferred simply and as error free as possible, one model of the system must easily relate to the next. This technique enhances traceability of the software requirements. Because the modeling process is viewed as a changing process, this technique also is useful for prototyping. A particularly interesting part or feature can be studied in advance. The developers make a prototype of the system, which can easily be changed. TABLE 11-1 lists the object-oriented analysis models.

*Table 11-1. Object-Oriented
Analysis Models*

- Object analysis model (OAM)
- Object information model (OIM)
- Object behavior model (OBM)
- Object process model (OPM)

An *object analysis model* (OAM) consists of all the analysis that's needed so the customer's software requirements can be understood. The model also contains information regarding all of the identified external interfaces, which are especially important for embedded systems. These interfaces are linked with external systems, as shown in FIG. 11-2. The graphic is drawn so that the customer's software requirements are understood in an unambiguous way.

The goal for OAM is that the software requirements be mutually understood and recorded in the software requirements specification document before further analysis or design activities can proceed. The definition of notations that are used in the graphic should be clearly defined and properly recorded in the specification document. The object data dictionary can be initiated at this level by recording the essential information.

The *object information model* (OIM) identifies the conceptual entities of the software requirements and formalizes the entities as objects and attributes. Complete and unambiguous understanding of the software requirements is the goal.

OIM is the beginning of the software requirements analysis phase. It identifies things about the objects and their relationships. Objects and associations are modeled here. The model should be simple enough so it can be easily read and understood. Significant emphasis is placed on formalizing relationships between objects. A model is developed and depicted graphically, as shown in FIG. 11-3.

In FIG. 11-3, abstractions of like items are grouped into sets. Items are alike if they behave in the same way and can be described by the same characteris-

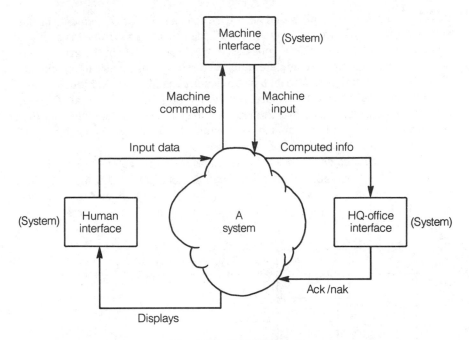

Fig. 11-2. OAM diagram.

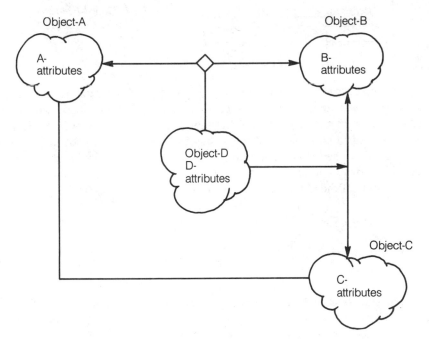

Fig. 11-3. OIM diagram.

tics. The first step is naming an object. Characteristics that all elements of the set have in common are called attributes of the object. An *attribute* is a single characteristic of an object that's possessed by all the entities in the group. The set of attributes must be complete, fully factored, and mutually independent. There's a dot notation for attributes. An example is "Object.Attribute."

The types of attributes are descriptive, naming, and referential. *Descriptive attributes* provide facts that are intrinsic to each object. The *naming attribute* provides a fact about the arbitrary name that's carried by each object. The *referential attribute* links one object to another object.

The *object behavior model* (OBM) formalizes the life or event histories of objects and relationships. Items go through various stages during their lifetime in the real world. The life cycle of an object is the behavior of an object during its lifetime. An example of the object lifetime diagram is presented in FIG. 11-4.

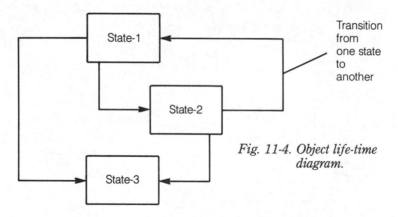

Transition from one state to another

Fig. 11-4. Object life-time diagram.

An object can be in only one stage at a time. The stages are mutually exclusive. These stages are discrete. Transitions can occur instantaneously. Transitions from one stage to another stage are not always allowed. Incidents can cause transition of items between stages. Some incidents cause a progression only when the item is in certain stages of its life cycle. Similar characteristics of real-world items have a common life cycle. Thus, the OBM is a formalization of the life cycle of an object in regard to the following parts:

- State.
- Events.
- Transitions.
- Actions.

The state of the OBM corresponds to the state of an object's life cycle. An event is an incident or action that causes a progression to another state or within the same state. The transition is the new state of an object after a particular event has occurred. The action is the function that's performed immediately when the object enters a new state. Each state can have only one action, but that action might consist of many processes.

A sample OBM is shown in FIG. 11-5. The boxes represent the states, and lines represent the events. The event causes the transition to the new state.

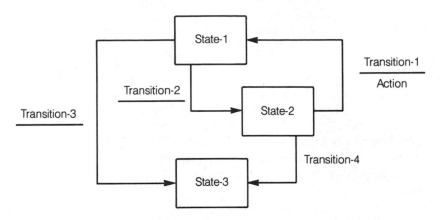

Fig. 11-5. OBM sample.

The *object process model* (OPM) makes use of data flow diagrams and develops the required processes that drive the objects through their event chains. The following list contains the processes for developing a data flow diagram for a single object.

- Develop an OBM that formalizes the behavior of an object over time.
- Analyze the action that's performed when the state is entered.
- Break the action down into a sequence of processes.
- Depict each process as a data-flow diagram.
- Place each action-data-flow diagram on a separate page.

The data of an object is represented as a data store in the data-flow diagram. The data store will be recorded in the object data dictionary, and the data store contains all data and attributes of the object. The instances of the object are created and stored in the data store. The data store is shared by all action-data-flow diagrams.

Object-oriented requirements analysis

Object-oriented requirements analysis is a method in which software requirements are examined from the perspective of "classes" and "objects" that are implied by or identified in the software requirements text. The specification document is produced in cooperation with the customer so the software requirements are understood and will be implemented in the design. TABLE 11-2 lists the object-oriented methods that are available for the software requirements analysis.

Table 11-2. Major Object-Oriented Methods

- Object-oriented methodology (OOM)
- Objectory
- Object-oriented structured design (OOSD)
- Hierarchical object-oriented design (HOOD)
- Object-oriented design (OOD)

An object-oriented requirements analysis combines a data structure approach with entity-relationship modeling and functional process modeling. This enables the goal to be reached and all the meaning of the software requirements to be captured in detail. The analysis accurately transfers the domain knowledge to the software engineers and communicates the requirements analysis in a form that's easily understood and mapped into an object-oriented design.

Software Productivity Solutions CASE tools

Software Productivity Solutions (SPS) has developed an Ada interface that permits transparent access between user programs that were created within its Classic-Ada software development tool and the ONTOS object-oriented database from Ontologic. The Classic-Ada/ONTOS interface allows Ada developers to effectively use the emerging object-oriented database technology that to date has been limited to those programming in C++.

Classic-Ada

Classic-Ada provides object-oriented constructs that are translated into Ada source code. An object is a set of encapsulated data and operations that manipulate the data. Interaction among objects is accomplished through message passing. Upon receipt of a message, an object responds by invoking the appropriate operation (method). The run-time determination of the method that was invoked is called *dynamic binding*. The set of messages to which an object can respond is called the object's *protocol*.

There are two types of objects: classes and instances. A class describes a set of similar objects by defining a template set of methods and instance variables that are common to all instances of the class. The state of an instance object is represented by its instance variables.

Inheritance allows new specialized classes to be built from existing classes by coding only what's different, instead of starting from scratch. (See FIG. 11-6.) Objects inherit methods and instance variables according to an inheritance hierarchy.

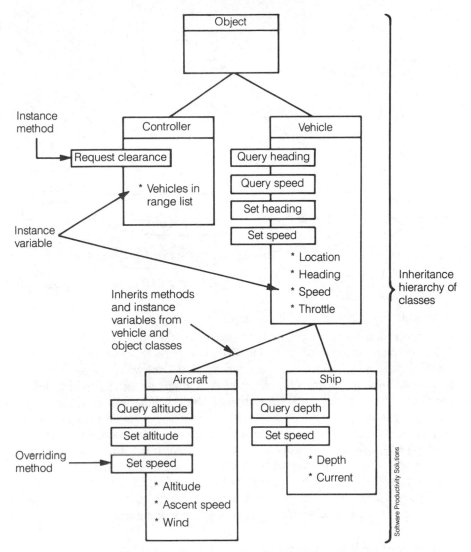

Fig. 11-6. Static view of a Classic-Ada program.

An instance object is referenced by a handle that was generated at the time of the creation of the instance object. Figure 11-7 presents dynamic binding of operations to objects, which is achieved by sending messages that contain the handle of the destination object. At run-time, the user application executive, which was generated by the Classic-Ada processor, routes the message to the appropriate object. Polymorphism, the use of the same interface protocol for different objects, promotes reusability by supporting the concept of interchangeable parts.

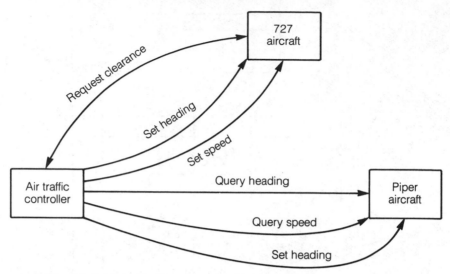

Fig. 11-7. Dynamic view of a Classic-Ada program. Software Productivity Solutions

Ada and object-oriented languages

Software Productivity Solutions (SPS) have taken the approach of performing object-oriented programming within Ada language. A collection of tools, called Classic-Ada, has been developed in which the software developer works in an object-oriented paradigm. A set of Ada language extensions has been developed that permits the specification of objects, inheritance lattices, and message passing. These extensions also support the incorporation of native Ada code, such as exception definition and standard Ada procedures, into the object specification. The output of the code generator is a system that's compiled with a polymorphic message-passing protocol and a specification of class that attributes inheritance, dynamic binding, and a definition of instance attributes. This code generator, which is coupled with advanced environment tools, forms the basis of the Classic-Ada development environment.

Classic-Ada with Persistence

Classic-Ada with Persistence stores and retrieves objects from ONTOS during the execution of a Classic-Ada user program. Objects are stored and persist in the object-oriented database across executions of the user program. (See FIG. 11-8.)

Eli: Automated Reusable Software Toolset

Eli, a reuse library system and set of cooperating tools, supports a software development process that's centered around the reuse of software assets instead

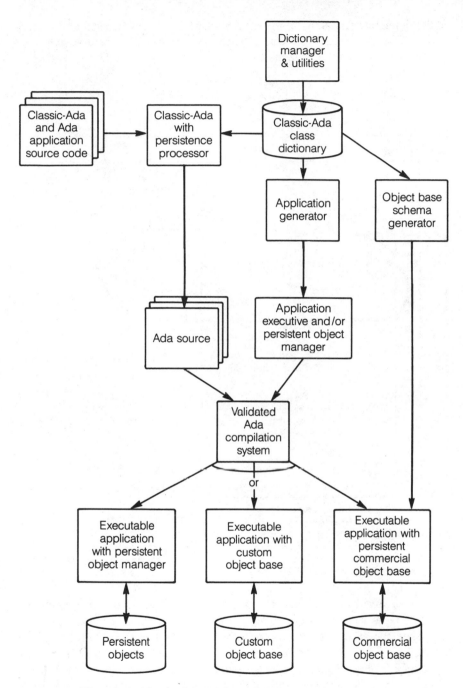

Fig. 11-8. Classic-Ada with persistence. Software Productivity Solutions

of development from scratch. Figure 11-9 shows Eli's open architecture mechanisms. The component information, such as characteristics, source code, and metrics can be stored and managed externally for the reuse library system in

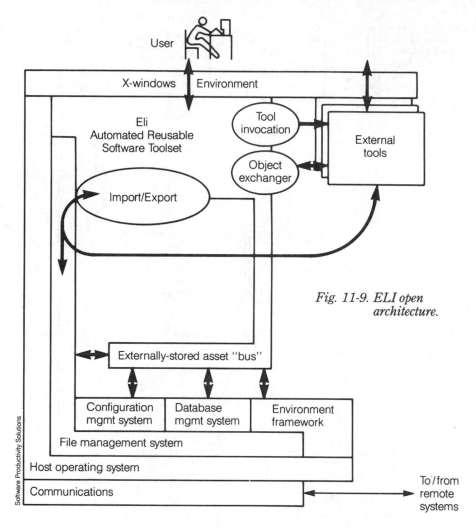

Fig. 11-9. ELI open architecture.

files, or database or configuration management systems in the user's environment. The user tools can share information with the reuse library system via published file exchange formats for import/export. The external tools can be invoked from within the reuse library system by the use of a transparent tool invocation facility. Cooperating tools can manipulate component information via a process-to-process communication mechanism with the reuse library system. The multiple distributed reuse library systems can share information via the file exchange mechanisms. The product's internal object-oriented database can be rehosted onto commercial or custom object management facilities.

12

Artificial
intelligence
methods

Artificial intelligence is a computer science that's concerned with analyzing requirements so intelligent computer systems can be built. This chapter covers basic artificial intelligence methods for requirements analysis and specification.

The basics of artificial intelligence

Systems using artificial intelligence exhibit a level of human intelligence. The ultimate aim for AI is to build computers that can perform in such a way that the machine's output is indistinguishable from that of a human mind. Thus, computers may become partners with humans in the enterprise of soaking up the lore of experts and gleaning knowledge from databases.

Humans acquire knowledge and exchange information through natural language. Artificial intelligence will discover these rules of the thumb known as heuristics and build them into computer programs. A prime goal of AI will be to enable computers to participate in dialogue with humans in natural language. Figure 12-1 illustrates the basics of AI, which are expert systems and knowledge-based systems.

Expert systems

Expert systems hold the hope of using artificial intelligence to capture and clone the skills and wisdom of experts. An expert system models a human expert's thought processes. Expert systems are tools that permit software developers to analyze, design, and implement customers' requirements. An

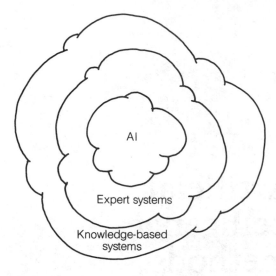

Fig. 12-1. AI basic system.

expert system can be used by an experienced software developer as a supplemental source of information.

Expert systems combine the knowledge and rules of several experts on a given subject and store this information in the computer. The computer thus becomes an expert on the subject by synthesizing the knowledge and rules that aid humans in decision making. Expert systems enhance the quality and availability of knowledge when it's required by decision-making professionals.

Expert systems involve user interfaces. The user interface doesn't intrinsically limit the capabilities of the expert system to reason. The user interface only enhances the ability of the user and computer so it can communicate and improve the quality of the user's understanding of the requirements.

The expert system shell also manipulates the information that's provided by the user in conjunction with the knowledge base and arrives at a particular conclusion. It's the shell that actually processes the information that's entered by a user, relates it to the concepts that are contained in the knowledge base, and provides an assessment, judgment, or solution to a particular requirement.

The structure of the shell is very similar to that of an interpreter, but richer and more capable of taking the facts, assertions, and conditions that are contained in the knowledge base and applying them to the input data. The shell also manages the user interface, which performs functions that range from the validation of numeric values that are entered on the screen to management of the mouse and the representation of the graphical objects.

Properties of an expert system

Properties of an expert system are: the effective use of knowledge, experience, intuition, hunches, good guesses, and creative leaps of mind. Some other properties of expert systems are: reasoning with knowledge, using heuristics methods, performing efficiently, explaining well for understandability, and remaining flexible for requirements changes. Understandability and flexibility are the requisite properties of software engineering.

The purpose of an expert system is to enhance the judgment of human beings. An expert system supplies knowledge and the reasoning of human experts on a given subject. Expert systems can provide a relatively naive user with a lucid and powerful assessment of the requirements. It can assess whether an expert system is available or whether it's practical for an expert to be involved in the decision. A typical expert system is composed of two parts, as shown in TABLE 12-1.

Table 12-1.
Expert System Parts

- Rules
- Inference

Rules are parts of expert systems, and they represent the knowledge of an expert on a given subject. These rules are a collection of knowledge in the application domain. The rules act upon the facts and information as they are fed into the requirements so a solution can be determined. The knowledge base is made up of facts and rules of thumb that are known as heuristics.

Because a knowledge base automatically handles the execution of rules or instructions, the analyst is relieved of this burden. In addition, the inferencing capabilities automatically establish and maintain the relationships between rules. Since the references between rules are automatically established, rules can be added, changed or deleted as the requirements need changing, without significant editing or maintenance.

The knowledge base stores the rules and definitions as they're needed by the system. It also keeps them available for use and provides facilities that assist in maintenance. The knowledge base includes knowledge about the facts and relationships that describe the requirements, as well as the judgment, knowledge, and rules of thumb that an expert would use in the development of a solution.

Inferences are the reasoning in rules. Inferences are the facility within a knowledge base that applies the rules to the requirements. This facility is also called an *inference engine*. An inference engine details how the rule base will act upon the data so a solution can be produced. The inference engine manipulates the information in the knowledge base and determines in what order associations and inferences will be made. This includes the way in which any solution search will be accomplished, what type of reasoning will be used, how pattern matching will be done, how uncertain information will be handled, and how a solution will best be defined. It determines the order in which rules are applied, freeing the analyst from the need to be concerned with this aspect of the system. The inference engine makes this determination, which is based on incoming data and information stored in the knowledge base. The inference engine includes experience and intuition, expressed as "if-then" rules.

Knowledge-based systems

A knowledge-based system (KBS) is an expert system that has evolved over the years due to ongoing research into artificial intelligence. A KBS involves judgment and assists in decision making. A KBS uses data to make judgments and procedural languages to process data. A KBS uses established methods and methodologies that analyze customer's requirements. They use rules that are processed by an inferencing mechanism that adapts to the facts of each case.

A KBS provides a new way of analyzing software requirements. A KBS uses natural language to explain the basic rules of reasoning for a software requirement. Then the KBS automatically employs these rules in the solution of the problem. The result is software that can apply the power of reasoning or judgment to the requirements.

A KBS allows the software developer to concentrate on the requirements while the system handles the details of processing the rules and facts. It's the implementation of the underlying inferencing, natural language, and object-oriented programming concepts that makes a KBS work.

Characteristics of a KBS

A KBS uses instructions that process data and obtain results. A KBS actually determines the sequence of rules that will be employed while the application is running. This is based on the available facts and the desired result. The KBS builds applications that evaluate a situation, apply a set of rules, and make a judgment or recommend a decision or action. The methodologies that are useful in the decision-making process are listed in TABLE 12-2.

Table 12-2.
Decision-Making
Methodologies

- Backward chaining
- Forward chaining
- Hypothetical reasoning

Backward chaining inferencing starts from the goal and works backwards. This is a technique of reasoning in which the desired solution is known, but the sequence of events or information that leads to the solution is not known. Backward chaining establishes subgoals until the input data supports those subgoals. It's also called goal-directed reasoning. A sample of backward chaining is shown in FIG. 12-2. The identification of a path that leads to a particular solution is the goal of the backward chaining.

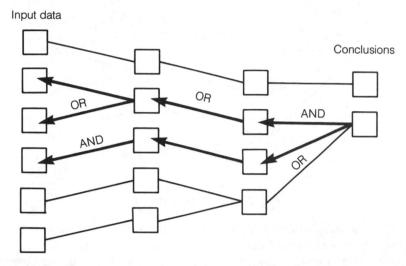

Fig. 12-2. Backward chaining.

This methodology is ideal for applications in which the possible conclusions are well defined. It's frequently used for classification-type requirements where the solution structure is well defined. The more you know about the process, the more likely that backward chaining will be the preferred methodology.

Backward chaining is a procedure that's used by the system to take the opposite tack. When it's given a conclusion, the system tries to prove it by following the logic chain backward. If D is the conclusion, the system will look for any rules that read "If C, then D," then for rules reading "If B, then C." When the system reaches a rule whose "if" portion is not the conclusion of another rule, it begins asking for specific information.

Forward chaining uses input facts that derive new facts until the goal is satisfied. It's also called data-driven reasoning. It's a technique of reasoning in which the data is specified, but the solution is unknown. It's commonly used when no one specific goal is defined, but rather any of a number of acceptable solutions could be appropriate, depending on changing circumstances. A sample of forward chaining is shown in FIG. 12-3. The goal is to determine a solution that's based on the available information and the specified constraints.

Forward chaining begins with data and reasons from it to a solution. In effect, the user enters information and then asks the system, "What conclusions can you draw?" If the user has entered fact A, for example, the system will search for a rule reading "If A, then B," then for one reading "If B, then C," and so on.

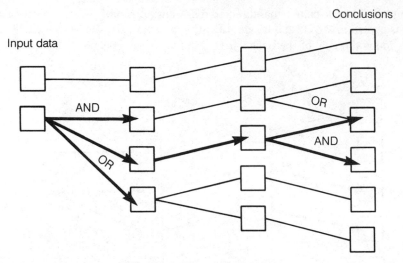

Fig. 12-3. Forward chaining.

Hypothetical chaining explores several different alternative solutions in parallel. It reasons about future alternatives and determines which sequence of steps will best attain a desired result. It's a method of looking at a variety of solutions to a problem that's based on the availability of different and sometimes contradicting information. Hypothetical reasoning is often employed in optimization problems, where solutions vary according to cost; it's also used in planning or modeling requirements in which the solution is a sequence of steps. It often explores how different combinations of resources will effect the final result.

Segments of KBS development

Segments are part of the process of developing knowledge-based systems. Segments are analogous to software engineering phases. The critical factor in building a KBS is the data. Segments of KBS development are listed in TABLE 12-3. KBS software development typically includes at least one throwaway prototype system. Such prototypes depict the eventual user interface and system software requirements.

Table 12-3. KBS Development Segments

- Knowledge acquisition
- Knowledge engineering
- Knowledge implementation environment

Knowledge acquisition involves obtaining the information about what the requirements are. This function is very similar to an analyst's role, which is to define a customer's needs and requirements. The goal is to extract the correct information about the domain into a form that's usable for inferencing. Availability of information is the key factor here. The question arises whether an expert is really available in a particular subject and can share experiences. If so, can the expert share the information, and at what cost and at what time?

The second important key is accountability. Who is to blame if something goes wrong in the KBS? How can you defend the knowledge provided and make a decision? This is a peculiar case if the knowledge has been provided by more than one source. Tracing the decision back to the original expertise is difficult. The third key factor is accuracy. Verifying the correctness and accuracy of the information obtained is not easy. This can easily jeopardize a decision-making process.

KBS tools that incorporate natural language technology help simplify this process because the customer or expert can define, maintain, and review the rules in ordinary English. Figure 12-4 shows a knowledge acquisition process. So a KBS can be created, a knowledge analyst taps expert know-how through

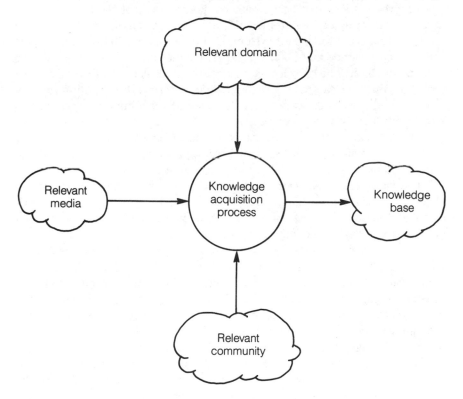

Fig. 12-4. The knowledge acquisition process.

relevant media, domains and communities. All the components of the knowledge system are then incorporated into a knowledge base. Through extensive observation and interviewing, the knowledge analyst analyzes all aspects of the requirements. So an expert's knowledge can be captured, even the most prosaic decisions must be broken down, analyzed, and then encoded step by step in natural language. Each task, when processed on a case-by-case basis, becomes a manageable component that forms the underlying structure for the development of the expert system. Frequent test cases help the knowledge analyst uncover any obscure information.

In the process of knowledge acquisition, the knowledge analyst and the expert work together and build an explicit model of the expert's implicit domain. The interviewing technique helps recreate the stimuli of where the expert was when he or she first learned the task.

Knowledge engineering is the actual system design phase where the selection of reasoning methodologies helps engineer the requirements. A knowledge engineer is like a system designer who is familiar with inferencing technologies and their application. He or she extracts knowledge from the subject matter expert and structures that knowledge into a sequence of rules or other representations that best simulates the process that the human expert uses in engineering the requirements. The knowledge engineer is usually the primary architect of the expert system. He or she works with a human expert and extracts every detail of how the expert handles different situations in the particular subject. The knowledge engineer then translates these details into a form the computer can readily manipulate and decides how the information can best be linked to the various mental associations a human expert makes when confronted with the requirements.

The knowledge engineer defines the knowledge by constructing a case analysis, encoding the knowledge, and testing the system's structure. While using an iterative approach, the knowledge engineer develops a prototype.

The *knowledge implementation environment* occurs in the implementation phase. This phase consists of coding the rules and incorporating the knowledge-based system into the computer environment. Computer feedback to a human expert verifies the intelligence of the system.

The customer's requirements verification determines that a piece of software does what it's supposed to do, and that the software does what the customer wants it to do. This is called validation. These are difficult phases of software engineering. Validation is facilitated by developing and demonstrating prototypes, since the feedback can be reflected in future versions of the software as requirements continue changing.

Establishing that a KBS meets its specifications under all circumstances is not an easy process. The number of decisions that a KBS can provide increases exponentially with the amount of data. It also increases with the number of rules and facts in the system. Verification that correct decisions are rendered regardless of input to the system is impractical for large amounts of data. This phase ensures that the KBS fits into the end user's software engineering environment.

AI CASE tools

AI CASE tools help develop knowledge-based tools that rely on semantic models of problem domains; AI CASE tools also help users produce complete, consistent, and correct requirements specifications. A problem domain model enables a knowledge-based tool, communicates with a user in domain oriented terms, performs semantic consistency checks, and guides the user according to the constraints of the problem domain. Because software development is knowledge intensive, knowledge-based tools should ultimately be more effective and cover more of the software life cycle. The key idea is to use knowledge acquisition techniques that formulate a semantic model of a problem domain. Once a computer-based model exists for a problem domain, then intelligent assistants can help users to develop requirements, specifications, and design.

There are basically two types of low-end tools for building expert systems. These are end-user tools, like expert system shells, and high-level programming languages that lend themselves to artificial intelligence uses. Which tool is best depends on a site's programming resources, the number of rules in the expert system, and budgets.

Expert system shells are AI tools that allow software developers to build a KBS. The reasoning methods and strategies that mimic decision-making and requirements-analysis techniques are used by experts and represented in the shell. The knowledge engineer formulates the "if-then" rules, which are rule-based expert system shells, and follows the process of how a human expert works.

Knowledge Base Management System tool

The Knowledge Base Management System (KBMS) tool was developed by AI Corporation for commercial applications. It's a comprehensive application development environment that extends conventional data processing practices to knowledge-based or expert system applications. (See FIG. 12-5.) KBMS is used for building and maintaining knowledge-based systems.

The KBMS environment

KBMS is written in the C language and operates on an IBM mainframe and personal computer platform, as well as Digital Equipment computer environments. Within each environment, KBMS adheres to key industry standards, such as IBM's SAA and AD/Cycle directions for mainframe and OS/2 systems. KBMS delivers automatic transparent database interfaces to DBMS systems and other data storage facilities. You can even access multiple databases con-

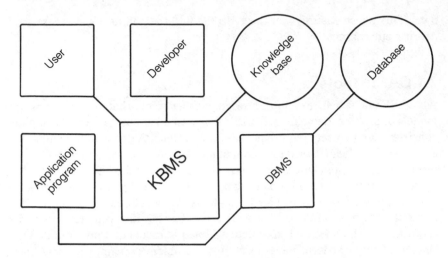

Fig. 12-5. KBMS development environment. AI Corp.

currently. KBMS supports most of the available operating systems, tele-processing and window management systems and databases.

KBMS major features

KBMS incorporates all the key reasoning methodologies in its inference engine. This allows automation of many applications by expressing them in the form of rules and then letting the KBMS inference engine dynamically determine the appropriate rule for the execution of a given situation. The inference engine is the heart of the KBMS system. It uses incoming data and information that's stored in the KBMS knowledge base and determines the order in which rules are executed each time a KBMS application runs.

KBMS features active objects that let you define sophisticated graphical user interfaces (GUIs) for many applications by just using "point and click." The knowledge base also stores data or objects that are relevant to the application area. The information in the knowledge base is used by the inference engine as it applies one or more reasoning methods before it reaches a solution. Menus, requests, and messages can be customized to your needs. Users can invoke KBMS sessions or question the knowledge base in conversational English. They can even get an English explanation.

KBMS has a graphics tool that enhances the productivity of application developers by delivering special graphical editing features that allow you to view the components of an application graphically. KBMS gives the developer a functional, intelligent editor that defines objects and enters rules. A custom format facility provides report formatting, screen painting and menu development. Online documentation and tracing and debugging tools expedite the programming process.

A custom format uses a unique SQL-based facility and communicates with procedural applications. It allows KBMS to be invoked from a procedural program. A general-purpose call-out facility is also provided so that KBMS applications can invoke user-written programs or access external devices as needed.

Cooperative processing allows KBMS applications to be efficiently distributed over multiple hardware platforms, from mainframes to VAX systems to personal computers. Applications can run on personal computers or workstations and still access corporate data as needed.

KBMS incorporates backward chaining, forward chaining, and hypothetical reasoning. The KBMS system handles the burden and determines when the rules should be executed. This inferencing capability frees the software developers so they will not have to code the order of rule execution or define the many interrelationships between rules. Because KBMS uses inferencing process so rules can be processed and judgment can be applied to data, it allows substantially more complex applications to be addressed than has been feasible with procedural languages.

KBMS provides a seamless interface into commercial database management systems. When a rule needs a data object, KBMS automatically retrieves it. There's no need for duplication of data structure that's already stored in an external DBMS. KBMS has extended knowledge base technology that:

- Allows for the operation of rules directly on database objects.
- Increases performance.
- Facilitates application portability.

KBMS automatically generates the SQL statement as it's needed for access or update of the data, and this process is completely transparent to the application. If the data is moved to a different storage facility, no changes to the application rules are needed. Prototype systems can be developed with rules that can access sample data and be stored in the knowledge base. Then, when the system is ready, it can be moved into production, where the rules require no modification for access to the live database records. Just tell KBMS what database the objects can be found in, and the rest is done automatically. KBMS includes its own relational data storage facility; in addition, it can access externally stored data. It allows for data to be stored and shared by multiple applications without requiring the overhead of an external DBMS.

13

Emerging
software requirements
analysis methods

It's well known that no two computer applications are identical. The requirements analysis approach to each system is unique. For each of these applications, an analyst must decide the most effective method or combination of methods for the software requirements analysis. Sometimes the contract dictates that a certain standard and method must be followed. Whatever an analyst decides, the method or methods must be recorded in the software engineering plan. The bottom line is that the customer must be satisfied with the result.

Fuzzy logic

Fuzzy logic means that some of the software requirements have been logically analyzed and are still not clear to the software developers. There are still some gray areas in understanding the requirements. The potential for misunderstanding and the resulting lack of logical precision frequently mean that the system will not really solve the customer's requirements in any satisfactory way. Those fuzzy requirements will be red-lined for further clarification in the design phase.

Selection criteria for a suitable model

Selection criteria for a suitable model depend on software requirements. The conventional model is as good as the modern model. The use of a model depends upon the customer's requirements, needs, budget, and schedule. It also depends on the degree of expertise of the analyst and the software developers and how familiar they are with the method. Here are some of the questions that must be asked. Is any CASE tool available for the method that will be used? Are enough education and training for that particular method available in the market? By using any immature method, the chances are that completion of the project will be delayed and cost more.

Effective dialogue

Effective dialogue must be established between the customer and software developer for harmony in completing the project. It's vital that both the software requirements and the method be understood. It's equally important that the customer is not left behind in this venture of education. So that the project will be completed successfully, it's important that there's an effective dialogue between the customer and the software developer all of the time. The dialogue should be conducted in simple and clear language. Irrelevant information should not be included in the dialogue. It's best that technical jargon not be included in the dialogue unless it's explained in a language that the user/customer fully understands.

The user's language is preferred for better communication. The software requirements document is still being formed, and any questions about the clarity of requirements can still be discussed with the customer. The dialogue should be expressed clearly in words, phrases, and concepts that are familiar to the user/customer. Information should be graphically visible, rather than searching the customer/user's memory. The dialogue should be consistent; otherwise, the user/customer will wonder whether different words, situations, or actions have the same meaning.

Rapid prototyping provides an environment for timely and effective interaction between the software developer and customer. The interaction is centered around discrete events such as the initial software requirements discussions, design reviews, and implementation phases. These communications are based on static representations of the proposed application system flowcharts, report layouts, and input formats. This approach helps eliminate misunderstanding among the software developers and the customer in understanding the software requirements. The primary communication vehicle becomes a working model of the actual system, which is a prototype, and discussion is focused in terms of the actual system rather than its static representation. The prototype establishes an effective dialogue between the software developers and the customer.

By the use of rapid iterative refinement of these prototypes, the customer and the software developer work together with a common understanding of the final functionality. This prototype evolution frequently permits system implementation that was agreed upon earlier in the software development cycle; the prototype allows the initial production experience to feed back directly into system refinement and thus resolve functional details in a timely and efficient way. Rapid prototyping, when it's correctly implemented, virtually ensures that the final system will meet the real needs of the customer.

The software developer should always keep the user/customer informed about what's going on through appropriate feedback within a reasonable time. Avoid clever shortcuts unless it's agreed upon by the software developer and the customer. Provide error messages in plain language that precisely indicates the problem. The messages should include constructive suggestions for a solution. Even better than good messages is careful software requirements analysis and design that prevents a problem from occurring in the first place. Customer satisfaction that the software requirements have been understood completely and unambiguously is the goal. And as these requirements models are understood, so will they be carried out in the software design phase.

Conventional model

A conventional model is shown in FIG. 13-1. Software development follows the basic waterfall model. This is a model that's commonly used for software requirements analysis, software requirements specification, software design, software implementation, software testing, and software maintenance. The requirements are usually stated in narrative fashion, rather than in a formal computer language, and the requirements express what the software will do. They're translated into functional specifications, and it is preferable if they are written in an executable computer language.

The design will encapsulate the structure of the software system and detail "how" the different parts of the program will be logically connected. Then the design will be turned into code, written in a computer language, and tested so bugs will be ferreted out.

There are numerous variations on the waterfall model, and parts of it are often repeated when problems are discovered as the software requirements change. Software engineers have recognized for years that this model is far from perfect, and different models are being explored. Some feel the waterfall model overemphasizes the production of documents, such as a requirements statement, but doesn't help the software engineers who produce them. Others feel that the process itself is sound, but leaves room for error in execution. For example, if the specifications don't accurately reflect the intent of the requirements, the end result may not be correct. Also, integrating a system's components can be extremely difficult when different teams of software engineers design and implement various pieces of a large system.

One alteration of the waterfall model favors creating prototypes. Prototypes are possible at just about any step in the waterfall cycle and can actually help produce most of the necessary documents. When more time is spent on the front end of the process and the problem is thought out so difficulties will be minimized in the later stages, then there is a hallmark of sound software engineering. Instead of focusing on writing code, engineers must look at how

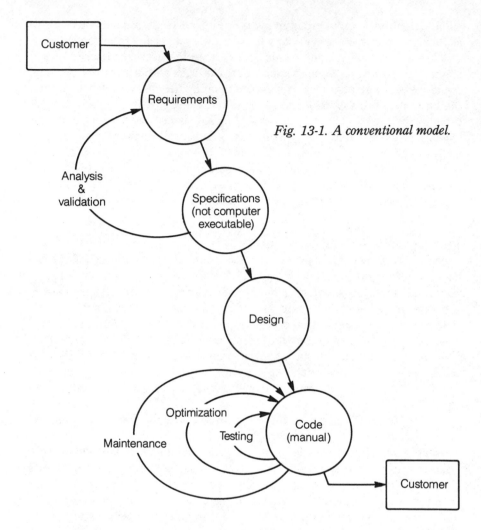

Fig. 13-1. A conventional model.

the program should be organized at a higher level so it can be more easily maintained. The implementation phase will go smoothly if the architecture is sound, and even more time will be saved during future versions.

Modern model

A sample of a modern model is illustrated in FIG. 13-2. The specifications are written in an executable computer language, which will allow rigorous validation of formal methods. The code is generated automatically in a process that incorporates the design stage. Testing is unnecessary because the specifications have been validated and the transformations that translate specifications into code have been checked for correctness. Maintenance is performed only for the requirements that are rewritten, and updated code is generated.

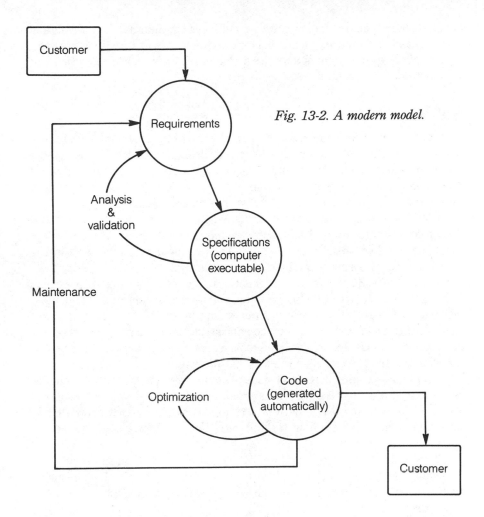

Fig. 13-2. A modern model.

Software engineering standards

Software engineering standards are used for discipline in software requirements analysis. The documentation produced assists in better control and dialogue during software requirements analysis and development. This documentation also assists during testing and maintenance phases. Use of these standards can ensure low-cost, high-quality productivity. There are many standards that are available in the computer industry. A list is provided in Appendix B.

When these standards are used, it's best to suitably tailor them to the software requirements. Some of these standards are generic and address varying concerns, which range from the very abstract to final technical details. Generic and abstract models establish conceptual frameworks and basic terminology. Technical standards typically evolve in more and more finite detail, which describes specific implementations of the generic model. These standards cover a generalizable model of software engineering, minimal documentation, development of diagramming symbols and techniques, software life cycle processes, software quality characteristics and metrics, technical specifications for requirements, design, and tests.

Software factory

The idea behind a software factory is to make use of the methods of mass production. These include standardized analysis, design, interchangeable components, and shared resources. Achieving a high degree of productivity and quality in the development of software is the idea. Use of a software factory means that productivity of quality software is enhanced. The root of the software factory idea goes back to the 1970s, when structured programming and design commenced. In the 1980s, software requirements analysis and development methodology ideas cropped up. CASE technology is emerging in the 1990s, so quality software productivity will improve.

Using the software factory concept can reduce project cost overruns, implementation delays, schedule slipping, and reduce the shortage of qualified workers. Software maintenance is an unending burden. The success story of the software factory in Japan has convinced the professionals that modern, structured methods, techniques, and tools can enhance quality and productivity. The results are less defect rates in the software.

The Japanese emphasis on advance planning and process analysis reduces the amount of coding necessary for a project. Figure 13-3 shows the resources allotted to various phases of software development efforts in the software factory environment. Throughout the software life cycle, there's a strict adherence to quality control.

There should be a postmortem after each project. This preserves the knowledge in the organization. You also learn from your mistakes, ensuring that you don't make the same mistake twice. Learning from experience is also

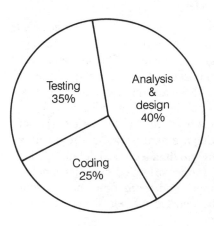

Fig. 13-3. Software development effort.

a good tool for education and training. But, the software factory concept is an anathema to people who have experienced developing software another way.

In a software factory, efficiency of the software developer increases. Efficiency is enhanced by the use of standards during analysis and design. The modeling schema are guidelines to reusable components. The factors that affect reusability are illustrated in FIG. 13-4. Formal testing and quality assurance procedures enhance productivity. In the software factory structure, the teams work as self-directed partners in the project instead of following any hierarchy. Analysts, software developers, and customers/users understand that the software factory concept will necessitate a commitment. The major costs of a software factory are reusable components and maintenance costs for a library of reusable software. You must invest up front to introduce the software factory concept into your environment.

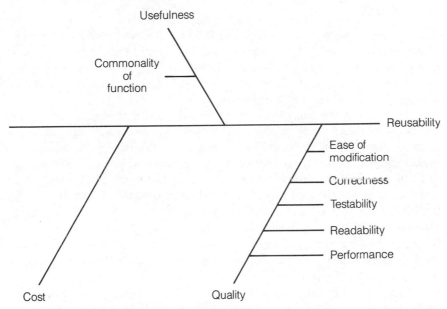

Fig. 13-4. Factors affecting reusability.

Hybrid object-oriented method

The hybrid object-oriented method is a home-grown approach. It's a combination of the object-oriented methods that were discussed in Chapter 11 combined with other familiar methods for the requirements analysis and design. The object-oriented method is an emerging method in the computer industry. Many professionals are not yet expert in this procedure. Many customers/users still have difficulty in understanding the concept of the object-oriented process. It's sometimes advisable to use a familiar method up front so the customer is assured that their requirements have been understood. This helps to establish a good rapport with the customer.

The model that is thus created may not be completely mapped into the object-oriented design. But the information is useful when an object-oriented design model is being created. In the design phase, the model is enhanced with the static and dynamic properties of objects. The static properties of objects define the objects and establish the relationships between them. The attributes of objects are also defined in the design phase. In essence, the internal behavior of objects is explored completely.

The dynamic properties of objects include operations on objects. They also include the relationships between operations. The applicability of operations is constrained by the attributes of objects. The object-oriented design model is mapped into the object-oriented programming phase.

Smart way

A smart way involves using object-oriented programming and KBS development tools that provide a hybrid knowledge and inference structure. They support both rule-based and object-oriented programming. These tools generally have a graphical interface, such as windows, and offer a graphical way of presenting the knowledge base to the software developer.

Many expert systems development efforts have now shifted from rule-based backward chaining to object-based hybrid systems that the new tools allow. Although small backward chaining systems may be written more easily initially, they can become more confusing as the system grows. In fact, heuristics and procedural control are all specified through the rules of a simple rule-based system. As the system grows, more control rules are required so the knowledge base can be managed. The system slows down because more rules require more inferencing, which takes more time and memory.

Because the structure of the domain that you represent consists of objects, the hybrid approach is simpler. Objects have the advantage of directly representing items that exist in the real world. The relationships among objects in a model are represented by linking them according to the object's class in a hierarchy. Pattern matching rules can examine all instances of an object class, which reduces the number of rules that are required. Once the objects and domains have been developed within the KBS, the knowledge engineer uses rule-based programming and specifies how the objects should behave along with the heuristics. In rule based programming, each rule specifies a set of conditions and a set of conclusions that can be made if the conditions are true. The conclusions may represent logical deductions about the knowledge base or specifications of how it changes over time. Each rule is independent, and the system can evolve gracefully over time by adding or modifying rules as appropriate. Both forward chaining and backward chaining may be used within an application.

Unified software requirements methods

The IBM AD/Cycle is considered a unified software requirements method. AD/Cycle is simultaneously a philosophy of software development, a structured framework for products, and those products themselves. The concept of integration is more important than the tools. The idea is to have an integrated suite of tools across the entire life cycle, backed up by a methodology for implementing systems.

AD/Cycle architecture

AD/Cycle architecture is built around the Repository. It's a specialized form of a database that's designed to store all information that's relevant to the application. The application building process includes business models, programming components, project plans, even intricate process flows that reflect how a particular organization goes about the job of application building. All of these live in the Repository. The Repository is actually two things, one concrete and one abstract. First is the Repository Manager, a DB2 program whose job is to accept, manage and release the information. The second is the Information Model. It's a tangible model of how that information is defined and structured. It's easier to understand the position of the Information model within the Repository if you see it in context as the third layer of a four-layer tier structure, as shown in FIG. 13-5.

Layer 1 is not actually part of the Repository. It contains production data, which is data that the enterprise needs so its work can be done: part numbers,

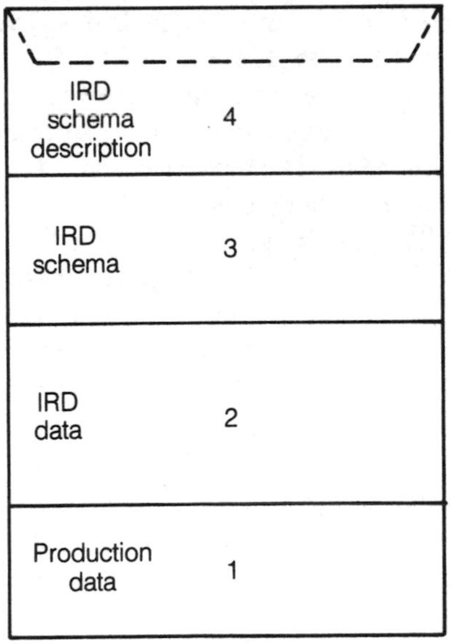

Fig. 13-5. Four-layer structure.

employee names, or, in the part of the enterprise dealing with application development itself, source code files and project plans. This data is stored in the enterprise database, not in the Repository.

Layer 2 is the International Resources Dictionary (IRD) layer. It contains metadata about the layer below. It defines, for example, how Layer 1 production data will be named and organized. Examples of IRD data are: "employee-number" and "object-module," plus a great deal more about each entity, such as field type and field length. While Layer 1 data remains in the enterprise database, Layer 2 information can be found in the Repository. This layer represents what most programmers today call the data dictionary.

Layer 3 is the IRD Schema layer or AD/Cycle Information Model. It contains metadata for Layer 2 data; it describes the data dictionary. Layer 3 metadata might be: "data-item," "validation-check," "value-range," or "process context." The Information Model is a full level that's removed from the things with which application programmers are concerned. These are actual data descriptions and program components. However, this is exactly the information that concerns CASE vendors and tool builders.

Layer 4 is named the IRD Schema Description. It deals with how the basic abstract application-building elements of Layer 3 are defined and organized. Even tool builders are not operationally interested in this layer. It's of interest only to definers of data dictionary architectures. Layer 4 is hard wired to the data dictionary architecture. A sample AD/Cycle architecture is shown in FIG. 13-6.

Synthesis CASE tool

Synthesis Computer Technologies case/ap is an integrated application development system. It's a CASE product that successively enhances an application prototype until the prototype becomes the final production version. Case/ap is designed to support software development in the rapid prototyping environment. The developer states that it's a tool for system software integration and development.

The case/ap uses an Iterative Refinement Process (IRP), as shown in FIG. 13-7. This process lets you build an initial prototype for the entire application, and then it's refined until you reach the application solution. The IRP approach dynamically involves the application's end users during the software development cycle. Thus, when the system goes into production, there are fewer unexpected problems.

Case/ap components

Case/ap combines several integrated components that increase software development speed and maintainability. The components include a central system dictionary, prototype construction, and iterative refinement. Each application system definition, which consists of data-dictionary and process specifications, is kept in a central system dictionary that's maintained by a specialized

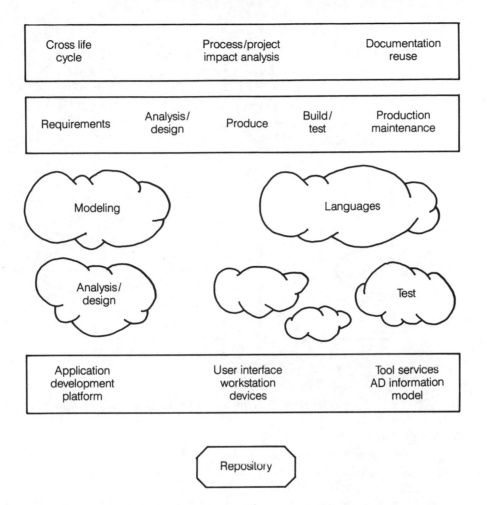

Fig. 13-6. AD/Cycle architecture.

"editor" interface. Updated processes and data model documentation can be generated at any time.

Prototype construction uses a flexible COBOL code generator. Initial program prototypes are built from the high-level data and process specifications. These prototypes are executed with the essential application functionality, but they don't include all the details of the eventual solution. Screen layouts and menu structures can be shown in the first prototype.

In iterative refinement, the prototypes are progressively modified and improved until the application is completed. The final prototype is the actual running system. The software developer can use case/ap productivity features, which will shorten development time and provide consistent standards that will significantly lower maintenance efforts.

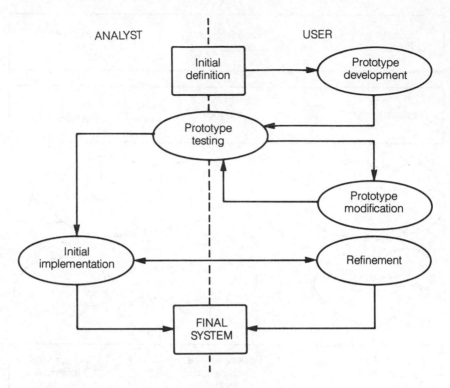

Fig. 13-7. The case/ap iterative refinement process. Synthesis Computer Technologies

Major features

The case/ap major features are interfaces for SQL/Rdb and SQL/Sybase, as well as performance enhancements that reduce compilation and execution times. The case/ap is written in C or COBOL.

Each case/ap prototype is a running application with screen layouts, report formats and interactive processes. The final prototype is the actual production system. No recording phase is required. A completed application requires only the case/ap run-time components on the target system, not the entire development environment.

The case/ap system includes data modeling facilities so that a logical data structure can be established for the application. An interface can directly import data models that are developed with front-end CASE tools. The system comes with a centralized repository that includes the data dictionary items, I/O specifications, processing requirements, and data validation conditions. It also includes library routines for data file access, terminal I/O, data arithmetic and audit trail logging.

Structured program modules allow additional C or COBOL code that will be merged with the generated application. A parameter table system automatically codes or decodes reference data. An access control system regulates data access at the logical-file or data-item level. A screen-form utility automatically generates terminal screen layout and lets you directly paint customer modifications.

The online, interactive product supports hierarchical and "many-to-many" data structures. It provides for the addition of user code and calls to foreign routines. It also provides an online tutorial and automatically generates complete system documentation. Two optional modules, case/ap QL (query language) and case/ap RG (report generator), provide unstructured data queries and interactive report generation functions respectively. The case/ap system can be used for stand-alone information systems or complex integrated applications. It runs on VMS V5.2.

Part III

Implementing software requirements

14

Documenting a software requirements analysis

A requirements specification document describes the behavior of a software. This behavior includes that of external and internal software interfaces. This also includes the user interfaces. This chapter covers the documentation of the software requirements specification, which establishes the baseline for software design and testing.

Software requirements specification

The software requirements specification (SRS) specifies all significant requirements, such as functionality, performance, design constraints, data elements, attributes, and the external, internal, and user interfaces. The SRS specifies the engineering and qualification requirements for a CSCI. The SRS includes the necessary requirements and ensures proper development of the CSCI. Each software requirement in the SRS is a statement of some essential capability of the software that will be developed. The SRS consists of methods that will be used so that software requirements can be expressed.

The SRS includes models that express complex requirements. Models can be mathematical, functional, and timing. Each interface will be uniquely identified by name. The SRS covers states and modes of a CSCI. Each input and output that's associated with a capability should be discussed. The capability may be further partitioned into smaller components so the customer's requirements will be satisfied. The internal interfaces thus created should be uniquely named. A narrative text summarizes the information that's transmitted over the interface.

The SRS document's data elements follow a certain industry standard. TABLE 14-1 lists suggestive parameters for the data elements that are internal to the CSCI. Any operational parameters must be mentioned in this document. Any installation instructions or/and adaption instructions must be explained.

Table 14-1. Data Element Parameters

- A unique name
- A brief description
- Unit of measure
- Limit/range of values
- Accuracy
- Precision

The SRS records the sizing and timing requirements of internal memory, along with the amount of processing time allocated to the CSCI. Timing models are quite useful for specifying the form and details of the software's behavior, particularly for real-time systems. This covers any software safety requirements, security requirements, software quality factors, and human engineering requirements.

The SRS discusses any software design constraints. The design constraints can be due to the use of evolving method/language. There may be no matured compiler available for that particular language. There may not be any CASE tool available for that particular method. Above all, there may be a lack of experienced professionals who can use the particular method and the language. The project may need more time and money so professionals can educate and train their own personnel and come up to a certain standard so the project can be completed successfully in time and within the budget.

The SRS should include a matrix and should prove that there's complete mapping to and from the system requirements specification. The system requirements specification that was discussed in Chapter 4 includes the customer's requirements for both the hardware and software. The system engineering document that was discussed in Chapter 6 filters out the hardware and software requirements. This SRS document contains only the software requirements. The relationships among all these documents are shown in FIG. 14-1.

Characteristics of a good SRS

The characteristics of a good SRS are listed in TABLE 14-2. *Unambiguous* means that the requirement stated in the SRS has only one interpretation. Each characteristic of the final product must be described by the use of a single, unique term. In cases where a term is used in a particular context, it could have multiple meanings. The term must be defined with a more specific expla-

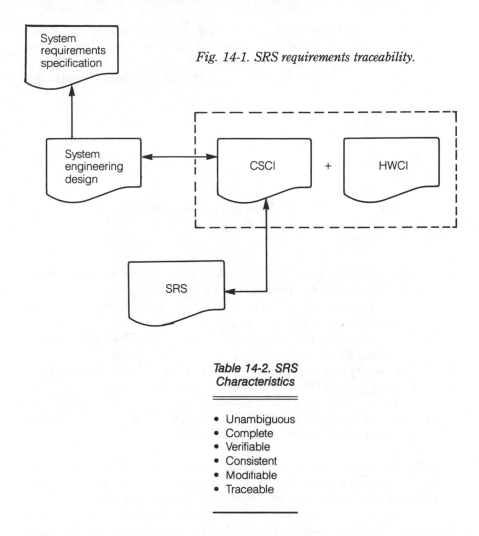

Fig. 14-1. SRS requirements traceability.

Table 14-2. SRS
Characteristics

* Unambiguous
* Complete
* Verifiable
* Consistent
* Modifiable
* Traceable

nation. One way inherent ambiguity can be avoided in the natural language is by writing the SRS in a formal requirements specification language.

Complete means that the SRS includes all significant requirements. The SRS defines responses of the software to all real classes of input data in all real classes of situations. It conforms to any SRS standard that applies to it. It includes full labeling and referencing of all figures, tables, and diagrams in the SRS. It includes definition of all terms and units of measure. It doesn't have a phrase "to be determined" (TBD). If TBD is occasionally necessary, then it should be accompanied by a description of the conditions that caused the TBD. It should also cover what must be done so the TBD can be eliminated. The phrase "not applicable" (N/A) should be discouraged unless it's a must, and in that case it really means "not applicable."

Verifiable applies when every requirement stated in the SRS can be verified. A requirement is verifiable if and only if there exists some finite, cost-effective process with which a person or machine can check that the software product meets the requirement. For example, the following requirements can't be verifiable.

- Human interface.
- Infinite loop.
- Maximum number.
- Forever.

Consistent means that the SRS has no set of individual requirements that are described in it and conflict with each other. The likely conflicting requirements are as follows:

1. Two or more requirements might describe the same real-world object but will use different terms for that object.
2. The format of an output report might be described in one requirement as tabular but in another as textual.
3. One requirement might state that all colors are blue, while another states that all colors are red.
4. One requirement might specify that the program will add two inputs, and another requirement will specify that the program will multiply them.
5. One requirement might state that A must follow B, while another requirement states that A and B occur simultaneously.

Modifiable means that the structure and style are such that any necessary changes to the requirements can be made easily, completely, and consistently. The SRS has a coherent and easy-to-use organization with a table of contents, an index, and an explicit cross referencing. The information in the SRS is not redundant. The same requirements should not appear in more than one place in the SRS.

Traceable means that the origin of each of the requirements is clear and can be referenced for documentation of future developments or enhancements. The backward traceability depends upon each requirement explicitly referencing to its source in previous documents, such as the System Requirements Specification and the System Engineering Design Document. Forward traceability depends upon each requirement in the SRS having a unique name or referencing number for the spawned documents, such as a Software Design Document. When a requirement in the SRS represents an apportionment or a derivative of another requirement, then both forward and backward traceability should be provided.

SRS benefits

One of the benefits of an SRS is that it establishes the basis for an agreement between the customer and the software developer on what the software product must do. It specifies the results that must be achieved by the software and not the means by which those results are obtained. It specifies what functions will be performed on what data and what results will be produced. The SRS gives a complete description of the functions that will be performed by the software, and the SRS will help the potential user determine if the specified software meets their needs.

The SRS facilitates a better understanding of the requirements before design begins. This reduces the development effort. Careful review of the requirements in the SRS can reveal omissions, misunderstandings, and inconsistencies early in the development cycle when these problems are more easily corrected.

The SRS provides a basis for estimating costs and schedules. The description of the product that will be developed as given in the SRS is a realistic basis for estimating project costs. The SRS also:

- Provides a clear description of the required software.
- Makes estimation easier.
- Plans the necessary resources.

The software engineering plan can be updated if necessary, and the SRS provides a baseline for validation and verification. The SRS document serves as a basis for enhancement, since it discusses only the product and not the project that developed it. Thus, the SRS provides a solid foundation for continued production evolution.

Interface requirements specification

The interface requirements specification (IRS) specifies external interfaces between one or more CSCIs. In case there's only one CSCI in a system, this document can be tailored.

The interface requirements specification identifies all of the interfaces by a unique name. The purpose of the interface is also included in the document. The IRS consists of data elements that are complete with definitions, units of measure, limit/range, accuracy, and precision. This should also include the source and destination of the interfaces.

15

The
software design
process

This chapter presents the logical internal structure of software design. It also discusses external data formats and the hierarchical partitioning of software requirements into manageable components. The design document is the only original document created by the software developer, and he or she uses the document to show the customer how the software will be designed.

Migrating from analysis to design

Migrating from analysis to design is a technique. The requirements are analyzed and specified in the software requirements documentation, and this provides a road map for migrating the requirements into the design. The correctness of the design depends on the degree of completeness of the software requirements analysis.

Each requirement must be traceable to one or more *design entities*. A design entity is a component of a design that's structurally and functionally distinct from other elements. The design entities result from logical partitioning of the software requirements. For example, a requirement is identified by "R1001" in the SRS. This is the same as assigned in the system requirements specification. Software engineers use unique creativity to differentiate their requirements into a subset of independent entities, such as:

R1001-01
R1001-02

.

.

R1001-n

A software engineer uses unique creativity that establishes logical design and links together these subset components. Any graphic representation such as the flow chart or hierarchy chart can be used to assist in the implementation of these components. In this venture, it's vital that no requirement is left unnoticed. At the same time, it's equally important that the software design be geared towards a zero defect strategy.

Zero defect strategy

Zero defect strategy attempts to create software design features that don't have any flaws. It's like a utopia; it may not exist in reality. There are always some design flaws, and these flaws will show up in coding and testing. The better the software design, the less these flaws will occur.

The software developer has so far only translated the customer's requirements. Now, all the how techniques will be included in the software design document. This is the first time the customer witnesses the real technical logic of the software design. The software developers will use their ingenuity and imagination to create a logical design. It's not an easy task. Their expertise will be needed to show that their software design logic will be free from any defect. This will be further proven in the coding and testing phase, where less errors will depend on the soundness of the design.

The number and type of entities that are required to partition a design are dependent on a number of factors, which are: complexity of the requirements, the design technique used, and the programming environment. The requirements should be allocated to a lower level of software design building blocks. These building blocks can be called architectural units. These are software modules, components, and units.

Balancing multiple views

Balancing the multiple views of the requirements model involves aligning all the essential aspects of the software design. Figure 15-1 presents multiple views of the requirements. This assists both the customer and the software developer to view the revolution of the requirements. The software developer should now focus on design details from a different viewpoint.

Each view represents a separate concern about the requirement. Together, these views provide a comprehensive description of the software design in a concise and usable form that simplifies information access and assimilation.

Software design document

The software design document (SDD) describes the complete design of a CSCI. This includes its logical components. The components include the logic and how they're connected with each other. The hierarchy covers computer

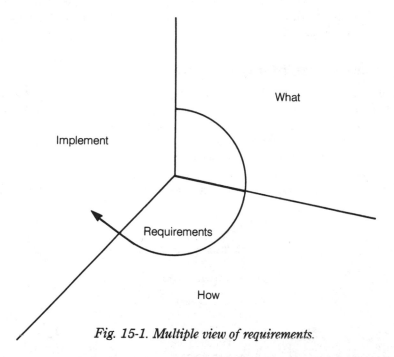

Fig. 15-1. Multiple view of requirements.

software components (CSC) and computer software units (CSU). It provides the internal organizational structure of the CSCI, which shows the sublevel of CSCs and CSUs. This includes the logical relationships among the CSCs. This also provides a logical relationship between a CSC and its CSUs. This presents the data that's transmitted via the interfaces.

The SDD identifies each system state and mode in which the CSCI operates, the CSC and CSU that executes in each state, and the mode. This also includes the allocation of memory and processing time to the CSC and CSU. The SDD consists of preliminary design and detailed design.

The *preliminary design* consists of CSCI architecture and all the external interfaces. The architecture should be partitioned and include all the CSCs and CSUs. The logical link between these components should be explored. The internal interfaces should be properly named and documented. Any real-time features should be highlighted.

The SDD includes memory and processing time allocation for each component. It includes the preliminary design of a CSC and its sublevel of all CSC/CSU. The logical relationships should be established for the design. The SDD includes any design constraints. All of the CSC should be named uniquely.

The *detailed design* consists of the logical relationship between a CSC and all of its sublevel components in the CSU. All the interfaces should be clearly and uniquely named and documented. All of the CSU should be uniquely named. The information recorded should be in a program design language, flowcharts, or any other graphic representation. It should include input/output data elements, interrupt and error handling, algorithms, logic flow, data structure, and data files or database.

Characteristics of a good SDD

Characteristics of a good SDD consist of design entity attributes. An *attribute* is a named characteristic in a design entity. An *entity* is an element of a design that's structurally and functionally distinct from other elements, and each is separately named and referenced. A design entity attribute provides a statement of fact about the entity. Some of these characteristics are listed in TABLE 15-1. All attributes are specified in each entity. Attribute descriptions include references and design considerations such as tradeoffs and assumptions, when they're appropriate.

Table 15-1.
Software Design
Characteristics

- Identification
- Type
- Purpose
- Function
- Subordinates
- Dependencies
- Interface
- Resources
- Processing
- Data

Identification means giving each entity a name. Two entities should not have the same name. The name should be meaningful and characterize an entity's nature.

Type is a descriptive kind of entity. The type attribute describes the nature of an entity. It may simply name the kind of entity, such as subprogram, module, procedure, process, or data store. Alternatively, design entities may be grouped into major classes that deal with a particular type of information and assist in locating an entity. There should be consistency in the naming convention and the entity's type.

Purpose is a description of why the entity exists. This provides the rationale for the creation of an entity. It should designate the specific functional and performance requirements for which the entity was created. The purpose attribute also describes special requirements that must be met by the entity that are not included in the software requirements specification.

Function is a statement of what the entity does. The function attribute should state the transformation that's applied by the entity to inputs to produce the desired output. In the case of a data entity, this attribute should state the type of information that's stored or transmitted by the entity.

Subordinates identify all entities that are composed of this entity. The subordinates attribute identifies the composed relationship for an entity. This information traces requirements to design entities and identifies the parent/child structural relationship.

Dependencies are a description of the relationships among this entity and other entities. The dependencies attribute identifies the uses or the relationships of an entity. These relationships are explained with graphic diagrams. This attribute describes the nature of each interaction and includes such characteristics as timing and conditions for interaction. The interactions involve initiation, order of execution, data sharing, creation, duplicating, usage, and storage.

The *interface* is a description of how other entities interact with this entity. The interface attribute describes the methods of interaction and the rules that govern those interactions. The methods of interaction include the mechanisms for invoking or interrupting the entity, communicating through parameters, common data areas or messages, and direct access to internal data. The rule that governs the interaction includes the communications protocol, data format, acceptable values, and the meaning of each value. This attribute also provides a description of the input ranges, the meaning of inputs and outputs, the type and format of each input or output, and output error codes. It also includes screen formats and a complete description of the interactive language.

Resources is a description of the elements that are used by an entity that are external to the design. The resources attribute identifies and describes all of the resources that are external to the design and are needed by this entity so its function can be performed. The interaction rules and methods for the use of the resources should be specified by this attribute. This attribute provides information about items of physical devices, such as printers, disc-partitions, and memory banks. This includes the software services of math libraries and operating services. This also includes processing resources such as CPU cycles, memory allocation, and buffers. The resources attribute describes usage characteristics such as the process time at which resources will be acquired and sized, which includes quantity and physical sizes of buffer usage.

Processing is a description of the rules that are used by an entity so its function will be achieved. The processing attribute describes the algorithm that's used by an entity to perform a specific task, which should include contingencies. This description is a refinement of the function attribute. This description includes timing, sequencing of events or processes, prerequisites for process initiation, priority of events, processing level, actual process steps, path conditions, and loop back or loop termination criteria. The error handling contingencies describe the action that will be taken in the case of overflow conditions or in the case of a validation check failure.

Data is a description of data elements that are internal to an entity. The data attribute describes the method of representation, initial values, use, semantics, format, and acceptable values of internal data. The description of data should enhance the data dictionary. Data information describes everything that pertains to the use of data or internal data structures by this entity. It includes data specifications such as formats, number of elements, and initial values. It also includes the structures that will be used to represent data such as file structure, arrays, stacks, queues, and memory partitions. The meaning and use of data elements should be specified. This description includes such things as static versus dynamic, whether the data element will be shared by transactions, used as a control parameter, or used as a value, loop iteration count, pointer, or link field. In addition, data information includes a description of data validation that's needed for the process.

Benefits of an SDD

Benefits of an SDD include examining early in the life cycle how the software developer will design the software. An incorrect interpretation of the requirement in the design can lead to disaster in the software product later on. An incorrect value of an attribute can result in a fault in the software that will be developed. The software developers should show their technical capabilities and that they have understood the requirements completely. They can now translate the requirements into a logical design. They should be comfortable in creating a good design that will be a guideline for programmers when they code. The software design document is just like a blueprint. It's a step ladder or guidance road map for the programmers so they can code successfully. Some of the benefits of a software design are listed below.

- Blueprint for software development.
- Identification of common software components.
- Identification of nondevelopment software components.
- Reusability of software components.
- Requirements traceability.
- Road map for testing.
- Guidelines for software integration.

The importance of blueprints is well known in the industry. Blueprints are needed as guidelines for the software development. These will also be used during the software maintenance phase. The customer's interface at the early stage in the "how" document ensures that any error can be corrected without its perpetual imprints. Blueprints ensure that the software developers have understood the requirements and that they will correctly translate them into design.

The cost of software development and maintenance directly depends on the correctness of the software design. It's the foundation of the software implementation phase. Any crack in the foundation will shake the software architecture. It's important that the software design logic is checked and is sound. This directly relates to the schedule of project completion. A good design helps the programmers implement the design effectively. If the software design is logically correct, the chances are that the product will be produced correctly, according to the customer's requirements.

The objective is to partition the software requirements into separate logical components that can be considered, implemented, changed, and tested with minimal effect on other entities. Each of these design entities will have a unique name, purpose, and function.

The design document is the only "how" document that the software developers will produce, and most of the time they're hesitant about it. The software developer must invent and design a foolproof software. This is an acid test that will verify the technical capability of the software developer.

What happened to the customer's requirements?

The software design document (SDD) describes how the software will be structured so that the requirements, which have been identified in the software requirements specification, are satisfied. The SDD is a translation of requirements into a description of the software structure, software components, interfaces, and data necessary for the implementation phase. All the requirements will be traced to and from an SDD. (See FIG. 15-2.) These require-

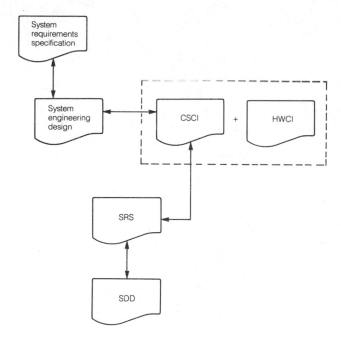

Fig. 15-2. SDD requirements traceability.

ments will be further tabulated in a matrix and will show their traceability to and from CSCs and CSUs. These are necessary for test purposes.

During the design, a requirement may be partitioned into a lower level and assigned to many different architectural units. Each of these requirements must be traceable from the software requirements specification to the lowest level architectural unit where it will be actually implemented.

The SDD is the blueprint for the implementation activity. The SDD bridges the gap between the SRS and implementation of the requirements. It's important that the bridge is technically and logically strong and approved by the customer before the software developer lets the SDD go into the coding phase.

16

The process
of implementing
software requirements

The process of implementing software requirements includes writing logical instructions so the computer can process them. The output result must match the requirements statement as specified in the SDD and SRS documents. In this chapter, I cover the importance of implementing software requirements. I also discuss the Logiscope CASE tool and the qualities and metrics of a well-structured computer program.

Software requirements implementation program

A software requirements implementation program provides logical instructions that are written so they can be processed by a computer. The use of a suitable computer language should have already been agreed upon by the software developer and the customer during the software engineering management plan. A program can be described as a computerized software system or any component of such a system. Thus, the term can be applied to a range of software products, namely, a module that encapsulates a data type, a procedure that formats a string, a database management system, or a distributed operating system.

These programs always respond to a requirements statement. The requirements statements have been identified in the SRS and the blueprint of the software design. Thus, the program consists of a set of logical instructions that the computer will process so the result will match the specified requirements statement. This requirements statement is also a testable statement. A programmer converts the SDD-specified requirement into detailed logic so it can be easily coded into the computer language. A programmer writes a sequence of logical instructions for the computer program and tests them for any error in logic. The programmer develops sample input data that will be processed by the computer for program adequacy. He or she basically focuses on the precision, consistency, and completeness of the requirement statement. Another concern is that there must be no error created in the logic. This contributes to effective maintainability of the program.

Verifying requirements specifications

Verification of a requirements specification demonstrates that the result of the program matches its requirements. A specification is a provable statement that describes properties that a program will possess. The major features of a program that can verify a specified requirement are as follows:

1. A well-structured program.
2. Correct logical loops.
3. A programming-logic concept.

A well-structured program

A well-structured program can easily verify the specified requirement. The correctness of a program is shown when the outputs generated by the program are consistent with the specifications of the program. Testing may reveal errors in either the specification or the code. The correct program should contain the correct data types. Data types can be listed in the categories stated in TABLE 16-1.

Table 16-1. Data Type Categories

- Data abstraction
- Data consistency
- Data implementation

Data abstraction means that the specification is correct if it's consistent and complete. Data abstraction can be based on either an abstract model or an algebraic approach. Under the abstract model approach, the operations of the data type are expressed in terms of operations of a simpler type, such as stack operations. On the other hand, the basis of an algebraic specification is a self-contained set of axioms. An implementation of the abstract data type is correct if it can be shown to be consistent with the specification.

Data consistency means uniformity when the data type is defined. Data should be consistent with the data model schema, which should be discussed in the software requirements specification.

Data implementation is verified with respect to its specification. There exists a relationship between an abstract operation and its implementation in terms of "abstract mapping" (1987 Hoare). This mapping from representation to abstraction must obey a commutative property. For example, when an abstract operation "f" is implemented by a concrete function "p" and denotes its function symbol by "P," then mapping R must obey the relationship:

$$R(P(x)) = f(R(x))$$

Intuitively, the left-hand side of this equation describes the result and finds the abstract value of the result by applying the implemented operation. The right-hand side describes the result by applying the abstract operation to the appropriate original abstract value.

Correct logical loops

Correct logical loops verify the specified requirements. The correctness of logical loops depends on parameters that are listed in TABLE 16-2. The proofs of programs that contain logical loops require a greater degree of creativity.

Table 16-2.
Loop Parameters

- Invariants
- Functions
- Procedures
- Goto
- Array

Invariants are conditions that hold at every entry to and every exit from the loop. For example, an invariant for a loop that accumulates the sum of the elements of an array A(1..n) as the value of variable "sum" is

$$sum = \sum_{i=1}^{k} A(i)$$

where k counts the times the loop has been executed. When the loop invariant is known and is closely related to the post condition of the loop, the verification of the loop is easy. Often this is not so, and the formulation of the loop invariant requires much creativity (1982 Gries).

Function describes a loop. In that case, the function is equivalent to an unrolled version of the loop. For example, let's suppose that you wish to find the function that's computed by "WHILE B DO S" (1988 Mills). You guess a function "f" and show:

$$f = [\text{IF B THEN S}] \circ f$$

where the square brackets denote "the function computed by." Additionally, you must show that the function correctly describes the case when the loop body is never executed. This is done by showing equivalence with the identity function for that special case. Rather than show that the loop terminates, you show that the domain of the function that is guessed includes the domain of the actual loop function.

Procedures provide another source for verification. For procedure calls without parameters or calls where the arguments match the parameters, the semantics of the call may be described by macro expansion. Substitution of parameters and recursion are the two main factors in procedures. You can introduce a rule of substitution that prohibits aliasing and side effects. The second factor proves that the procedure is correct whenever there are no recursive calls. Assuming that the procedure is correct for "n," recursive calls show that it's correct for "n + 1" recursive calls.

Goto and exit increase the complexity of the programs that use them with unrestricted transfer of control. A well-structured program dictates that such transfers will be used only in special cases.

Array, records, and pointers include the left-hand side of assignments in a programming language. It's assumed that the variable on the left-hand side of the assignment is a simple identifier, and a substitution for a simple identifier is easily defined. The usual method introduces functions that perform the appropriate substitution and selection.

A programming-logic concept

A programming logic concept can verify that a requirements statement is a logical consequence of axioms. This requires a framework of reasoning that the language of logic provides. Syntactic rules define which combinations of the symbols of this language are well-formed formulas (WFF) and which WFF are clauses. Every WFF can be expressed as a set of clauses. Depending on how restrictive or permissive the syntax, you obtain different logics: propositional logic, first-order predicate logic with equality, and second-order predicate logic. Some of the programming logic parameters are listed in TABLE 16-3.

Table 16-3.
Logic Parameters

- Interpretation
- Inferences

Interpretation of a WFF is a requirement statement. It's interpreted by the assignment of a meaning to every constant symbol and free variable in it. Different interpretations of the same WFF transform it into different statements. Semantic rules of the logic permit the evaluation of a statement. The evaluation of a statement yields the value true or false. A WFF is valid if and only if it evaluates true for every interpretation; it's satisfiable if and only if it evaluates true for at least one interpretation. It's nonvalid if and only if it evaluates false for at least one interpretation; and it's unsatisfiable if and only if it evaluates false for every interpretation. An interpretation in which a WFF evaluates true is a model for this WFF. The notion of a model can be extended to any arbitrary subset Q in the set of WFFs: an interpretation is a model of Q if every WFF in Q evaluates true under this interpretation. A WFF w, which need not belong to Q, is a logical consequence of Q if it evaluates true under every interpretation of Q.

Another example is IF-THEN-ELSE and WHILE logical constructs. Each of these constructs is interpreted by a proof rule. The rule uses some form of the expression {P}S{R}, which reads

"If statement P is true before execution of S, then,
provided S terminates, R will be true after execution of S."

If this expression is true, then P is a precondition of S, and R is a postcondition.

The nature of the proof of program S is as follows. The programmer supplies statements P and R, which supposedly describe the intended purpose of the program. Statement P defines properties of the input of the program; R defines properties of the output. Expression {P}S{R} is then the hypothesis that must be proven.

Inferences are natural deductions. Calculus is a set of axiomatic schemas and a set of inference rules that generate WFFs with a particular property. For example:

$$\frac{a \rightarrow c,\ b \rightarrow c,\ a \lor b}{c}$$

The notation asserts that if the expression above the line is true, then the expression below the line is also true. Here's the assertion: "If a implies c, and b implies c, and a or b is true, then c is also true."

The Logiscope CASE tool

Logiscope is an automated source code analyzer. The CASE tool provides complexity analysis and test coverage analysis. It assists in measuring software quality during source coding and testing. It's a product of Verilog, France. American Management Systems (AMS) is its licensed distributor. The vendor claims that it supports the software life cycle during development, testing, maintenance, and reverse engineering activities.

Logiscope calculates and reports more than thirty different metrics, which include McCabe, Halstead, and Mohanty metrics. These metrics measure the complexity of the module and evaluate the size and hierarchical leveling. The metrics also determine if the code is relatively well structured. A list of selected metrics and their definitions appears in TABLE 16-4 and TABLE 16-5.

Table 16-4. Modular-Level Complexity Measures

Comments/statements ratio (COM_RAT or T_COM)—The ratio of comment blocks to executable statements, which indicates the level of internal documentation.

Control density (C_D)—The average number of decisions per node in the module [(NB_ARCS-NB_NODES)/NB_NODES)] or [(VG-1)/NB_NODES].

Cyclomatic number (VG)—The maximum number of test cases required to execute every executable statement in the module at least once. This value has a high correlation with the number of errors, maintenance effort, testability, and good programming practices (NB_ARCS-NB_NODES + 2).

Estimated number of errors (NB_ERROR)—The predicted number of errors (bugs) in the module based on the complexity of the algorithm represented by the module (EFFORT$^{2/3}$/3000).

Intelligent content (INT_CONT)—Represents the complexity of the algorithm being performed in a module, as a function of module length and volume (P_LENGTH∗P_SIZE).

Language level (L_LEVEL)—Gauges the aptitude of the language to represent the algorithm as implemented, and is an indicator of verbosity and ambiguity in the language (P_LEVEL^2∗P_VOLUME).

Length ratio (LEN_RAT)—The ratio of the estimated program length, as defined by Halstead, to the computed length (P_LENGTH).

Maximum number of degrees (NB_DEG)—The maximum number of arcs converging on a single node in a module's control structure (a critical node through which a large number of execution paths pass).

Maximum number of levels (NB_LEV)—The maximum number of structure nestings (e.g., nested IF-THEN-ELSE statements) within a module.

Mental effort (EFFORT)—The number of mental discriminations required to program a module. A high value indicates a potential for increased maintenance time and a greater risk of error in maintenance or enhancement operations on the module (P_VOLUME/P_LEVEL).

Number of arcs (NB_ARCS)—Number of transfers of control within a module from one node to the next.

Number of comments (NB_COM)—The number of comments in the module. LOGISCOPE™ treats contiguous multi-line comments as one comment block.

Number of nodes (NB_NODES)—Number of sequential blocks of code within a module.

Number of pending nodes (P_NODES)—The number of additional entries of exits from a module, other than the normal start/end flow.

Number of statements (NB_STMT)—The number of executable statements in the module.

Operand occurrences (N_2)—The total number of uses of operands in the module. This includes variables and literals passed as parameters to a procedure or function.

Operator occurrences (N_1)—The total number of uses of operators in the module. The actual symbols counted as operators varies based on the language being analyzed, but can essentially be thought of as the reserved words of the language plus the names of any user-defined procedure or function calls.

Program length (P-LENGTH, N)—The length of the module, expressed as the sum of the number of operator occurrences and the number of operand occurrences, N_1 + N_2 (as described above). This value is used in subsequent calculations of module complexity.

Program level (P_LEVEL)—The level of the module, an indication of the comprehensibility of the module relative to the implementation of the language [V∗/V or (2/ETA_1) ∗ (ETA_2/N$_2$)].

Table 16-4. Continued.

Program size (P_SIZE)—Estimation of the size of the module, used as an indicator of the potential number of faults in the module, $[(ETA\_1 * \log_2 (ETA\_1 + ETA\_2 * \log_2 (ETA\_2)]$.

Programming time (P_TIME)—The estimated number of seconds required to program a module, using Halstead's determination that an experienced, concentrating programmer can make 18 mental discriminations (EFFORT) per second (EFFORT/18).

Program volume (P_VOLUME)—The size in bits required to specify a program using uniform binary encoding. Measures the conciseness of the representation of the algorithm $[N(\_1 + N\_2) * (\log_2 (ETA\_1 + ETA\_2)]$ or $[P\_LENGTH * \log_2 (V\_SIZE)]$.

Unique operands (ETA_2)—The number of unique operands in the module (e.g., variables or constants).

Unique operators (ETA_1)—The number of unique operators (e.g., $+$, $-$, user-defined functions, etc.).

Vocabulary size (V_SIZE)—The size of the vocabulary used in the module, expressed as the sum of the number of unique operators and the number of unique operands, $ETA\_1 + ETA\_2$ (as described above). This value, like program length, is used in subsequent calculations of module complexity.

Logiscope produces graphs (control graphs, kiviat diagrams, and call graphs). These visually depict how well structured the modules are, and they give reports that provide fine detail. Logiscope visualizes the structure of over thirty-five different languages, which include ADA, C, COBOL, Fortran, Pascal, and PL/1. Logiscope provides two types of analysis: static and dynamic.

Table 16-5. Architectural/Hierarchical Complexity Measures

Hierarchical complexity (H_CPX)—Average number of modules per level (NB_NODES/NB_LEV).

Number of arcs (NB_ARCS)—Number of transfers of control (calls) in the call structure.

Number of calling paths (NB_PATHS)—Number of unique paths in the call structure from a specific root module to all called modules (leaves).

Number of nodes (NB_NODES)—Number of modules (e.g., functions, subroutines) within the call structure.

Number of levels (NB_LEV)—Number of hierarchical levels in the call structure.

Mohanty's accessibility of a module (A(M))—Measures the probability of activating a module (M) from the entry module if all modules are equiprobable.

Mohanty's testability of a path (TP(P))—Testability of a path in the system ball structure is characterized by the depth of the path (number of levels) and the extent of calls (width) made by the modules in the path.

Mohanty's testability of a system (TS(P))—Testability of the system is based on the number of paths in the system and the difficulty of testing each path.

Structural complexity (S_CPX)—Average number of calls per module. (NB_ARCS/NB_NODES).

Schutt's control entropy (ENTROPY)—Provides a measure of the disorder of the call graph. The degree of disorder can also be determined by simply reviewing the call graph.

Static analysis

Static analysis is a review of source code that is done prior to compilation and execution. The review provides graphical and tabular output that describes the complexity, structure, testability, and maintainability of code. The three levels of static software analysis are listed in TABLE 16-6.

Table 16-6. Static
Software Analysis
Levels

• Modular level
• Synthesis level
• Architectural level

The *modular* level of the static analysis provides analysis for an individual module that is a uniquely identifiable piece of source code that has both starting and stopping points. The modular level of static analysis provides complexity measures in the form of structural and textual metrics. It evaluates software code on the basis of metrics. These metrics are not an absolute measure of software quality; rather, they provide relative measurements. Metrics should be used in conjunction with other metrics, not in isolation, for a comprehensive code evaluation. The result of modular static analysis is displayed in graphical and tabular form in FIG. 16-1. The control graphs plot the flow of control through a module from left to right and graphically depict each of the main control structures. These control structures are sequential statements,

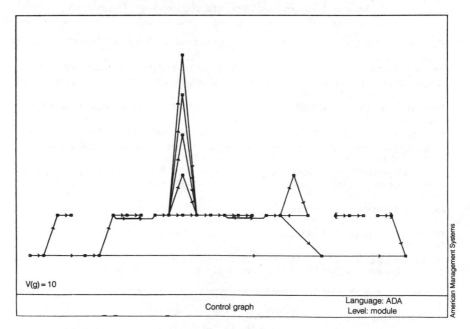

V(g) = 10

Control graph

Language: ADA
Level: module

American Management Systems

Fig. 16-1. Control graph.

IF THEN ELSE, WHILE loop, REPEAT UNTIL loop, case, GOTO, EXIT, and EXCEPTION WHEN. Good structure and characteristics of poor structure, such as abnormal exits and GOTOs, can be identified by control graphs.

Figure 16-2 exhibits the kiviat diagram. This displays the results of all the metrics for a module in one place. The table in the upper left identifies the

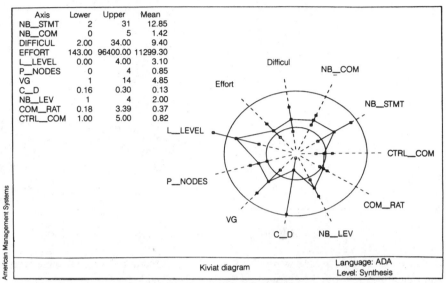

Axis	Lower	Upper	Mean
NB_STMT	2	31	12.85
NB_COM	0	5	1.42
DIFFICUL	2.00	34.00	9.40
EFFORT	143.00	96400.00	11299.30
L_LEVEL	0.00	4.00	3.10
P_NODES	0	4	0.85
VG	1	14	4.85
C_D	0.16	0.30	0.13
NB_LEV	1	4	2.00
COM_RAT	0.18	3.39	0.37
CTRL_COM	1.00	5.00	0.82

Kiviat diagram

Language: ADA
Level: Synthesis

American Management Systems

Fig. 16-2. Kiviat diagram.

short name for the metric, the lower bound, upper bound, and the value of each metric for the module. A kiviat diagram plots a module's metric values radially along a set of spokes. These values should fall between the two concentric circles, which represents acceptable lower and upper bounds. The metrics table complements the kiviat diagrams. The table includes the metric long name, short name, and value of each metric for the module. In addition, a "*" appears in the last column when the metric value is above or below the specified upper or lower bounds.

Figure 16-3 shows a criteria graph. This identifies metric values that are outside acceptable limits for a set of quality criteria. A quality criterion is represented by a set of metrics. The graph is used for both the module level and the architectural level. Two concentric circles are shown on the graph, and they correspond to the defined metric limits. Each criterion is assigned a portion of the graph with corresponding plotted metric values. Values plotted in the region between the two circles are within bounds, and those values outside of this region exceed the acceptable bounds, and those values outside of this region exceed the acceptable range. This graph helps quickly identify those metrics that may affect the reusability of the code.

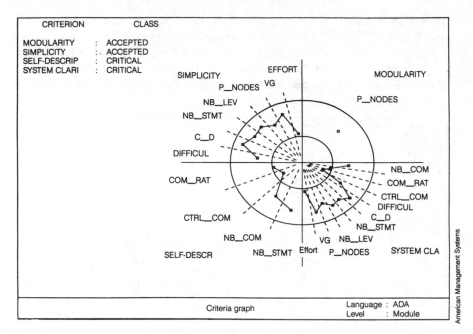

Fig. 16-3. Criteria graph.

Synthesis static analysis provides summary information that's based on modular-level results. Synthesis analysis results provide means, standard deviations, ranges, and distributions for each software complexity measurement (metric) that is computed from the code. It also relays the percentage of the code that meets the specified software quality standards. The outputs include metrics distributions, as shown in FIG. 16-4. It shows the distribution of an individual metric among a group of modules. For each metric there's one distribution. The vertical axis represents percent modules. The horizontal axis represents the value of the metric.

Figure 16-5 illustrates a statistical table that can establish standards for a given programming environment. This table lists each metric's short and long name, the mean value for each metric, the minimum and maximum values that are observed among the modules for each metric, and the percentage of modules whose metric values met the quality standards. In addition, the synthesis level provides kiviat diagrams that are similar to the modular level diagrams. This displays the metric results for a group of modules.

Architectural analysis displays the module hierarchy and call structure that illustrates the relationships between the modules. Architectural analysis allows and explores the complexity of the overall design of the system. Figure 16-6 exhibits a call graph that depicts the calling structure or global architecture of a program. It identifies the unique paths through the call structure, and thus illustrates the minimum number of tests that will be performed so complete interface testing will be ensured. The call graph of a well-designed sys-

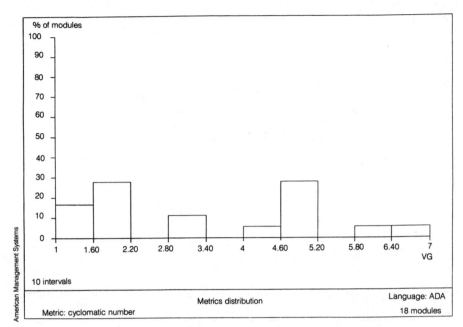

Fig. 16-4. Metrics distribution.

Metrics	Ident	Mean	Standard deviation	Min Value	Max Value	% in
Number of statements	NB__STMT	11.55	7.95	0.00	31.00	89%
Program size	P__SIZE	96.66	61.45	44.82	276.50	100%
Intelligent content	INT__CONT	24.89	13.42	8.63	68.04	75%
Estimated number of errors	NB__ERROR	0.07	0.08	0.01	0.32	94%
Program level	P__LEVEL	0.14	0.10	0.03	0.39	88%
Program difficulty	DIFFICUL	11.67	8.00	2.52	30.54	88%
Mental effort	EFFORT	4857.25	7725.60	202.04	29932.27	100%
Language level	L__LEVEL	4.35	6.24	0.47	26.93	88%
Number of arcs	NB__ARCS	11.33	8.10	1	29	100%
Number of nodes	NB__NODES	10.38	6.71	2	24	100%
Number of pending nodes	P__NODES	0.44	1.01	0	4	94%
Cyclomatic number	VG	3.38	1.82	1	7	100%
Control density	C__D	0.19	0.10	0.00	0.33	50%
Maximum number of levels	NB__LEV	3.00	1.45	1	6	83%
Maximum number of degrees	NB__DEG	3.11	1.04	1	4	100%
Comments rate	T__COM	0.42	0.20	0.08	0.71	88%
Unique operands	ETA__2	11.83	8.17	0	33	89%
Operand ocurrences	N__2	22.55	21.40	0	84	83%
Unique operators	ETA__1	10.55	6.41	0	24	83%
Operator ocurrences	N__1	26.16	22.01	0	84	89%

Statistic table

Language : ADA
Modules : 18

Fig. 16-5. Statistic table.

tem has well-ordered relationships, top-down hierarchy of calls, and some
separation between mainline processing and exception handling. A poorly
designed system has a call graph with erratic structures, recursive conditions,
and unnecessary jumps between multiple levels. A global graph shows the

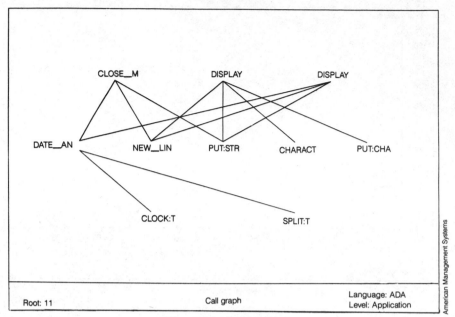

Fig. 16-6. Call graph.

relationship between all modules used in the system. It will provide a list of disconnected modules.

Dynamic analysis

Dynamic analysis is the analysis of executing code. The purpose of dynamic analysis is to check the status of the testing process against established testing goals and to ensure that the test cases that are being used are sufficient so all the decision paths and procedure calls in the system can be tested. Dynamic analysis supports the software testing process by providing aids for the development of test cases and information about the completeness of test coverage. It analyzes the effectiveness of both unit and integration testing efforts. Logiscope dynamic analysis reveals all tested and untested paths. It also enables programmers and/or testers to construct tests that exercise all paths in the software.

Logiscope provides test coverage results that measure the effectiveness of test cases. It provides both graphical and tabular output that identifies the decision paths that are covered (unit-level test coverage), procedure calls that are made (integration-level test coverage), and the paths not tested.

This information is coordinated with the test aid's output and allows programmers to quickly identify portions of code that were not tested and update the test cases as necessary. Test coverage at the module level measures the coverage of unit tests. The output shows the extent to which the possible paths through the module have been tested. Test coverage at the architectural level measures the coverage of integration/system tests. The output shows the extent to which the possible paths through the system have been tested.

Figure 16-7 exhibits a dynamic control graph that's similar to the control graph for static analysis, except that the solid lines show the tested paths, and

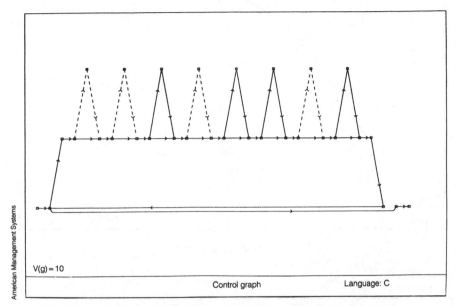

Fig. 16-7. Control graph.

the dashed lines identify untested paths. The dynamic call graph is illustrated in FIG. 16-8. This is similar to the call graph for static analysis. In addition, the solid lines show the tested paths, and the dashed lines identify untested paths. An asterisk identifies instrumented code. Figure 16-9 presents a decision-to-decision path (DDP) coverage-rate table. This graph supplies data for a group of tests and assists in determining module-level test coverage. For each test, it provides the number of times each DDP was exercised and the coverage rate for the module. For all tests combined, it provides the total number of times each DDP was exercised and the global coverage rate of the test battery for the module. Coverage is determined by counting number of DDPs that are exercised at least once, and dividing by the total DDPs. A DDP coverage-rate histogram is exhibited in FIG. 16-10. This shows the distribution of coverage rates among modules for a test group. The vertical axis represents the percentage of modules that are tested. The horizontal axis represents the percentage of DDPs that are tested.

Logiscope benefits
The complexity analysis provides complexity measures, module structure, and overall architecture. Complexity analysis gives the software developer the

American Management Systems

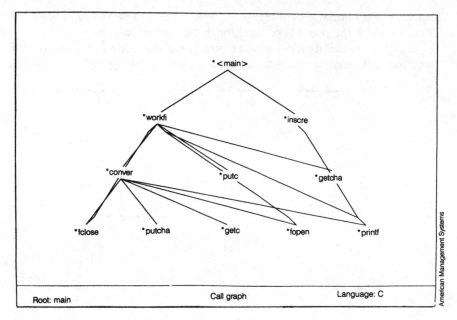

Fig. 16-8. Call graph.

Module	Nb of DDP	Nb of calls	% executed DDP
main	1	1	100%
inscreen	1	1	100%
workfile	7	1	85%
convert	19	0	0%

Application :   Language : C   Group tests :
DDP global coverage rate for the group of tests

American Management Systems

Fig. 16-9. DDP table.

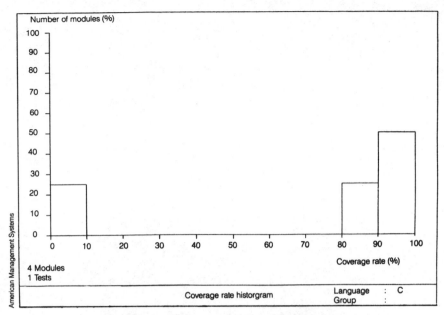

Fig. 16-10. DDP coverage-rate histogram.

visibility and control that's required for well-structured programming. Test coverage analysis is performed during unit and integration testing, through instrumentation of source code, program execution, measurement, and graphical representation. Coverage analysis as it's provided by Logiscope includes decision-to-decision paths, and calls between modules.

17

Validating
and verifying
software requirements

Building a system is a technique that should integrate all the correct and tested software components in accordance with the software design blueprints. Software that has been well received always begins with requirements that have been well written. Through acceptance tests, the customer validates and verifies the software product for correctness and fulfillment of the requirements.

Integrating software units/components

Software units/components integration involves a systematic integration of all correct and tested units into a component. Then these tested components are combined into a system. At this time, it's important that the software design blueprints be consulted again for the necessary guidance to logically link these units and components. When the software requirements specifications are revisited, you can verify the usefulness, viability, and requirements compliance of all the software. This schema is illustrated in FIG. 17-1. Tests are conducted for all coded units that are threaded in a component. This technique consists of static testing, desk checking, code walk-through, and dynamic testing. All successful test results are documented in a database file for reference and records.

   The next step is to logically combine all the computer software components, which are composed of verified, tested units. Again, the software design blueprint can guide you through the logic, and then you can follow with integration. When the system requirements specifications are revisited, they will help you further conform to the customer's specified requirements for the system. These tested components will be threaded together so a CSCI can be formed. This phase is composed of a series of tests that demonstrate how the

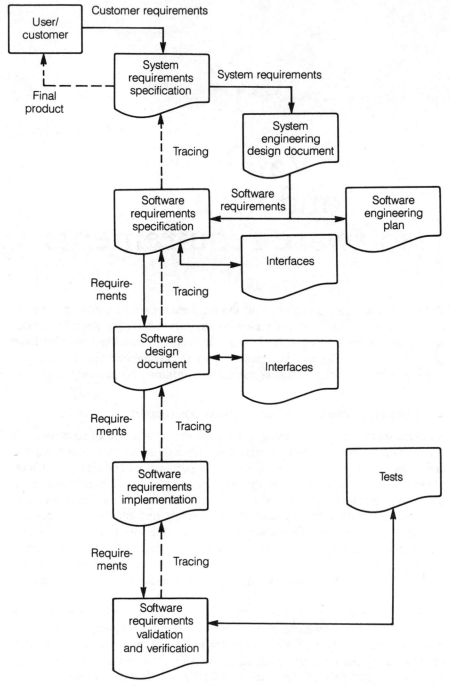

Fig. 17-1. Building a system schema.

system software performs the desired requirements; then the system is ready for formal review and extensive testing.

T tool

T tool is an integrated set of techniques, metrics, and standards. It's the product of PEI testing methodology. The methodology concentrates on five improvement techniques, which are listed in TABLE 17-1. With this methodology,

Table 17-1. T Tool Improvement Techniques

1. Defining requirements for testability
2. Designing software for testability
3. Designing tests for most probable errors
4. Designing tests before code is designed
5. Performing reviews, inspections, and walk-throughs

software developers can define requirements, define tests that will demonstrate requirements, and then design the software. (See FIG. 17-2.)

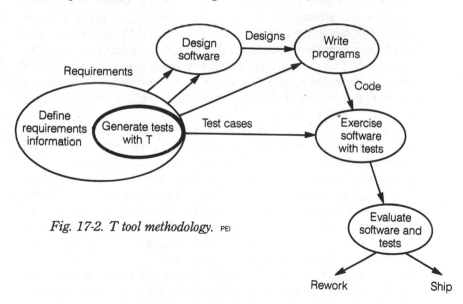

Fig. 17-2. T tool methodology. PEI

1. Defining requirements for testability means that you understand what the customer expects of the software. Each of the software requirements must be uniquely identified in the software requirements specification so the requirements can be traced for testability later. T tool can make software requirements writing easier. T tool asks that the soft-

ware developer record these requirements so test cases can be created by automatic means. The software developer defines functions, processes, states, conditions, data, and events for these tests. All this information is entered on fixed-form screens. T tool will take care of documents, paragraphs, sentence structure, graphic placement, verb tense agreement, inconsistent use of terms, and sentence ambiguities. If there's any inconsistency, T tool will report it for correction. T tool makes sure that software requirements are testable and up-to-date. Then, when they're needed, T tool can create test cases directly from the requirements.

Having correct software requirements is the most important thing the software developer can do so the customer will approve of the delivered software product. Well-received software always begins with well-written requirements.

2. Designing software for testability requires well-documented requirements that should have test cases. These test cases will demonstrate every software requirement and the absence of probable error. The T tool vendor states that their users can design out errors and design in quality by creating products that pass T test cases. In this environment, the software requirements are allocated to architectural units, modules, and subsystems. A requirement is sometimes partitioned into lower-level requirements and assigned to many different architectural units. Occasionally, an architectural unit's created so other units can be controlled. The methodology states that each requirement must be traceable from the system to software requirements specification and software design, and then to the lowest-level architectural unit where it's actually implemented.

3. Designing tests for most probable errors is another feature of the T tool. Test cases that are created according to the methodology will cause all software requirements to be exercised for values of inputs that would detect the most probable errors. If the software developers know how the product will be tested before coding begins, they will likely design out the most probable errors. The recommended rules for software requirements are the use of a standard format, a checklist, prototype models, simple sentences, user's vocabulary, data dictionary terms, and externally visible nouns and verbs.

4. Designing tests before code is another feature of T tool. Every software requirement is separately traceable. Every interface is separately verifiable. Every unit is separately testable. Doing the solid work in the forefront makes the coding progress easier.

5. Performing reviews, inspections, and walk-throughs checks the correctness of the code implementation. Approval of every completed walk-through is required before unit testing. Building integration testing involves putting together architectural units and testing them as a single entity. Software units are strung together so the output of one

unit is the input to the next one until the final output is visible outside the build. Interface problems may be solved at this time. Testing finds errors and demonstrates that the product functions as it is specified.

Software requirements validation and verification

Software requirements validation and verification determines that the software product fulfills the customer's requirements. It also determines that the software product is free of defects and meets the customer's expectations. The main concern is to confirm that the software product meets the requirements. The result of the product should be correct in accordance with the specified requirements. The result should be consistent and accurate. It's necessary and sufficient that such a result should be produced. Software requirements validation and verification uses input-output assertions, structural induction, regression, transaction flow analysis, stress analysis, failure analysis, concurrency analysis, and performance analysis techniques.

The *input-output assertions* technique uses the assertions that are associated with the entry point, exit point, and the intermediate points in the source code. The composition rule of logic lets the conjunction of assertions form along particular execution paths. This confirms that if all intermediate assertions along a given execution path are true, then the truth of the input assertion implies the truth of the output assertion for the given path.

Structural induction is based on the principle of mathematical induction. An illustration of this principle is a set S. Let's presume P is TRUE for the first element in the set S. If P is less than or equal to N for the first element in set S, then P is TRUE for the (N + first element) in set S. Structural induction generally applies to recursive data structures.

Regression is the retesting of the software component that detects errors when they're introduced during modification. The software modification mandates that regression testing should be performed. It's important that the older capabilities of the software be tested since the customer is dependent on these, rather than testing the new capabilities that are provided by the modification. Regression tests are supplemented with other specified tests for the modifications. Step-by-step testing of each affected component is of prime importance. This testing allows the logical flow of the software design model. It involves retesting, starting from the lowest-level components, and then incrementally combining these into the CSC and CSCI, which are ultimately threaded into the system.

The *transaction flow analysis* identifies the transactions by drawing data-flow diagrams after integration testing, which models the logical flow of the system. This analysis will be compared and confirmed with the software design model.

Stress analysis involves the behavior of the system when its resources are saturated, and it assesses whether or not the system requirement for stress satisfies its specification. It's important that the resources are identified and that they can be stressed. Some of the resources for the stress test cases are file space, memory, input-output buffers, processing time, run-time, and interrupt handling. Stress analysis forces a view of the software product under unforeseen conditions that may not have been anticipated.

Failure analysis is an examination of the software product's reaction to various types of potential failures due to hardware or software. The product's specifications are examined, and they determine precisely which types of failures must be analyzed and what the product's reaction must be. This process assists in the detection of the software product's ability to recover from errors such as lost files, lost data, and duplicate transactions.

Concurrency analysis examines the interaction of the tasks that are being simultaneously executed within the software product, which ensures the satisfaction of the system specifications. Concurrent tasks may be executed in parallel or have their execution interleaved. This analysis is performed during the software design phase and identifies such issues as potential contention for resources, deadlock, and priorities. A concurrency analysis for implementations takes place during system testing. Tests should be designed, executed, and analyzed so the parallelism can be exploited in the system and can ensure the satisfaction of the specifications.

Performance analysis ensures that the product satisfies its specified performance objectives. Performance analysis is applied during each of the product's validation and verification activities. Performance objectives are analyzed to ensure completeness, feasibility, and testability. The performance requirement is evaluated on each component during the software design and determines whether or not the customer's requirement has been satisfied. Prototyping, simulation, and modeling are applicable techniques. Again, performance analysis takes place during each level of testing. Test data should be constructed to correspond with scenarios for which the performance requirements are specified.

System integration

System integration consists of systematically analyzing and combining product components. These individual components have already been examined for correctness. Integration testing is conducted to verify usefulness, viability, and requirements compliance of all the components that compose the CSCI. This phase is composed of a series of tests that demonstrate how the system software performs the desired requirements, and that the system is ready for formal review and extensive testing.

Functional integration tests are conducted extensively at the informal levels; these tests ensure that module-level and unit-level testing is successful. The software components of a system are integrated individually in top-down, bottom-up, big-bang, or threaded manner. The bottom line is that the software developer must prove that the test results demonstrate the components' correctness and interfacing capability; these tests verify that the software design and performance satisfy the requirements of the software specifications. System testing exercises the entire system, from beginning to end.

Revisiting system requirements tracing

Revisiting system requirements tracing is a technique that ensures that the product, as well as the testing of the product, addresses each of the product's requirements. Reference can be made to the system requirements specification, software requirements specification, software design document, and software engineering development plan documents. A sample of requirement tracing is presented in FIG. 17-3. Another approach for requirement tracing is the use of matrices. Sometimes these methods can be used as a supplement to one another. This may be a useful approach for complicated systems.

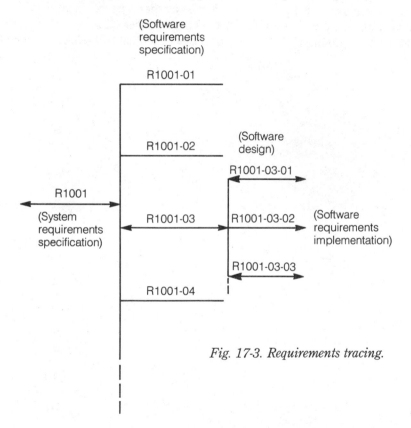

Fig. 17-3. Requirements tracing.

There are generally three types of matrices that map the requirements. One type of matrix maps requirements to software modules, units and components. Construction of this matrix ensures that all requirements are properly addressed by the product. The second type of matrix maps requirements to test cases. Construction of this matrix ensures that all requirements are properly tested. The third type of matrix maps requirements to their evaluation approach. This evaluation approach consists of various levels of testing, reviews, and simulations. The requirements evaluation matrix ensures that all requirements will undergo some validation and verification.

System requirements validation and verification

System requirements validation and verification confirms the satisfaction of the customer's criteria as they were specified in the system requirements specification and statement of work, which verifies the completion of all audits, such as functional and physical configuration. Many of the techniques that are discussed for software requirements validation and verification are applicable in this situation also. Once the customer is satisfied, the certification of verification and validation is signed. Before accepting them, the customer ensures that the software product, source code, object code, and all related documents are complete.

Appendix A

Abbreviations and acronyms

ACAP	Analyst capability
ADL	Ada design language
AEXP	Application experience
AI	Artificial intelligence
ANSI	American National Standards Institute
APSE	Ada programming support environment
CASE	Computer aided software engineering
CDR	Critical design review
CDRL	Contract data requirements list
CFD	Control flow diagram
CM	Configuration management
COCOM	Constructive cost model
COTS	Commercial-off-the-shelf
CPM	Critical path method
CPU	Central processing unit
CSC	Computer software component
CSCI	Computer software configuration item
CSDM	Computer software development methodology
CSU	Computer software unit
DBMS	Database management system
DD	Data dictionary
DFD	Data flow diagram
DID	Data item description
DOD	Department of Defense
DSD	Data structure diagram
EC	Estimated cost
ELOC	Estimated line of code

ER	Entity relationship
EST	Eastern standard time
EV	Earned value
FCA	Functional configuration audit
FQT	Formal qualification testing
FSE	Forward software engineering
GFS	Government furnished software
HOOD	Hierarchical object oriented design
HWCI	Hardware configuration item
ICT	Intelligent CASE tools
IDD	Interface design document
IEEE	Institute of Electrical and Electronics Engineers
I/O	Input/output
IORL	Input/output requirements language
IORTD	Input/output relationships and timing diagram
IRD	International resources dictionary
IRP	Iterative refinement process
IRS	Interface requirements specification
ISO	International Standards Organization
IV&V	Independent verification and validation
JSD	Jackson system development
JSP	Jackson structured programming
KBMS	Knowledge base management system
KBS	Knowledge base system
LOE	Labor of efforts
LRM	Language reference manual
MAGEC	Mask and Application Generator and Environment Controller
MANPRINT	Manpower and Personnel Integration
MMI	Man-machine interfaces
NDS	Nondevelopment software
OAM	Object analysis model
OBM	Object behavior model
OIM	Object information model
OML	Object management library
OOD	Object oriented design
OODB	Object oriented database
OODM	Object oriented design method
OOM	Object oriented methodology
OOP	Object oriented programming
OOSD	Object oriented structured design
OPM	Object process model
OSF	Open Software Foundation
OSI	Open system interconnection
OTS	Off-the-shelf

PCA	Physical configuration audit
PCAP	Programmer capability
PDL	Program design language
PDR	Preliminary design review
PERT	Program evaluation and review technique
PPD	Predefined process diagram
PSA	Program statement analyzer
PSL	Program statement language
P-Spec	Process specification
PST	Pacific standard time
QA	Quality assurance
RDM	Requirements definition model
RE	Resoftware engineering
RELY	Required software reliability
RFP	Request for proposal
RM	Refinement method
ROM	Read only memory
RSE	Reverse software engineering
RSI	Report specification interface
RSL	Requirements statement language
RT	Requirements tracer
RTE	Run-time environment
RTL	Run-time library
RUSE	Required reusability
SA	Structured analysis
SADT	Structured analysis and design technique
SBD	Schematic block diagram
SCR	Software cost reduction
SD	Structured design
SDD	Software design document
SDF	Software development file
SDL	Software development library
SDP	Software development plan
SDR	System design review
SECP	Software engineering conversion plan
SED	Software engineering design
SEDD	System engineering design document
SEDP	Software engineering development plan
SEI	Software Engineering Institute
SEMP	Software engineering maintenance plan
SERA	Software engineering requirements analysis
SOW	Statement of work
Spec	Specification
SPM	Software programmer's manual
SPS	Software product specification

SQL	Software query language
SREM	Software requirements engineering methodology
SRR	System requirements review
SRS	Software requirements specification
SSA	Structured system analysis
SSD	Strategies for system development
SSDD	System/segment design document
SSR	Software specification review
SSS	System/segment specification
STD	State transition diagram
StP	Software through pictures
STR	Software test report
STT	State transition table
SUM	Software user's manual
TAGS	Technology for the automated generation of systems
TRR	Test readiness review
UC	User cases
UCRA	User-centered requirements analysis
UI	User interface
VDD	Version description document
VDM	Vienna development methodology
VEXP	Virtual machine experience
VMVT	Virtual machine volatility target
WBS	Work breakdown structure

Appendix B

Software development standards

ANSI	American National Standards Institute
ANSI/IEEE Std 729-1983	IEEE Standard Glossary of Software Engineering Terminology
ANSI/IEEE Std 730-1984	IEEE Standard for Software Quality Assurance Plans
ANSI/IEEE Std 828-1983	IEEE Standard for Software Configuration Management Plans
ANSI/IEEE Std 829-1983	IEEE Standard for Software Test Documentation
ANSI/IEEE STD 830-1984	IEEE Guide to Software Requirements Specifications
ANSI/IEEE Std 983-1986	IEEE Guide for Software Quality Assurance Planning
ANSI/IEEE Std 990-1986	IEEE Recommended Practices for Ada as a Program Design Language
ANSI/IEEE Std 1002-1987	IEEE Standard Taxonomy for Software Engineering Standards
ANSI/IEEE Std 1008-1987	IEEE Standard for Software Unit Testing
ANSI/IEEE Std 1012-1986	IEEE Standard for Software Verification and Validation Plans
ANSI/IEEE Std 1016-1987	IEEE Recommended Practices for Software Design Descriptions
ANSI/IEEE Std 1042-1988	IEEE Guide to Software Configuration Management
ANSI/IEEE Std 1058.1-1987	IEEE Standard for Software Project Management Plans

ANSI/IEEE Std 1063-1987	IEEE Standard for Software User Documentation
BSI	British Standards Institute
DOD-STD-2167A	U.S. Defense System Software Development
DOD-STD-2168	U.S. Defense System Software Quality Program
DOD-STD-7935	Automated Data Systems Documentation Standards
EEC	European Economic Community
EN	Euro Norm 29000 Series of Standards
GOSIP	U.S. Government Open System Interconnection Profile
IEEE Std. 982.1-1988	IEEE Standard Dictionary of Measures to Produce Reliable Software
IEEE Std. 982.2-1988	IEEE Guide for the Use of IEEE Standard Dictionary of Measures to Produce Reliable Software (IEEE Std. 982.1-1988)
IEEE Std. 1028-1988	IEEE Standard for Software Reviews and Audits
IEEE Standards	To provide recommendations reflecting the application of software engineering principles to the development and maintenance of software.
ISO	International Organization for Standardization
JTC1	Joint Technical Committee 1 on Information Technology
MIL-STD-286	Tailoring Guide for DOD-STD-2168
MIL-STD-287	Tailoring Guide for DOD-STD-2167A
MIL-STD-480A	Configuration Management Practices for Systems, etc.
MIL-STD-480B	Configuration Control Engineering Changes, Deviations Waivers
MIL-STD-483A	Configuration Management Practices for Systems Equipment Munition and Computer Software
MIL-STD-490A	Specification Practices
MIL-STD-499A	Engineering Management
MIL-STD-882B	System Safety Program Requirements
MIL-STD-1521B	Technical Reviews and Audits for Systems, Equipments and Computer Programs

MIL-STD-1750A	U.S. Military Standard for microprocessor
MIL-STD-1803	Software Development Integrity Program
MIL-STD-1815A	Ada Programming Language
NIST Standards	U.S. National Institute of Standards and Technology
OSI	Open Systems Interconnection
SCUSA	Standards Council of the United States of America (proposed)

Appendix C

References

Abbott, R.J. 1986. *An integrated approach to software development*. New York, N.Y.: John Wiley.

ACM. August, 1991. *Communications*.

ACM. May, 1991. *Communications*.

ACM. December, 1990. *Software Engineering Notes*.

ACM. May, 1990. *Software Engineering Notes*.

ACM. January, 1991. *Software Engineering Notes*.

ACM. April, 1991. *Software Engineering Notes*.

ACM. September, 1990. *Software Engineering Notes*.

AI Expert. August, 1990.

Allworth, S. T., and R.N. Zobel. 1987. *Introduction to real-time software design*. New York, N.Y.: Springer-Verlag.

Agresti, W. W. 1986. *Tutorial: New paradigms for software development*. Los Angeles, Ca.: The Computer Society Press.

Ardis, Mark A., and Alfs T. Berztiss. 1988. Formal verification of programs. SEI curriculum modules.

Bauer, F. L. January, 1976. Programming as an evolutionary process. Proceedings of the 2nd International Conference on Software Engineering, IEEE Computer Society, pp. 222-234.

Bergland, G. D., and R. D. Gordon. 1981. *Software design strategies*. Washington, D.C.: IEEE Computer Society Press.

Birrell, N. D., and M. A. Ould. 1985. *A practical handbook for software development*. New York, N.Y.: Cambridge University Press.

Bjorner, D., and C. B. Jones. 1982. *Formal specifications and software development*. Englewood Cliffs, N.J.: Prentice-Hall.

Blank, J. and M. J. Krijger. *Software engineering: methods and techniques*. New York, N.Y.: Wiley Interscience.

Boehm, B. December, 1976. Software engineering. IEEE Transaction, *Computers*, pp. 1226-1241.

_____. 1981. *Software engineering economics*. Englewood Cliffs, N.J.: Prentice Hall.

_____. May, 1988. A spiral model of software development and enhancement. *IEEE Computer*.

Bohm, C., and G. Jacopini. May, 1986. Flow diagrams, turing machines and languages with only two formation rules. *Communications of the ACM*.

Booch, G. 1982. *Software engineering with Ada*. Menlo Park, Ca.: Benjamin/ Cummings Publishing Co.

_____. February, 1986. Object-oriented development. *IEEE transactions on software development*, pp. 211-221.

Brackett, John, W. December, 1988. Software requirements. SEI curriculum module SEI-CM-19-1.0.

Budde, R., K. Kuhlenkamp, L. Mathiassen, and H. Zullighoven. 1984. *Approaches to prototyping*. New York, N.Y.: Springer-Verlag.

Budgen, David, and Richard Sincovec. July, 1987. Introduction to software design. SEI curriculum module SEI-CM-2-1.2 (Preliminary).

Buhr, R.J.A. 1984. *System design with Ada*. Englewood Cliffs, N.J.: Prentice-Hall.

Cameron, John, JSP & JSD. 1989. *The Jackson approach to software development*. Washington, D.C.: IEEE Computer Society Press.

Case, A. 1990. *Team system analysis*. Englewood Cliffs, N.J.: Prentice-Hall.

Chen, P. P. March, 1976. The entity-relationship model—toward a unified view of data. *ACM transactions on database systems*, pp. 9-36.

Clement, P.C., R.A. Parker, D.L. Parnas, J.E. Shore, and K.H.Brit. July, 1989. *A standard organization for specifying abstract interfaces*. Washington, D.C.: Naval Research Laboratory.

Collofello, James S. July, 1987. The software technical review process. SEI curriculum module SEI-CM-3-1.2 (preliminary).

_____. 1988. Introduction to software verification and validation. SEI curriculum module.

Computer design. May, 1991.

Computer design. June, 1989.

Connor, M. F. May, 1980. Structured analysis and design technique (SADT) introduction. Engineering Management Conference Record, *IEEE*, pp. 138-143.

Cross, N. 1984. *Development in design methodology*. New York: N.Y.: 1984.

Davis, C. G., S. Jajodia, P. A. Ng, and R. T. Yeh. 1983. *Entity-relationship approach to software engineering*. New York, N.Y.: North Holland.

DEC professional. August, 1991.

DEC professional. September, 1991.

DeMarco, T. 1979. *Structured analysis and system specification*. Englewood Cliffs, N.J.: Prentice-Hall.

Dijkstra, E. W., F. Dahl, and C. A. R. Hoare. 1972. *Structured programming*. New York, N.Y.: Academic Press.

DOD Ada Joint Office. November, 1982. Ada methodologies: concepts and requirements. (Methodman Doct.)

Druffel, L. April, 1983. Software technology for adaptable, reliable systems —program strategy. *SIGSOFT software engineering notes.*

Embedded systems. April, 1991.

Fairly, R. 1985. *Software engineering concepts.* New York, N.Y.: McGraw-Hill.

Firth, Robert, Bill Wood, Rich Pethia, Lauren Roberts, Vickey Mosley, and Tom Doice. November, 1987. A classification scheme for software development methods. Technical report. Software Engineering Institute, Carnegie-Mellon University.

Fox, J. M. 1982. *Software and its development.* Englewood Cliffs, N.J.: Prentice-Hall.

Freeman, Peter, and Anthony Wasserman. 1983. *Tutorial on software design techniques.* Washington, D.C.: IEEE Computer Society.

Gane C., and T. Sarson. July, 1977. Structured systems analysis: tools and techniques. *Computer.*

Gommaa, H. July, 1986. Software development of real-time systems. *Communication*, pp. 657-668.

Goodenough, John B., and Mark W. Borger. Fall, 1990. Ada usage/performance specification. *ACM Ada letters.*

Gries, D. 1982. A note on a standard strategy for development loop invariants and loops. *Science of Computer Programming.*

Harel, D., A. Pnueli, and R. Sherman. June, 1987. On the formal semantics of statecharts. Proceedings of the 2nd IEEE symposium on logic in computer science. New York, N.Y.: IEEE Press.

_____. 1988. *STATEMATE: A working environment for the development of complex reactive systems.* New York, N.Y.: IEEE Press.

Hatley, D. and Pirbhai, I., Strategies for Real-Time System Specifications, Dorset House, New York (1987).

Heitz, M. November, 1987. HOOD: Hierarchical object oriented design for development of large technical and real-time software. CISI Ingenierie, Direction Midi Pyrenees.

Hoare, C.A.R. September, 1987. An overview of some formal methods for program design. *Computer.*

Hori, S. 1972. CAM-I long range planning final report for 1972. Chicago: Illinois Institute of Technology Research.

HP professional. November, 1990.

Husa, J.D., Stimulating software engineering process - A report of the software engineering planning group, ACM SIGSOFT software engineering notes, Vol 8, No 2, April 1983.

Humphrey, Watts S. October, 1989. CASE planning and the software process. Technical report. CMU/SEI-89-TR-26.

IEEE computer. February, 1991.

IEEE expert. Fall, 1989.

IEEE software engineering standards. 3rd Edition. 1989. N.J.: IEEE.

IEEE software. January, 1991.

IEEE spectrum. January, 1991.

IEEE spectrum. October, 1990.

IEEE transactions on software engineering. March, 1991.

IEEE transactions on software engineering. November, 1990.

Jackson, M. 1978. The jackson design methodology. Infotec state of the art report, structured programming.

Information center quarterly. Winter, 1991.

Information week. July, 1991.

Johnson, A. L. August/September, 1986. Software engineering combines management and technical skills. *SEI bridge*.

Jorgensen, Paul C. July, 1987. Requirements specification overview. SEI curriculum module SEI-CM-1-1.2 (preliminary).

Katzan, Harry. 1976. Systems design and documentation. New York, N.Y.: Van Nostrand Reinhold.

Lee, Kenneth J., and Michael S. Rissman. 1989. An object-oriented solution example: A flight simulator electrical system. *SEI technical report*.

Leveson, N. G. June, 1986. Software safety: Why, what, and how. *ACM computing surveys*.

Liskov, B. and S. N. Zilles. April, 1974. Programming with abstract data types. *ACM SIGPLAN Notices*, pp. 50-60.

Martin, Charles F. *User-centered requirements analysis*. Englewood Cliffs, N.J.: Prentice-Hall.

McMenamin, S. M., and J. F. Palmer. 1984. *Essential systems analysis*. New York, N.Y.: Yourdon Press.

Mills, Everald E. October, 1987. Software metrics. SEI curriculum module SEI-CM-12-1.0..

Mills, H. D. June, 1988. Stepwise refinement and verification in box-structured systems. *IEEE computer*, pp. 23-36.

Mills, H.D., M. Dyer and R. C. Linger. September, 1987. Cleanroom software engineering. *IEEE software*.

Palmer, J. F. August, 1987. Integrating the structured techniques with JAD: Leveled systems development. Working paper presented at the 12th Structured Methods Conference.

Parnas, D. December, 1972. On the criteria to be used in decomposing systems into modules. *Communication of the ACM*.

Parnas, D. L., P.C. Clements, and D.M. Weiss. March, 1985. The modular structure of complex systems. *IEEE transactions on software engineering*.

Partsch, H., and R. Steinbruggen. September, 1983. Program transaction systems. *Computing surveys*, pp. 199-236.

Pedersen, J. S. 1988. Software development using VDM curriculum module SEI-CM-16-1.0. Software Engineering Institute, Carnegie Mellon University.

Peters, L. J. 1981. *Software design: Methods and techniques*. New York, N.Y.: Yourdon Press.

Rombach, H. Dieter. October, 1987. Software specification: A framework. SEI curriculum module SEI-CM-11-1.0.

Ross, D. T. April, 1985. Applications and extensions of SADT. *IEEE Computer*, pp. 25-34.

_____. Douglas Ross talks about structured analysis. *IEEE computer*, pp. 80-88.

Royce, W. W. 1987. Managing the development of large software systems. Proceedings of the 9th International Conference on software engineering. *IEEE computer society*, pp. 328-338.

Rush, G. October, 1985. A fast way to define system requirements. *Computerworld*.

Sathi, A., T. Morton, and S. Roth, Callisto. 1986. An intelligent project management system, *AI magazine* 7 (5): 34-52.

Scacchi, Walt. October, 1987. Model of software evolution: Life cycle and process. SEI curriculum module SEI-CM-10-1.0.

Shlaer, Sally and Stephen J. Mellor. 1988. *Object oriented systems analysis: Modelling the world in data*. Englewood Cliffs, N.J.: Yourdon Press.

Sodhi, Jag. 1991. *Software engineering methods, management, and CASE tools*. New York, N.Y.: McGraw-Hill.

_____. 1990. *Computer systems techniques: Development, implementation, and software maintenance*. Blue Ridge Summit, Pa.: TAB Books.

_____. 1990. *Managing Ada projects using software engineering*. Blue Ridge Summit, Pa.: TAB Books.

_____. 1989. Evaluation of teaching SERA. Seventh annual national conference for Ada technology.

_____. November, 1988. Overview of Ada features for real-time systems. *Defense science*.

Sodhi, Jag, and K. M. George. 1989. Objects with multiple representations in Ada. Seventh annual national conference for Ada technology.

Software. February, 1991.

Software. November, 1990.

Software. March, 1991.

STARS Joint Services Team. October, 1985. Stars software environment (SSE) operational concept document (OCD). Proposed Version 001.0, Department of Defense.

Stevens, W. P., G. J. Myers, and L. L. Constantine. May, 1974. Structured design. *IBM systems journal*, pp. 115-139.

Teichrow, D. January, 1989. PSL/PSA: A computer aided technique for structured documentation and analysis of information processing systems. *IEEE transactions on software engineering*, pp. 41-48.

U.S. Department of Air Force ESD implementation guide for DOD-STD-2167A system software development standard. January 30, 1989.

The starts guide. NCC. Manchester M1 7ED.

U.S. Department of Defense. Military standard, defense system software development. DOD-STD-2167A. Washington, D.C.

Ward, T. Paul, and Stephen J. Mellor. 1985. *Structured development for real-time systems*. Volumes I, II, and III. Englewood Cliffs, N.J.: Prentice-Hall.

Warnier, J.D., and Kenneth T. Orr. 1977. *Structured systems development*. New York, N.Y.: Yourdon Press.

Wasserman, A. I., P. A. Pircher, and R. J. Muller. January, 1989. An object-oriented structured design method for code generation. *SIGSOFT software engineering notes*, pp. 32-55.

Wirth, N. April, 1971. Program development by Stepwise refinement. *Communications of the ACM*, pp. 221- 227.

Wood, William G., John P. Long, and David P. Wood. August, 1989. Classifying software design methods. Technical report, CMU/SEI-89-TR-25.

Yourdon, Edward, and L. Larry Constantine. 1978. *Structured design*. New York, N.Y.: Yourdon Press.

Yourdon, E., Editor. 1979. *Classics in software engineering*. New York, N.Y.: Yourdon Press.

Zave, P. May, 1982. An operational approach to requirements specification for embedded systems. *IEEE transactions on software engineering*, pp. 250-269.

Appendix D

Vendors and products

AI Corp.
138 Technology Drive
Waltham, MA 02254
617-891-6500
KBMS

American Management Systems
1777 North Kent Street
Arlington, VA 22209
703-841-5507
Logiscope

Cadre Technologies
222 Richmond Street
Providence, RI 02903
503-690-1300
RqT
Teamwork

Cisi-Ingenierie
2, Rue Jules Vedrine
31400 Toulouse
France
(33) 6120 4324
HOOD

Dansk Datamatik Center
Lundtoftevej 1 C
DK-2800 Lyngby
Denmark
VDM

GEC-Marconi
12110 Sunset Hills Road
Reston, VA 22090
703-648-1551
GECOMO PLUS

George Mason University
School of Information Technology &
Engineering
4400 University Drive
Fairfax, VA 22030-4444
703-323-3530
DARTS

Goddard Space Flight Center
Greenbelt, MD 20771
301-286-7631
GOOD

Grady Booch
C/O
Rational
835 S. Moore Street
Lakewood, CO 80226
303-986-2405
OOD

i-Logix Inc.
22 Third Avenue
Burlington, MA 01803
617-332-8678
STATEMENT

IBM Corporation
P.O. Box 700
Suffern, NY 10901
914-578-3535
S-JAD
AD/Cycle

Interactive Development
Environments, Inc.
595 Market Street
12th Floor
San Francisco, CA 94105
415-543-0900
StP

AL Lee & Associates
P.O. Box 260319
Plano, TX 75026
214-248-0823
MAGEC

Meta Systems, Ltd.
315 E. Eisenhower
Suite 200
Ann Arbor, MI 48108
313-663-6027
PSL/PSA

Michael Jackson Systems Ltd.
22 Little Portland Street
London WIN 5AF
United Kingdom
(01) 499 6655
JSD

PEI
4043 State Highway
Tinton Falls, NJ 07753
201-918-0110
T Tools

Project Technology, Inc.
2560 Ninth Street Suite 214
Berkeley, CA 94710
415-845-1484
OOA

Sage Software
1700 NW 167th Place
Beaverton, OR 97006
503-645-1150
PolyMake

Software Development Concepts
424 West End Avenue 11 E
New York, NY 10024
WARD/MELLOR

Software Productivity Solutions
122 N Fourth Avenue
Indialantic, FL 32903
407-984-3370
Classic-Ada/ONTOS
Ali

Synthesis Computer Technologies
5199 E. Pacific Coast Highway
Long Beach, CA 90804
213-494-4069
case/ap

Teledyne Brown Engineering
Cumming Research Park
300 Sparkman Drive NW
P.O. Box 070007
Huntsville, AL 35807
800-633-4675
RT
TAGS

Transform Logic Corp.
8502 East Viade Venture
Scottsdale, AZ 85258
800-872-8296
DesignAid II

Index

Other Bestsellers By The Author